D0048983

· · · · · · · · · ·
About Island Press

ISLAND PRESS is the only nonprofit organization in the United States whose principal purpose is the publication of books on environmental issues and natural resource management. We provide solutions-oriented information to professionals, public officials, business and community leaders, and concerned citizens who are shaping responses to environmental problems.

In 1994, Island Press celebrated its tenth anniversary as the leading provider of timely and practical books that take a multidisciplinary approach to critical environmental concerns. Our growing list of titles reflects our commitment to bringing the best of an expanding body of literature to the environmental community throughout North America and the world.

Support for Island Press is provided by Apple Computer, Inc., The Bullitt Foundation, The Geraldine R. Dodge Foundation, The Energy Foundation, The Ford Foundation, The W. Alton Jones Foundation, The Lyndhurst Foundation, The John D. and Catherine T. MacArthur Foundation, The Andrew W. Mellon Foundation, The Joyce Mertz-Gilmore Foundation, The National Fish and Wildlife Foundation, The Pew Charitable Trusts, The Pew Global Stewardship Initiative, The Rockefeller Philanthropic Collaborative, Inc., and individual donors.

· · · · · · · ·
About the Lincoln Institute of Land Policy

The Lincoln Institute of Land Policy is a nonprofit and tax-exempt educational institution established in 1974. Its mission as a school is to study and teach land policy, including land economics and land taxation. The Institute is supported by the Lincoln Foundation, established in 1947 by John C. Lincoln, a Cleveland industrialist. Mr. Lincoln drew inspiration from the ideas of Henry George, the nineteenth-century American political economist and social philosopher.

Integrating the theory and practice of land policy and understanding the forces that influence it are the major goals of the Lincoln Institute. The Institute explores the fundamental forces affecting land use and development: governments' strategies for managing change, community and individual rights and responsibilities, taxation and regulation, the functioning of markets, patterns of human settlement and economic production, and transportation systems.

Land Use in America

This book is the report of the Sustainable Use of the Land Project.

Land Use in America

Henry L. Diamond and Patrick F. Noonan

Lincoln Institute of Land Policy

ISLAND PRESS

Washington, D.C. • Covelo, California

Library of Congress Cataloging-in-Publication Data

Land use in America / [edited by] Henry L. Diamond and Patrick F. Noonan.
      p. cm.
      Includes bibliographical references (p.   ) and index.
      ISBN 1-55963-464-2 (pbk. : alk. paper)
      1. Land use—United States—Planning. 2. Land use—Environmental aspects—United States. 3. Land use—Economic aspects—United States. I. Diamond, Henry L. II. Noonan, Patrick F.
HD205.L357 1996
333.73'13'0973—dc20   95-47012
                                                                 CIP

Printed on recycled, acid-free paper ✪

Manufactured in the United States of America

10 9 8 7 6 5 4 3 2 1

Contents

· · · · · · · · ·

. . . .

Contributed Papers

Foreword

. . . .

More than a century and a half ago, a French visitor to our then new country, Alexis De Tocqueville, observed that Americans seemed to prefer to solve problems without waiting for their government to act. So it is with this report prepared under the guidance of Henry Diamond and Patrick Noonan, who drew on a group of advisers knowledgeable in the field of land use.

So it was, too, with *The Use of Land: A Citizens' Policy Guide to Urban Growth,* published in 1973 and the inspiration for this current effort. I had the opportunity to chair the Task Force on Land Use and Urban Growth, which produced *The Use of Land.* In heralding a "new mood" with respect to land conservation and development, an embodiment of the environmental rally that had swept the country at the time of the first Earth Day in 1970, the authors of *The Use of Land* held out hope that significant changes in the pattern of land use might result in more humanly satisfying communities, more accommodating of natural systems, less wasteful of resources.

A great deal has happened for the better since 1973. The new mood has affected land use. Development is scrutinized now for its range of impacts, and many private developers are building with increased environmental sensitivity, for they have learned that it is not only good citizenship but good business.

A series of environmental laws has been passed. Air quality in virtually all American cities is better and in many places water quality also has improved. Resource lands and other lands important to outdoor recreation are more plentiful and better protected. Indeed, as a nation we have made tremendous strides in achieving the goals laid out by the 1963 national Outdoor Recreation Resources Review Commission—a Commission I also had the privilege to chair—for national systems of wilderness, rivers, and trails.

Yet, as important as these accomplishments are, we cannot rest. Too many productive lands and natural resources are still imperiled. Sprawling, haphazard development too often still contributes to a gradual, cumulative degradation of the landscape and the loss of distinctiveness in our settlements, even as Americans seem to yearn for a greater sense of community that can nurture and support families and traditional values.

Decisions about land use are now being made in a climate rather different from that of two decades ago. Our nation now seems caught in the throes of a new current fueled by frustration with government and government regulation, which has also grown in a haphazard fashion, particularly since the early 1970s. A property rights movement has emerged to counter what its adherents argue is excessive government zeal in constraining the use of public and private lands. Many landowners, including those who are and want to be responsible stewards, find the regulatory maze cumbersome and confusing at best, and for some, small landowners especially, even threatening to their very livelihood. As a society, we must assure that all our citizens are treated fairly even as we pursue the essential goal of safeguarding the environment. This report seeks to take an even-handed look at that problem.

Some of the controversy surrounding this matter is reminiscent of earlier battles as old as the Republic over water and timber, fisheries and farmland, mining and grazing. How will we use the natural bounty with which our great country is blessed? Who benefits? Who loses out? How do we weigh today's needs against the needs of future generations of Americans or the community's interest against those of the private landowner? Who decides?

No one should doubt that the prosperity and future well-being of our country depends on healthy, functioning natural systems, productive forests, fertile soils, wildlife, waters and estuaries, minerals, and the like. This is a realization that should readily transcend politics and ideology and differing policy perspectives, no matter how passionately held.

Gifford Pinchot, the founder of the U.S. Forest Service and the father of what we think of as conservation—in his mind, the greatest good for the greatest number of people over the longest period of time—once wrote, "A nation deprived of its liberty may win it, a nation divided may unite, but a nation whose natural resources are destroyed must inevitably pay the penalty of poverty, degradation, and decay." It remains for each generation to reaffirm or rediscover this wisdom and to act accordingly. The particular challenge of our generation is to apply these principles not only in our forests and parks but in our cities and suburbs as well.

The spirit of citizen involvement De Tocqueville sensed during his trip across America so long ago is alive and well today in our land, not only in countless conservation organizations and the burgeoning local land trust movement but in efforts like that of Henry Diamond and Pat Noonan. Theirs is an endeavor with no official sponsorship. It attempts to take account of what has occurred in land use since the original report was pub-

lished and to present an analysis of the situation today, as well as an
agenda for tomorrow.

Henry Diamond served as New York State's first Commissioner of Environmental Conservation under my brother, Governor Nelson Rockefeller, and has subsequently developed a national law practice that spe-
cializes in environmental issues. He was an active member of the task
force from which came *The Use of Land*. Pat Noonan has spent his entire
professional life, first as President of The Nature Conservancy and now as
founder and Chairman of The Conservation Fund, vigorously pursuing
the conservation of lands with biological, scenic, and historical importance. He has emerged as one of the most effective, even-handed leaders
in today's conservation movement.

They are well qualified to comment and to help us all reaffirm the importance to our nation of a land base that is healthy, productive, and satisfying of human needs.

Laurance S. Rockefeller

Preface and Acknowledgments

• • • • • • • •

This project draws its inspiration from *The Use of Land: A Citizens' Policy Guide to Urban Growth*. Since the book was published in 1973, enormous progress has been made on many environmental fronts. But land use has been neglected. Why? What has happened since *The Use of Land* to turn around the report's heralded "new mood in America," the hopeful message that communities had within their grasp the power to take charge of their destiny? Because land is so central, it is important to understand why efforts to rationalize land use have not moved forward in step with the rest of the environmental agenda. This book is the result of our inquiries.

We sought out the best people we could find to help, including not only planners and conservationists but governors, mayors, corporate chief executives, builders, farmers, and policy advocates. Their views are presented in boxes distributed throughout the report and in the papers that make up the second part of the book. We drew heavily on the insights and experience of our advisers and contributors to develop the agenda, but the ideas, recommendations, and proposals are our own. The advisers and paper contributors do not necessarily endorse our views, nor do we necessarily endorse all the views expressed in the contributed papers.

The paper contributors are listed in the table of contents. The advisers are listed on page 335. There is considerable overlap. The usual caveat about affiliations being listed for identification purposes only applies.

This report is intended for those who care about land in this country and how its use affects the quality of life Americans enjoy. This includes public officials, business and civic leaders, landowners, lenders, environmentalists, and interested citizens from all walks of life and all political persuasions. There is nothing liberal or conservative in caring about this land.

We deliberately did not address public lands issues—mining, grazing, and timber sales on the vast public holdings in the West. These are important matters worthy of serious treatment in their own right, but the public domain is not our focus. Although we do reference some public lands issues in the text—the growing demand for outdoor recreation, for instance, is fulfilled in part on public lands—this book is primarily about the use of private lands in and near communities.

Nor is this a technical manual or "how-to" book. The Urban Land Institute, the American Planning Association, the National Trust for Historic Preservation, and other groups already have useful manuals and books available or works in progress that address the needs of professionals. The Lincoln Institute of Land Policy regularly publishes excellent papers and other publications. So, too, our publisher, Island Press, has a wide selection of books on a full range of topics that are invaluable for professionals and citizens alike.

At the core of this report is an agenda to guide the use of land in 21st century America. It is based on review of the events of the past quarter-century, the contributed papers, and our own observations. Our purpose is to help communities throughout the country rise to the challenge of accommodating growth in better, more environmentally sound, more fiscally responsible ways.

This book is also a report card reviewing progress in land use over more than 25 years. The tools available to citizens and planners to aid them in making informed decisions have become better and more sophisticated. Scientific knowledge is greater. Experience with environmental impact reviews and other techniques is substantial. Yet many of the issues and questions paramount today are essentially the same as those laid out in *The Use of Land*. Indeed, we find they are even more urgent and difficult.

Many friends and colleagues have helped. We are grateful to each of them. They have provided invaluable insight and expertise, and they have served as a reminder of why we are doing this. Many people share with us the belief that exercising good stewardship of the land is crucial for our nation to prosper and grow in environmentally sound ways.

Although this was a small operation, we had outstanding staff who carried out the review and analysis that helped create the agenda. Alan Fox was the project's principal researcher at the start, responsible for helping us progress through the difficult formative stages. Gordon L. Binder played the instrumental role first as one of our informal advisers; then, over the last months of the project, he functioned as chief of staff to bring it to completion. Wendy S. Millet served as project coordinator and carried out a wide range of tasks and Douglas S. Lea was a major contributor to the research and writing. Nancy J. Jones, Robert J. McCoy, and Linda Chalfin contributed extensively—research, writing, editing, and other functions that are necessary to produce a report. We are grateful to our advisers who have been especially generous with their time, reviewing, commenting, and critiquing the manuscript along the way.

This book was enriched by the ideas and perspectives that appear in the contributed papers, and we are grateful to the paper authors.

We want to acknowledge, too, the assistance, comments, and information provided by those who helped informally and unofficially and who are too numerous to list. Indeed, we owe a debt to the good work of many organizations whose materials have provided the foundation on which this book rests. Resources for the Future, The Conservation Fund, and Beveridge & Diamond, P.C. provided crucial institutional support and in-kind contributions of space, computers, and technical help for which we are especially grateful.

We also want to thank the Lincoln Institute of Land Policy for hosting and supporting two significant review meetings for parts of our advisory group and for the institute's own expert staff. Duke University's School of the Environment also sponsored a very helpful review session with selected attendees at their March 1995 conference, "The Use of Land in a New Context," for which we are grateful. These sessions proved critical in the evolution of our thinking, as they provided the chance for peer review.

Lastly and perhaps most importantly, we gratefully acknowledge those without whose financial support this project would have been impossible: Ambassador Laurence W. Lane, Jr., the David and Lucile Packard Foundation, Environment NOW, the Henry M. Jackson Foundation, the Irvine Foundation, and, in particular, Jackson Hole Preserve, Inc., and its Chairman, Laurance S. Rockefeller, whose vision and encouragement have been essential.

Henry L. Diamond and Patrick F. Noonan

The Agenda

. . . .

This report concludes that better land use is essential to the health and well-being of America's communities. Clean air, clean water, and livable communities cannot be achieved without good land use: Yet land use has been the neglected part of environmental efforts, because it evokes deep emotional responses and because it is so complex governmentally. Therefore, a land use agenda for America's communities is important.

AGENDA ITEM #1
Local governments must take the lead role in securing good land use. Initiatives in land use planning and growth management need to be anchored in a community-based process that develops a vision for the future.

Local communities are the key to better land use. But first, each must define a vision for the future. This vision includes an inventory of resources, respect for established traditions, and articulation of community values. To realize a vision, local leaders must enlist all sectors in devising land use plans and execute those plans with greater efficiency and flexibility. No community retains its character by accident.

AGENDA ITEM #2
State governments must help local governments by establishing reasonable ground rules and planning requirements, assisting small and rural areas, and providing leadership on matters that affect more than one local jurisdiction.

States are uniquely positioned in the American system of governance to blend local initiatives and investments in infrastructure with state and national objectives and to address the demands of commerce, the constraints of natural systems, and the need for equitable taxation. Although one solution does not work everywhere, at a minimum states must establish general rules for land use planning and provide leadership to encourage communities to deal with complex problems regionally. States have a special role in helping small, poor, or rural jurisdictions prepare for growth.

AGENDA ITEM #3
The rules governing land development need to be overhauled. They need to be more efficient and more flexible, encouraging—not hindering—new approaches to land development and conservation.

The rules governing the use of land must become more adaptable while they provide predictability to developers. The rigidity of traditional tools—single-use zoning, pro-forma subdivision ordinances, formulaic impact reviews—stifles innovation and encourages inefficiency in public investments and degradation of natural systems.

AGENDA ITEM #4
Landowners must be treated fairly and oppressive regulations fixed. But making government pay in order to apply environmental safeguards for the common good is a bad idea.

The rights of landowners must be taken seriously. Resentment of government intrusiveness threatens environmental programs, the management of future growth, and the stability of communities. Crucial to an easing of tensions are a review of egregious situations, exemptions for small landowners, timely decisions on permits, and expeditious appeals. Proposals to require government to follow abstract formulas in paying for alleged reductions in value would create unwarranted, and potentially disastrous, financial burdens and administrative chaos.

AGENDA ITEM #5
Many government policies and actions—agricultural, highway, and environmental programs—impact land use. If they are not better coordinated, they will continue to result in land use policy by accident.

In the absence of explicit land use policies, the cumulative impacts of government actions on a variety of issues create a de facto regime for land use. These policies are often confusing and conflicting, and their effects on the use of land are destructive. Cooperation among agencies and coordination among policies are essential to achieving better land use practices.

AGENDA ITEM #6
In selective situations, public land acquisition is needed, and a reliable source of funds must be available to pay for it.

Selective acquisition of land is still necessary. Certain places and their surroundings are so strategically located or vulnerable that public ownership is essential. With public funding to purchase land becoming so scarce, partnerships with the private sector can multiply the value of public investments. A federal trust fund for assisting acquisition is needed to provide states and local jurisdictions with funds and predictability so they can plan ahead.

AGENDA ITEM #7
Older areas in cities and suburbs must become a focus for renewal. Government policies should help fill in vacant land in already built-up areas and renew older properties rather than promote unplanned expansion at the urban fringe.

The potential of older urban areas must be developed if metropolitan regions in the United States are to realize their role as the engines of economic growth and entrepreneurship in the global economy. To exploit these idled land assets, by redeveloping vacant and deteriorating areas, a clearing of the regulatory thicket is needed, especially those rules that unnecessarily encumber the reuse of land with a history of hazardous wastes. Once cleanup attains the standard for a projected use, liability should be limited. Private capital should be channeled toward decaying cores with tax incentives and other inducements. Regulatory reviews should be simplified for developers willing to consider building in designated zones.

AGENDA ITEM #8
As most land is privately held, private landowners must be galvanized to assure a healthy land base. Corporate and individual stewardship must be encouraged by providing education, tax incentives, and other benefits.

Without the stewardship of property-owning corporations and individual landholders, the future of the American landscape is bleak. Private initiatives for conservation and quality development require a mix of incentives: tax deductions to encourage donations of land and easements; reduced estate taxes and property assessments to promote long-term stewardship; safe harbors from liability tied to the restoration of habitat and damaged lands; and other inducements. Relief from regulation should be exchanged for agreements to manage for habitat enhancement.

AGENDA ITEM #9
A constituency for better land use is needed based on new partnerships that reach beyond traditional alliances to bring together conservationists, social justice advocates, and economic development interests. These partnerships can be mobilized around natural and cultural resources that people value.

In the absence of a committed constituency, few land use proposals will succeed. Strategies that focus on geographic features of the landscape people value will mobilize a constituency. Within the geographic framework, new alliances among government officials, business and civic leaders, environmentalists, developers, farmers, and residents of urban areas become possible. Local land trusts, in particular, are an effective means of bringing this geographic focus to bear, and must be encouraged as a means of citizen collaboration in the 21st century.

AGENDA ITEM #10
New tools are required to meet the new challenges of land use. Land use disputes should be solved through negotiation or mediation rather than through confrontation and litigation. Geographic Information Systems (GIS) and other advances in technology also offer new opportunities for improving land use decision making.

Mediation, negotiation, and other techniques for resolving disputes offer new opportunities for avoiding the expense and animosity that accompany prolonged rulemaking, tedious appeals, and endless litigation. When disputes and conflicts are being resolved cooperatively, the government role often changes to that of convener and facilitator, and the resourcefulness of citizens in devising common sense solutions can be tapped.

New computer technologies now make it possible to amass, organize, and present vast amounts of data. GIS, in particular, can map and help monitor natural systems and identified lands suitable for development and conservation. These technologies are already transforming the planning process and should be widely used by both the public and private sectors.

This book is a call to action. Its rallying cry is a new commitment to land stewardship, quality development, and environmental progress. These are the goals that the American people must embrace, and public officials and community leaders must speak to constructively, consistently, and frequently. Across the nation, community by community, Americans must make a commitment to good land use practices and pursue an agenda for the 21st century that will improve land use much as the environmental agenda of the past quarter-century challenged every segment of society to accomplish extraordinary environmental goals. With change comes opportunity, and the future guarantees abundant occasions for citizens, elected officials, community organizations, corporations, and others to take the initiative in developing a shared vision and collaborative approach that will guide growth in the 21st century.

· · · · · · · ·

Healthy Land
Makes Healthy Communities

Following World War II, an explosion of population and economic activity transformed America's cities, suburbs, and countryside. This unprecedented transformation has accelerated dramatically since the early 1970s and now amounts to a virtual recasting of traditional settlement patterns (see figure 1).

The seismic aftershocks of explosive growth have registered in the American hinterlands—in distant wilderness preserves, wildlife refuges, and parks; in deserts, prairies, forests, and mountain ranges; and in the agricultural communities and rural horizons that once defined the American experience. The vast American countryside, the fountainhead of national myth, memory, and identity, is beginning to lose its distinctiveness.

Today, in greater and greater numbers, Americans live, work, and play in suburban settings (see figure 2). For some, the suburban transformation has been an unmitigated boon, providing convenient access to better, more spacious housing, good schools, better recreation, and convenient shopping. For many others, however, the suburban expansion imposes real—if often camouflaged—burdens on the texture, continuity, and depth of social life, as well as on the diversity, beauty, and health of the surrounding landscape.

The cumulative impact of current land use practices is troubling in a great many places. In Chicago, Los Angeles, Philadelphia, and virtually every other major metropolitan area, countless uncoordinated development decisions have caused expansion at a far faster rate in land consumption than in population growth (see figure 3). Throughout America, the cost of financing road and sewer extensions and providing other public services has guaranteed an unending tug on scarce public dollars at the same time infrastructure in some parts of the community continues to decay. Center cities founder helplessly in the wake of outward expansion. Many urban neighborhoods, once teeming with people and commerce, have become derelict. Development on floodplains along the Mississippi

Since World War II, and accelerating over the past 25 years, an explosion of population and economic growth has transformed the American landscape. Today, a majority of Americans live, work, and play in suburban settings. Courtesy of Land Ethics, Annapolis, Maryland.

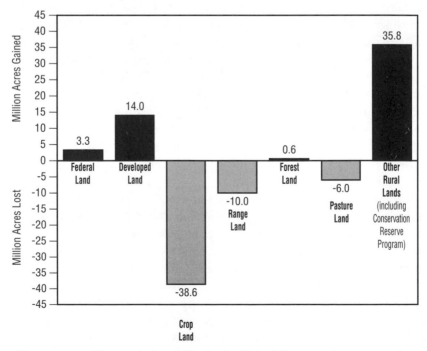

FIGURE 1   Changes in Land Use in the United States, 1982 to 1992. *Source:* U.S. Soil Conservation Service, National Resources Inventory, 1992.

Population (in thousands)

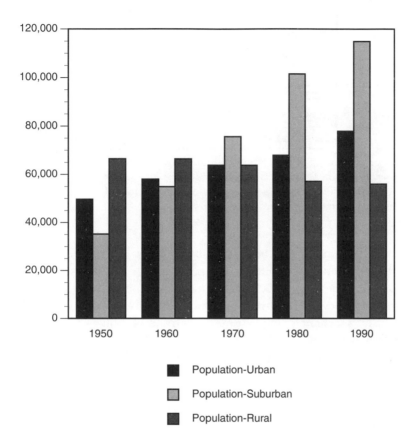

FIGURE 2   U.S. Population in Urban, Suburban, and Rural Areas, 1950 to 1990. *Source:* U.S. Bureau of the Census, *Population Censuses, Number of Inhabitants, U.S. Summary, 1950–1990* (1991).

River and on steep slopes and fire-prone sites in Southern California has escalated taxpayers' exposure in disaster relief when floods or mudslides arrive. Failure to curb pesticides and other pollutants draining off farmland threatens the groundwater supplies of Long Island and other communities. In the face of these and other problems, America's land is not yielding the full measure of benefits that people desire.

For many people today, dissatisfaction goes beyond physical change in the landscape and the attendant costs. They are searching for roots, a sense of place, a sense of community. Their discontent may stem from economic uncertainties or reflect unease about the nature and pace of change

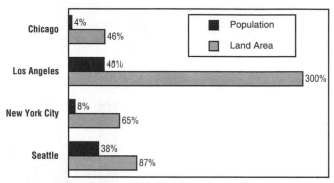

FIGURE 3   Expansion in Population and Land Area for Selected Metropolitan Areas, 1970 to 1990. *Source: Planning and Zoning News,* January 1993; Leinberger, Christopher B., "Metropolitan Development Trends of the Late 1990s: Social and Environmental Implications" (1995).

generally. Their anxiety may be sparked by an influx of newcomers, incidents of street crime, maddening traffic jams, or deteriorating schools. It must seem to some Americans that they have lost control over their communities, maybe even their lives. Many undoubtedly yearn to recapture from the past a seemingly simpler time, with tranquil suburbs or thriving, friendly urban neighborhoods.

For too long the land in this country has been neglected and, as a consequence, the quality of life that Americans might enjoy has suffered. But neither degraded land nor ugly, unsatisfying communities need be inevitable in 21st century America. Nor is it inevitable that the country be locked into the rising costs of extending public facilities or of providing disaster relief because of inefficient land use patterns that do not respect natural forces, especially the flow of water. Rather than treating land as an afterthought incidental to the quality of life, Americans should recognize that land stewardship—promoting efficient use of the land and rational decision making about its use—is central to realizing their desires for a strong economy, a healthy environment, and livable communities. This concern readily cuts across political lines, uniting all Americans who care about the future of their country.

· · · · · · · ·

Today's Land Use Challenges

Throughout the nation's history, a crisis or disaster has galvanized people. Such was the case, for example, with the environmental revolution. Life-threatening smog in Donora, Pennsylvania, in 1948 signaled the need for cleaning up the air. A river catching fire, the Cuyahoga in Cleveland in 1969, launched a serious effort to clean up the nation's water. No equivalent event has awakened the American public to the need to improve the way land is used—although in the late 1970s, the dramatic discovery of a toxic waste dump underlying the Love Canal neighborhood of Niagara Falls, New York, came as close as any single event to doing so. In spring 1993, record floods in the Midwest prompted the question why development was located in floodprone areas to begin with, leading to federal buyouts of some especially vulnerable properties and even entire towns.

Yet today there is no national outcry about land use. Except for those directly involved, controversies over logging in the national forests or preservation of wetland acreage remain beyond Americans' everyday concerns. Locally, controversies do erupt over siting unpopular facilities—landfills, billboards, group homes, airports, new highways, and so forth. There are innumerable neighborhood groups concerned about local land use issues, traffic, crime, open space, and the like. More often than not, however, office parks, shopping centers, and subdivisions creep into existence with little fanfare. They may consume a lot of farmland at the urban fringe, they may be nondescript or even ugly, yet they generate little protest. Gradual changes to the landscape make it difficult to catch the attention of people bombarded with environmental and other alarms, only some of which have had a direct impact on them.

Abandoned toxic waste sites, high property taxes reflecting the costs of extending public services over a large area, the mounting price of disaster relief, deteriorating conditions in older urban cores, the loss of fertile agricultural lands, polluted waterwells—these are wake up calls demanding a response. They are directly tied to prospects for the productivity of the land and the nation's economic health.

Today's land use challenge appears in various places in various guises, transcends the usual categories of political debate, and resists the easy stereotypes and high drama that capture media attention. It is, in short, a silent crisis, a quiet specter, but nonetheless a challenge that affects the well-being of virtually every American.

At the heart of the current predicament lies the increasing obsolescence of the American system for making decisions about land use. In a 1992 paper entitled "Growing Smart: A Program for Modernizing America's Laws Affecting Planning and the Management of Change," the American Planning Association summarizes the situation in these words:

Although amended from time to time, the basic legal con-
structs found in state enabling legislation have changed very
little over the past 50 years. Today, many communities continue to rely on a legislative framework that was created for a
very different pre-World War II America. As a result, the planning and growth management mechanisms in force in most
states in the 1990s are woefully out-of-step with the times.
They frustrate nearly everyone—developers and business
people, conservationists and preservationists, community and
regional planners, design professionals, housing advocates, environmentalists, and citizens.

Still, over the past two decades the record on land use has seen impressive gains even while important land use planning objectives have not always been realized. Strong support for planned growth is evident in many
places across the nation, although this support is often mixed with a backlash against government regulation. The backlash, sometimes characterized as a property rights movement, arises in part from the economic
downturn of the late 1980s and early 1990s and in part from a reconsideration of the role of government. Its emotional force derives from a
deeply rooted value in American culture: the belief that one's house and
property are the equivalents of one's castle and kingdom. Thus, it has
proved extraordinarily difficult for public officials to deal with such issues
as building in floodplains or other places prone to natural disasters like
wildfires and mudslides, which means major problems may result from individual choices directly relating to the inefficient use of land.

The communities that were the flashpoints of growth in the 1960s and
1970s continue to experience conflicts, but growth and its attendant problems, fueled by powerful demographic forces, have pressed outward in the
last 20 years. Many more communities now feel the impacts of traffic
congestion, unsightly development, diminishing open space, and natural
resource constraints—all closely linked to the way people settle the land
and the quality of life they enjoy.

Since the early 1970s, some communities and regions have seen immigration from foreign countries become a highly significant factor in population growth, particularly states like California and Florida. Meanwhile, Colorado and other states in the mountainous West have become
the destination of choice for ex-Californians and others fleeing problems
in their home states.

Yet there is another side to what is happening. In many places, there is a new understanding of a basic attitude: "If you build it, they will come." In no area is this more true than in transportation. Consequently, tying transportation improvements to land use planning appears to be vital, both in directing growth to appropriate areas and in supporting the establishment of greenways, wildlife corridors, and other amenities and conveniences. There is a growing recognition that development should be steered to areas with access to infrastructure and municipal services, areas with sufficient water and other resources to support growth, and areas less likely to be affected by natural disasters. This saves open space, floodplains, steep slopes, and other sensitive environmental areas. Some fast-growing communities are beginning to use a set of effective tools, such as land acquisition, easements, transferable development rights, performance zoning, and incentive packages to encourage more compact urban growth, infill, and redevelopment. New scientific and technical aids like Geographic Information Systems (GIS) are helping officials and citizens make better decisions.

Good Land Use Is Achieved by Good Planning

Long-term planning is central to achieving better land use and growth management. Failure to recognize that does not eliminate land use decision making. Land use is a fact of life, whether explicitly recognized or not. In the absence of planning, land use decisions are made haphazardly or by default. Without planning, the impacts of land use decisions are still felt and their costs are still borne by the community.

Land use planning has not been popular in this country. In many quarters, it has been viewed as foreign, even totalitarian. But planning is not radical doctrine. It is rational decision making. It is time the country gives up its fear of planning and embraces its benefits.

Some knowledgeable observers argue that unplanned land use patterns are no accident. When all the conflicting and competing variables are thrown in—public services, police protection, commuting to work, a host of other activities that are part of daily routines—diffuse, sprawling development patterns, they maintain, reflect an optimal urban form for a society that puts a high premium on individual choice and decentralized decision making. They caution against trying to impose land use plans and controls, through inappropriate and ineffective planning, in effect an artificial discipline, on a market that now serves consumers and the community reasonably well.

But orderly planning can benefit the whole community, for planning ensures that sufficient land is earmarked for a community's housing, jobs, schools, and open space. It provides the framework for long-term enhancement of the environment and community character, which is increasingly essential to economic growth. And planning rationalizes expenditure of public funds for roads, sewers, parks, schools, and the community's other common needs.

Planning also minimizes the destruction of natural systems and accommodates human settlements to the natural world. Understanding the efficiency of natural systems, where and how water drains from the land, for example, can help keep homes and businesses out of harm's way from flooding and other hazards.

As important as the efficient use of resources is, land use planning also means building and maintaining a quality America, protecting the country's heritage and landmarks, making sure the countryside and the places people live do not become ugly and unpleasant.

Planning enables communities to adapt to changing conditions by monitoring and anticipating trends. Nothing in life is static, neither natural systems nor human activities. Understanding past changes in the landscape may help explain current conditions and guide future decisions. Community values also change with time. In the 1950s, the vast interstate highway system was designed in part to meet civil defense objectives during the Cold War, to be able to evacuate cities and move military equipment around the country. If the system was intended to evacuate people from cities threatened by nuclear attack, it also worked in reverse. People could live outside cities and commute in. In Boston, the massive Central Artery, hailed in the 1950s as a symbol of modern city building, today is coming down in a $7 billion project to reroute traffic and reclaim downtown.

There is another reason why greater attention must be paid to land planning. Planning prevents haphazard conservation, which can be as bad as haphazard development. Saving a small wetland without paying attention to its setting, only to see it surrounded by incompatible development, is a Pyrrhic victory at best. Conservationists' appeals to set aside habitat for a single endangered species, coming late in the life of a development proposal, generate enormous ill will that can undermine the valid purpose of trying to save the species. In contrast, a broad, consensus-based plan for protecting habitat for a diversity of endangered or threatened wildlife before development proposals are made is a much more sensible and effective approach. Planning for conservation, every bit as much as planning for growth and development, can add predictability to the land use

The devastating spring floods in the Midwest in 1993 drew attention to the issue of development in floodprone areas and prompted federal buyouts of some vulnerable towns and properties. Understanding the efficiency of nature, the functioning of watersheds generally, and the importance of wetlands in particular can help accommodate human settlements to the natural world, keeping homes and businesses out of harm's way. Photo by Stephen D. Levin. Courtesy of Rails-to-Trails Conservancy, Washington, D.C.

Community values change over time. In the 1950s, Boston's Central Artery was hailed as a symbol of modern city building. Today, it is coming down as part of a $7 billion project to reroute traffic and reclaim downtown. Courtesy of the Central Artery/Tunnel Project, Massachusetts Highway Department, Boston, Massachusetts.

process, eliminating costly delays. If government agencies have an obligation to lay out their long-term priorities, the American land conservation movement, too, has an obligation to set forth its long-term priorities for areas to be protected.

A strong economy, a healthy environment, and an enjoyable quality of life—all depend on the land. In the past, land has provided food, timber, wildlife, minerals, and other natural resources that have helped build this country and kept it strong. In the future, the productivity of the land will be no less central. Moreover, a high quality of life, also dependent on land, is increasingly a requisite for maintaining and strengthening the community's economic base in the postindustrial, knowledge-based economy.

New strategies, tools, and partnerships already are beginning to reshape how this country is growing. Ultimately, it will be the political determination of citizens and their elected leaders, who must turn from business as usual, to assure that America in the 21st century manages its land for the benefit of people today and future generations. To achieve this end, an ethic of land stewardship must be cultivated among landowners, communities, states, and every segment of society across the nation.

· · · · · · · ·
Making More Efficient Use of the Land

Land use has been a slow starter relative to environmental progress on air, water, and waste during the past quarter century, although there has been progress in some places and on some issues. States and communities now have a wide variety of tools at their disposal, ranging from environmental impact assessments to sophisticated computer technology, and these have improved some land management decisions. But too often land development continues in costly, inefficient patterns, and the quality of the outcome still leaves many residents unsatisfied.

To those informed about land use, the lack of real progress over the past quarter century comes as no surprise. The challenge in land use is different from pollution control, on which the country has made great strides. Land is unique. It has a possessive, emotional appeal, as well as an economic dimension, and decisions about its use are seldom made on a purely rational basis. How, in the first place, can one quantify what rational land use means or measure how well communities work for people?

The use of land is subject to many disputes—prominent among them, competing or clashing views about how a community should develop and the relationship between public and private interests. How should homes, workplaces, shopping, and recreation be organized with respect to one another? Which parts of the community should grow and which should be preserved? What about the appearance of new buildings? How should they be integrated into the existing character of a place? How should the need for short-term profits by those who develop the land be balanced against broader community needs? Too few traditions or methods exist to reconcile the thoughts of a diverse citizenry when these and related questions are raised.

As the United States struggles with land use issues today, a profound tension is emerging. What is increasingly seen as good science does not necessarily conform to what is seen as good governance. On one hand, the desire to develop more effective, more scientifically rigorous strategies for protecting natural systems has prompted decision makers to widen their horizons geographically, to advance the region, the watershed, and the ecosystem as the sensible and proper scale for making decisions about land use and growth. On the other hand, these systems usually cut across the boundaries of political jurisdictions, while most land use decisions are made locally, a jealously guarded prerogative that is unlikely to change. Moreover, devolution of responsibilities from the federal government to other levels is now on the national agenda, notably in the environmental area but in many others areas affecting land use as well. Such shifts posit a stronger, reinvigorated role for states and for the counties, municipalities, towns, and special authorities that constitute local governments. But there may also be intensified conflicts over which level of government, state or local or regional, has responsibility for which matters affecting the use of land. What makes sense scientifically for a region or watershed is only one of the factors that will determine the sorting out of responsibilities.

.   .   .   .

Florida: A Status Report

If states are the laboratories of democracy, then Florida is a preeminent setting for land use experiments. (Florida was one of four sites looked at in *The Use of Land* in 1972; see boxes on the other three—Long Island, California, and Colorado.) In the early 1970s, Florida was on the front lines of development wars; its exposure and vulnerability inspired one of the strongest growth management movements in the country. South Florida, Tampa–St. Petersburg, and Orlando (home of Disney World, which opened in 1971) were three of the fastest-growing regions in the country. At the time, the state was attracting 223,600 residents annually, more than 28,000 to Dade County alone. Concern for Florida's natural resources, buffeted by the intense pressures of explosive growth, resulted in the 1972 passage of some of the strongest land and water management laws ever to clear a state legislature. These included the Environmental Land and Water Management Act, the Florida Land Conservation Act, the Florida State Comprehensive Planning Act, and the Florida Water Resources Act.

Today, more than two decades later, Florida is still a leader in land use planning, building on its legacy even as it continues to struggle with a booming population and the challenge of balancing growth with constraints on the exploitation of natural resources. Now home to nearly 14 million people, Florida is still growing at a rate of about 230,000 people a year. In addition, nearly 40 million others visit the state annually. Dade County's population, which topped 2 million in 1994, jumped nearly 20 percent from 1980 to 1990 alone.

Significant growth pressures today have expanded beyond Dade County. In 1972, Martin County, 75 miles north of Miami, was home to about 40,000 people. *The Use of Land* characterized it as a quiet, rural backwater, with orange groves, cattle ranches, and summer cottages along its Atlantic beaches—and a population likely to more than double by 1990. In fact, the county was home to more than 100,000 people in 1990 and added yet another 9,000 by 1994.

In South Florida, water, some experts predict, ultimately will determine just how many more people can be supported. The authors of *The Use of Land* observed, "Ironically, the ubiquitous presence of water is not evidence of a plentiful, clean supply but, rather, of a vulnerable, sensitive ecosystem that has been violated by development." Since then, rampant growth has underscored the need to rethink land use policies, with particular emphasis on protecting both the quality and the quantity of water—both for human use and for natural systems. Nathaniel Reed, a well-known Florida conservationist and businessman, who serves on the South Florida Water Management District and in 1986 founded 1,000 Friends of Florida—a statewide growth management advocacy group—believes that Florida's future "is truly about the control of water. Water will control land use. Water will control our economy." In South Florida, there is a general recognition that this will entail three fundamental actions: restoring the natural sheet of north to south flows from central Florida through the Everglades; storing rainfall to support natural, municipal, and agricultural uses during periods of drought; and ensuring that water quality is pure enough to sustain natural systems.

Beyond water, there is also a growing recognition of the need to link land use planning with transportation and other critical factors. The Commission for a Sustainable South Florida is preparing recommendations for a five-year action plan "that will bolster the regional economy, promote quality communities, secure healthy South Florida ecosystems, and ensure today's progress is not achieved at tomorrow's expense."

Long Island (1973–1995)

In the years following World War II, the population of Long Island, New York, exploded. Its two counties—Nassau and Suffolk—were among the fastest growing in the United States. The pressures were so intense that, according to long-time Long Island Regional Planning Board Executive Director Lee Koppelman, "By 1960, there was a realization that if a handle was not developed to control land use, then Long Island would be virtually paved over from shore to shore." Today, Long Island's population hovers around 2.6 million, the same as it was in 1973. In fact, while Suffolk County increased its population by a modest 2.9 percent from 1980 to 1990, Nassau County actually dropped 2.6 percent, offsetting Suffolk's gain. Although the population has stabilized, open space continues to give way to sprawling commercial and residential development. The situation is exacerbated by the island's balkanized governmental structure; each town makes land use planning decisions independently of its neighbors, undermining county and island-wide efforts to promote regional planning.

With Nassau and western Suffolk counties developed almost to capacity, the remaining question is what will happen in eastern Suffolk County. There has even been a move on the part of five towns in that region to break away from Suffolk County to preserve the rural character of the eastern end of the island, where a flourishing vineyard and winery industry brings in sufficient revenues to keep some of the land in agricultural use.

The first initiative involving regional cooperation at the town level of government has been focused on Suffolk County's 100,000-acre Pine Barrens preserve and the huge supply of drinking water beneath it. In 1993, New York State's Pine Barrens Protection Act created a 52,500-acre core preservation area, surrounded by a 47,500-acre area designated for compatible growth to protect the watershed. Even after the act's passage, however, its implementation has continued to be a source of contention among builders, property owners, and environmentalists in the towns of Brookhaven, Southampton, and Riverhead. In January 1995, a five-member Pine Barrens Commission composed of town, county, and state officials approved a plan favoring acquisition and limited transfer of development rights in the core area, while regulating development in an adjacent compatible growth area. Koppelman urged a ratio of 75 percent acquisition to 25 percent transfer of development rights "because there are a lot of sensitive lands outside the core." Under the plan, the state would provide $50 million for land purchases and administration, while Suffolk

County would contribute $25 million over a period of several years. The fate of the plan, however, rested on approval from the three towns. There also has been concern that attempts to balance New York State's budget might result in funding cuts. In late June 1995, Governor George Pataki signed a plan designating the Long Island Pine Barrens as New York State's third forest preserve.

At the western end of the island, potability of groundwater and saltwater intrusion have been issues. Possible contamination of drinking water supplies is one among several concerns behind a four-year study by the National Cancer Institute to determine the links between environmental contamination, diet, and other factors and breast cancer. The $10 million Long Island Breast Cancer Study Project, in which 3,200 Long Island women will participate, was mandated by Congress at the urging of a coalition of Long Island groups concerned about the island's higher than normal breast cancer rate.

Long Island's tremendous number of political jurisdictions, 110 in all, each dependent on the property tax for revenues and, therefore, in competition over the tax base has further complicated land use planning. Some experts argue that larger lot zoning resulted in a tendency to favor single-family, detached housing that quickly gobbled up land. That still happens, although a recent decision by the Southampton Planning Board to permit 3-acre lot development of a 31-acre farm, instead of cluster development, has been challenged by a local environmental group. According to Koppelman, as early as 1957 a study sponsored by the Long Island Builders Institute recommended cluster zoning. Initially, residents were suspicious that open lands preserved through clustering would later be developed. Today, however, all of the island's communities with the exception of Shelter Island have mandatory cluster zoning, although each has the option to waive the requirement and permit traditional, larger lot development. And at Shelter Island, the town was able to place one-third of the community's 2,220 acres in permanent open space through a Nature Conservancy acquisition of a private estate.

The politics of Long Island are also unique because of the very affluent, highly educated composition of the population. Support for land use planning and environmental protection remain strong in contrast to the backlash elsewhere in the nation. At the same time, the island's residents are charged by some with elitist and exclusionary policies that have frustrated efforts to provide low- and moderate-income housing.

Still, Long Island has made some progress in addressing the lack of affordable housing over the last 20 years, despite what the *Long Island*

Business News called "Long Island's well-known NIMBY[Not In My Back Yard]ism." In 1994, Long Island created a second economic development zone in North Bellport, in a neighborhood where one-third of the residents had incomes below the poverty level and 40 percent received some type of public assistance. A nonprofit alliance, the Long Island Housing Partnership of Hauppauge, broke ground on the first 13 single-family, three-bedroom houses there. The houses were to be sold to qualifying first-time homebuyers at modest prices.

Long Island's first economic development zone was in Central Islip. By 1994, that community had sold the last of 380 houses in an award-winning, single-family urban renewal housing project totaling $50 million. The project was credited with redeveloping one of Long Island's most blighted communities, Carleton Park, into a vital neighborhood.

After decades of struggle to balance unavoidable growth with protection of open space and vital resources, Long Island has a checkered record of success and failure. Despite progress, many question whether the island's unwieldy political structure will continue to inhibit meaningful regional planning and development. The Pine Barrens offers perhaps the first real opportunity and the first real test.

John DeGrove, a commission member and a nationally known planning expert, suggests that South Florida's ability to handle the growth projected over the next 20 years—including an estimated increase of 2.5 million people in Dade, Broward, and Palm Beach counties alone—will require a new approach to water management. He believes success will depend on directing growth away from water recharge areas and sensitive natural systems and toward compact, designated development zones. Among the incentives DeGrove cites as necessary to encourage infill and redevelopment are simplifying the permit process to offer one-stop shopping; providing public funding to repair and upgrade deteriorating or inadequate urban infrastructure, such as sewer and water lines; removing cleanup liability for past pollution; and energetically working with banks and other lending institutions that are more accustomed to, as well as more comfortable with, making loans for outlying suburban development.

A new political and economic climate, as elsewhere in the country, adds to the difficulty of the growth management task. The economic downturn in the early 1990s led some to target growth management controls as a primary cause of Florida's problems. Property rights became a source of

For more than two decades, Florida with its rapid growth and vulnerable natural systems has been a preeminent setting for land use planning innovations.
Even with pioneering growth management laws, however, the state must continue to try new policies, streamline procedures, and create new programs
and incentives to accommodate expected growth. Courtesy of A. Nelessen
Associates, Princeton, New Jersey.

contention as well. As a consequence, groups such as 1,000 Friends of
Florida worked last year with state legislators to develop language to protect property owners' "vested" uses of their land, while at the same time
distinguishing those rights from "speculative" uses. The collaboration secured passage of a law that gives owners with vested rights—investments
in permits and architectural or engineering plans, for example—the right
to pursue dispute resolution with government regulatory agencies if passage of a new law or regulation encroaches on those rights and the owner
can prove an "inordinate burden." If the two parties fail to reach a compromise within 180 days, the law requires the judiciary to rule on compensation. If compensation is awarded, the government in return receives
an interest, such as a conservation easement on the property.

James Murley, executive director of 1,000 Friends, believes that other
techniques offer promise as well. He cites the purchase of development
rights in the Green Swamp and the less than fee acquisitions proposed for
a Hillsborough River Greenway as practical solutions to the objections
raised by property rights advocates.

California (1973–1995)

Twenty-odd years ago, California already faced tremendous growth pressures. Even then, it was the one state, according to *The Use of Land*, "which is everyone's archetype of rapid growth and unrestrained development—California, the home of Los Angeles, itself a symbol to many of how urbanization should not take place." Still, California had taken a number of important steps to control growth. The state granted tax abatements for land kept in active agricultural use. The San Francisco Bay Area Conservation and Development Commission was created in 1965 through citizen efforts. San Diego elected Pete Wilson as mayor in 1971 on a slow growth platform. In November 1972, California voters authorized the state to regulate all development along the coast with the passage of Proposition 20, which established a state coastal zone conservation commission and six regional commissions to grant permits, review environmental impact statements, and prepare a comprehensive coastal use plan for consideration by the legislature.

Today, California is still the example of both what to do and what not to do. Sprawling development patterns continue. *Beyond Sprawl*, a February 1995 report of the Bank of America, Resources Agency of California, Greenbelt Alliance, and Low Income Housing Fund, observed that "the 'new' California—with 32 million people and counting—is using land and other resources in much the same fashion as the 'old' California, with only ten million people." The report identified many of the trends associated with growth over the past 20 years: new housing developments encroaching farther into agricultural and environmentally sensitive areas; increasing dependence on automobiles; isolation of older communities, including central cities and the first wave of post-World War II suburbs. In clear and certain terms, the report also identified the costs—to taxpayers, businesses, new suburban residents, residents of central cities and older communities, farmers, and the environment. Current development patterns, *Beyond Sprawl* says, by reducing the quality of life in California, have made the state a less desirable location for businesses and their employees. In Los Angeles, quality of life concerns were already prompting an exodus in the late 1980s, before the economic downturn. A 1989 *Los Angeles Times Magazine* special report began: "Los Angeles County, 1943, population 3.1 million and growing: *Life* magazine reports that 'almost everybody who lives in Los Angeles believes that someday it will be the largest city in the world.' Los Angeles County, 1989, population 8.5 million and growing: Nearly half of Los Angeles residents say they have considered moving away in the past year."

Compounding the pressures created by massive population growth and natural resource constraints have been the changing economic and political climates within the state. Said William Fulton in the *Sacramento Bee*, "For all of the '80s and '90s, local planning in California has been dominated by the politics and fiscal realities of the Post-Proposition 13 era." With Proposition 13's imposition of a 1 percent per year cap on the increase in property taxes, localities turned to up-front development fees to cover the cost of growth. Outrage over increasing traffic congestion further fueled growth management concerns throughout the 1980s. Then the bottom fell out of the economy, and the political momentum seemed to stall. Reported Fulton, "[As early as] June [1988], voters rejected broad-ranging growth management proposals in Orange and San Diego counties. In November of that year, Riverside voters followed suit." When the recession hit with full force in 1990 and intensified the pressures surrounding growth and development decisions, Fulton said, "the joke within the [Governor Pete] Wilson administration was that everybody was praying for a little growth to manage."

For many, not only is an overall quality of life at stake, but in particular, Californians' treasured coast and productive lands. Michael Fischer, former executive director of the California Coastal Commission (the permanent body created by the state legislature in 1976 as an outcome of Proposition 20), as well as the Sierra Club, sees economic pressures eroding local political support for coastal protection. Fischer, who is now head of the California Coastal Conservancy, says that part of the success of the state's coastal program is that the local coastal programs meet statutory requirements, including keeping Route 1, the coastal highway, a narrow and winding scenic road. Without a freeway along the coast, and absent state and federal funding for sewer and water treatment facilities, the coastline has been protected. But Fischer is worried that the current commission, which he feels is dominated by local officials, is friendlier to development and wonders what impact that will have on the future.

Inland, the state has not fared as well as it has in conserving lands along the coast. Richard Wilson, California's Department of Forestry and Fire Protection chief, who chaired a statewide land use task force in 1975, sees farmers being squeezed harder and harder as development moves into Fresno County and the San Joaquin Valley, where some of the country's most productive farmland is located. Moreover, says Wilson, growers who produce such high-value crops as wine grapes are faring better than those who cultivate citrus and fruits or raise cattle or sheep. Increasingly, new bedroom communities are replacing agricultural lands as the population surges.

California has made enormous strides over the past 25 years in restoring San
Francisco Bay and protecting its spectacular coastline. Yet the state continues
to face substantial growth pressures, prompting even greater efforts to devise
innovative strategies that can reconcile development and conservation needs.
Courtesy of National Park Service, San Francisco, California.

On the positive side, in his current position, Wilson foresees an end to
the time when those who build in disaster-prone areas such as forest fire
zones will receive compensation for property loss. Already, he says, 85 percent of insurance underwriters in the state have stopped writing fire insurance policies. And he believes community stakeholders must take responsibility through better zoning and construction practices, with lower
insurance rates and reasonable bank loans the reward for building homes
with safer materials and in safer locations. "There is an awareness," says
Wilson, "that growth is no longer a free ride."

To succeed in the future, *Beyond Sprawl* asserts, California must forge
broader constituencies and alliances among environmentalists, inner-city
community advocates, business leaders, government experts, farmers, and
suburbanites—not an easy task. "To build a strong economy and retain a
good quality of life for the 21st Century," the report concludes, "we must
move beyond sprawl to a new vision of community in the few remaining
years of the 20th Century."

Despite challenges and hurdles, there are signs that Florida's quarter-century commitment to land use planning is paying off. Murley credits the state's success to both mandatory planning and aggressive land acquisition. The 1972 legislation authorizing the designation of areas of critical concern allowed the state to acquire more than 800,000 acres in Big Cypress Swamp, 323,000 acres in the Green Swamp, and almost 70,000 acres in the Florida Keys. Although Florida has not designated a new area of critical concern in the past 10 years, it has continued to fund land acquisitions, an investment now totaling more than $400 million a year, supplemented by another $100 million in county funds. The 10-year total of $3.8 billion is the largest state program for purchasing environmentally sensitive lands in the nation. Acquisition and environmental programs are all being evaluated with an eye to how they can be used to advance the concept of ecosystem management.

In January 1993, Governor Lawton Chiles established the Florida Greenways Commission and directed it to create a statewide network of greenways linking Florida's parks, open spaces, and communities, with a focus on protecting riparian corridors (corridors along waterways). Launched with grants from the Surdna Foundation, the John D. and Catherine T. MacArthur Foundation, and the U.S. Fish and Wildlife Foundation, and sponsored by The Conservation Fund and 1,000 Friends of Florida, the statewide project has started with four greenways linking state and national parks and wildlife refuges. The Loxahatchee Greenways Network, a prototype, is sponsored by the MacArthur Foundation and is being established on MacArthur and other properties in southern Palm Beach and northern Martin counties. The Apalachee Greenways Network will focus on six counties surrounding Tallahassee. The Suncoast Greenways Network is establishing river-based wildlife corridors and recreational greenways for the Tampa Bay area. In addition to the others, the Cross Florida Greenway will eventually become a 110-mile-long recreation and conservation area along the right-of-way of the abandoned cross-Florida Barge Canal.

Florida's willingness to revisit, refine, and build on its original legislative package has been key to its continued success. An Environmental Land Management Study Committee, convened in the early 1980s, gave birth to the laws known collectively as the 1985 Omnibus Growth Management Act. This legislation provided the teeth and funding to require and enforce land use planning at the city and county levels—which had been required by legislation first approved in 1975—and within 11 specially designated regions of the state. The act concentrates on three basic principles: control of coastal development, promotion of compact urban development, and concurrency. Coastal rules prohibit building in coastal areas that are at risk due to erosion or to having been inundated within the past 30 years and also specify building design in areas susceptible to hurricane damage. Compact development, although only vaguely defined in the Florida statute, has become a driving force in planning for transportation and other infrastructure.

Ironically, one of the difficulties in containing urban sprawl under the law has been its most significant feature — "pay as you go" infrastructure requirements, widely known as concurrency. Simply stated, infrastructure must be in place before growth can occur. Florida's concurrency provisions were designed to be strictly enforced; yet the planning law was enacted without direct linkages to funding sources for the necessary infrastructure. Consequently, as road and infrastructure capacity was consumed downtown, and money was unavailable to expand capacity within the rigid concurrency requirements, excess capacity on the urban fringe and in rural areas lured commercial and residential development. Gradually, it became clear that the requirements to ensure uncongested traffic flow by automatically limiting further development in urban and heavily built-up areas had unintentionally driven growth to outlying and rural areas where excess capacity still existed. Revisions to the law have allowed higher traffic volumes in urban areas to encourage infill and redevelopment.

In 1993, the Florida legislature approved another Environmental Land Management Study Committee bill, which included a 5 cents per gallon, local-option gasoline tax to pay for transportation improvements and a state Intermodal Surface Transportation Efficiency Act (ISTEA) that mirrors the 1991 federal legislation and links transportation to land use planning. The state also authorized a revision of the state comprehensive plan and local comprehensive plans.

Nevertheless, even with these planning advances, many Florida communities are struggling to provide services and keep up with growth. Broward County faces a $1.5 billion shortfall to meet projected growth in school populations over the next five years. The county commission and school board are putting together plans to slow down housing construction until schools are built. Dade and Palm Beach counties face similar shortfalls.

Cautious optimism mixes with lingering questions in Florida. Will there be enough water? Can future growth avoid damaging vital natural systems on which humans and wildlife depend? Indeed, Florida may well be in the vanguard of yet another milestone in the evolution of managed growth—a general awareness that natural systems impose their own constraints. Notes one astute observer of growth management, Steven McCrea, "In 1971, Governor Reubin Askew wondered whether Southeast Florida had exceeded its capacity to support its growing population. Since then, we've added about a million residents between Jupiter and Key West. We've endured another drought, four riots, three recessions, a more than $25 billion hurricane, boatlifts, and other challenges." Given Florida's quarter-century struggle to manage growth in the face of continued population increases and intense pressure on natural resources, the quest for sustainability takes on new urgency.

Most importantly, Florida is exploring new policies, streamlining procedures, and creating new programs and incentives to accommodate future growth. The state's challenge is to engage its citizens, find workable new approaches, and resolve conflicts through consensus building and cooperative action.

The rest of the country can benefit from Florida's leadership. The Sunshine State's saga is hardly unique. The struggle with the unintended byproducts of runaway growth has surfaced in other states, numerous regional groupings, and countless local jurisdictions. Their common and particular experiences, combined with federal interventions gathered under the rubric of environmental protection, and a series of severe economic dislocations, are bringing land use management into the focus it needs.

. . . .

State Planning and Growth Management

In 1926, the U.S. Supreme Court upheld the validity of comprehensive zoning. By 1940, virtually every state had adopted major features of the U.S. Commerce Department's Standard Zoning Enabling Act of 1926 and Standard Planning Enabling Act of 1928. These model statutes encouraged states to empower cities, towns, and counties to prepare comprehensive plans and to adopt zoning, subdivision regulations, and other land use measures. The legal justification was the constitutional authority of states to protect public health, safety, and welfare.

Most states continue to delegate substantial portions of this broad regulatory authority to local governments. Beginning in the 1970s, however, a number of states, prompted by environmental concerns and a desire to curb the excesses of urban growth, attempted to provide localities with a comprehensive framework for managing growth and protecting assets. These growth management programs—like that of Florida have met with varying degrees of success. Yet all offer promise and have proved important in building awareness and strengthening local capabilities to manage growth and development.

The extent of direct state involvement in local development decisions varies greatly from state to state. Every state exercises the power of the purse. Transportation funding, sewer projects, park acquisitions, and a host of other state programs, including economic incentives and tax policy, cast a long shadow over local discretion. Yet more than a dozen states have already gone beyond indirect leveraging to pass laws that assume at least some level of state review and approval for specific projects or in specific areas that affect state interests.

During the 1970s, seven states, starting with Vermont, passed legislation affecting local land use, planning, and growth management. Oregon's law, passed in 1973, covered the entire state. California and North Carolina laws concerned only coastal areas. Colorado, like Florida, took a statewide approach but did not adopt a comprehensive growth management program, instead restricting oversight to specific areas of concern or projects of statewide importance. (Hawaii has enjoyed statewide land use planning since 1967. The Hawaii law is limited in scope, however, and is now under review by the state legislature for amendments that would expand its objectives, enforcement, and funding provisions.)

In the 1980s, a new wave of growth management laws took a more comprehensive approach in terms of both lands covered and objectives included. Although retaining a traditional environmental thrust—supporting the creation of green space and parks, preservation of forests and farmlands, protection of sensitive ecological systems, clustered patterns of development—these more recent enactments also address a broad array of other matters, including housing, infrastructure, economic development, and urban form. (Many states without statewide growth management programs nonetheless have developed programs for the protection of specific areas and regions, such as the Adirondacks of New York, Cape Cod in Massachusetts, and the Lake Tahoe Basin in California and Nevada.)

As of 1995, Florida, Georgia, Maine, Maryland, New Jersey, Oregon, Rhode Island, Vermont, and Washington had statewide growth manage-

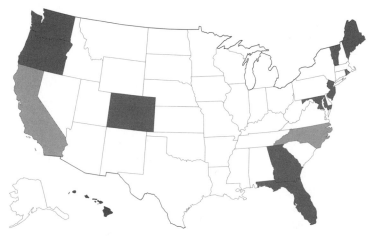

■ States with Statewide Growth Management Programs

□ States with Laws for Coastal Areas Only

FIGURE 4 States with Land Use or Growth Management Programs. *Source:* Florida Atlantic University/Florida International University Joint Center for Environmental and Urban Problems. *Note:* About a dozen states have adopted some version of a comprehensive statewide land use or growth management program. California's and North Carolina's programs focus on coastal resources. Colorado's law addresses development with regional impacts.

ment laws in one form or another (see figure 4). Four other states, California, North Carolina, Pennsylvania, and Virginia, have recently considered new legislation; Connecticut in 1992 enacted a Policies Plan that designated certain areas as suitable for different types of development. All of these states are on the East and West coasts, where growth over the last two decades has been significant.

Statewide growth management laws typically establish a set of goals: reduction of congestion, redevelopment of urban areas, preservation of pristine lands and other natural resources, conservation of agricultural lands, reduction of pollution and infrastructure costs, provision of affordable housing, and improvement in the quality of life. State programs usually require local jurisdictions to comply with statewide goals and to preserve significant public resources, including natural and historic landmarks. Generally, they require localities to develop land use plans and regulations containing consistency provisions tying state programs to these plans; delineated rural and urban areas, with incentives for compact development; and requirements for citizen participation.

Colorado (1973–1995)

In the past few years, Colorado's Front Range, a 40-mile-wide region stretching from Fort Collins in the north through Denver and south to Colorado Springs, has seen population grow by leaps, as have the state's mountain valleys. Douglas County, the fastest-growing county in the state and the second fastest in the nation, saw its population skyrocket nearly 900 percent from 1970–1993, from 8,400 to 83,360. During that same period, Jefferson County doubled its population; Boulder grew by 88 percent; and, in the mountains to the west, Summit County's population swelled five-fold to 14,631.

In the wake of such growth, many of Colorado's citizens want to make sure that their home state's beauty and natural resources do not go the way of once desirable places. Widespread concern led to a statewide growth summit and a series of regional summits headed by Governor Roy Romer during the first half of 1995. But the summits underscored what some have termed Colorado's "schizophrenic" approach to land use planning: Colorado citizens desperately want to protect their state; just as fiercely, they resist state land use controls. Although one of the first states to create a land use commission (in 1970), Colorado has never endorsed statewide land use regulations. The most popular and successful statewide initiative is Great Outdoors Colorado (GO Colorado), which passed in 1992 with 58 percent of the vote. It reallocates lottery monies originally designated for conservation in 1980, then diverted by the state legislature to prisons and other capital expenditures, back to protection of parks and open space. By 1998, when the reallocation is complete, GO Colorado will provide about $40 million annually for acquisition, easements, and other conservation measures.

Locally, land use planning measures vary tremendously. The city of Boulder and Boulder County are in the vanguard. There, a wealth of expertise and historical experience in land use planning are coupled with vigorous community support. With a resurgence of growth in the past few years, the city and county are working jointly to direct new growth toward suitable locations and to keep mountain vistas free of development. The Boulder Valley Comprehensive Plan includes a land use map that divides the community into service areas. The first is the city itself; the second, an inner ring also considered eligible for the full range of city services, with the intent of encouraging infill and discouraging leapfrog development. Another key component of the plan is the designation of greenways and other areas to

Colorado's Front Range has seen rapid growth over the past 25 years. In the 1950s the city of Boulder had precluded development above a base elevation to protect the scenic beauty of the mountains. Today, the community enjoys an extensive system of greenways and mountain parks, protected largely through acquisition. Courtesy of The Conservation Fund, Boulder, Colorado office.

buffer communities from one another and to protect open space and agricultural lands. Boulder's greenways and mountain parks are so extensive—approximately 22,000 acres protected largely through acquisition, less often through purchase of development rights—that they receive more visitors annually than the Rocky Mountain National Park. Boulder also still adheres to a "blue line" ordinance established in the 1950s to preclude provision of city services above a base elevation in order to preserve the scenic beauty of the mountains.

In 1995, the city and county began a comprehensive rezoning process to downzone certain areas and develop a transferable development rights program. State statute dictates a minimum lot size of 35 acres in unincorporated areas, unintentionally causing the construction of huge (up to 6,000 square feet) "prairie palaces" far from any city or commercial services. The rezoning effort is designed to direct development away from the mountains and open plains, clustering growth around existing communities that would be designated "receiving sites." A citizen initiative to limit commercial growth in the city of Boulder was slated to appear on the ballot in November 1995.

By contrast, many Colorado counties are just beginning to confront the

effects of growth and are not nearly as far along as Boulder in shaping and directing development. Some have a divided citizenry, not as wholeheartedly behind managing growth as people in Boulder. On the other hand, Jefferson County has realized that regulating growth in the high-country mountain, would expose fewer people to the risk of fire, a significant concern where dry timber abounds.

Despite mixed support in various places, there is some evidence of a statewide constituency emerging for land use planning in Colorado. In 1995, the newly formed 1,000 Friends of Colorado named Steve Pomerance, a former Boulder city council member, its president. The organization's goal is to develop statewide land use policies much like those in Florida, Oregon, and Washington and to encourage their passage by the state legislature.

Colorado's popularity as a destination for new settlers is unlikely to wane soon. Like other Rocky Mountain states, Colorado is on the new frontier. Its population of 3.6 million is expected to increase to about 4 million by the year 2000. Projected growth estimates for the Front Range show Douglas County growing by more than 700 percent in the next 50 years; Jefferson, by nearly 100 percent; Boulder, by 140 percent. Colorado must prepare now to avoid the costly lessons of other places around the country where development has overwhelmed attractiveness.

Wide variability is evident among state growth management laws. At one end of the spectrum, the laws of Georgia and Rhode Island are primarily goal statements; at the other, Oregon and New Jersey delineate areas for specified land uses and establish growth boundaries.

The state of Oregon has taken a notable approach to growth management, mandating all local jurisdictions to develop land use plans in conformity with state standards that include urban growth boundaries. The Oregon plan stands out not only because it was the first truly statewide comprehensive land use law, but also because it requires all 241 cities to establish urban growth boundaries outside of which urban development is restricted. Areas outside the boundaries have been rezoned for agriculture and forestry, with 25 million acres now designated exclusively for these purposes.

Land management in Oregon is also unique in requiring that jurisdictions in the Portland metropolitan area earmark vacant land in residential areas for affordable housing. To promote a greater diversity in the housing located inside the boundary, vacant, single-family lots were

scaled back to more affordable sizes. More land was set aside for multi-family units. As a result, the capacity of the same base of land within the growth boundary increased from 129,000 to 305,000 units in four years, drawing homebuilder support to the program. Farmers and foresters, too, support the program because it assures that lands outside the growth boundaries are reserved for their needs.

New Jersey takes a different approach. It designates development centers where growth is encouraged and densities are expected to increase. It also identifies areas where density decreases are required in the interest of conserving land. This approach is intended to balance growth and preserve lands without adding to state and local service costs. The New Jersey Pinelands Commission, set up in 1979 through complementary federal and state legislation, protects the Pine Barrens in southern New Jersey. The commission developed an areawide comprehensive plan and devised a tradable land credit system. In exchange for restrictive covenants on their properties, landowners in conservation zones obtain credits they can sell to landowners in growth zones. The state augmented the program in 1985, setting up the Pinelands Development Credit Bank

Along this road runs an urban growth boundary—directing urban development to one side, protecting open space on the other—as required by Oregon's statewide land use law, established in the mid-1970s. This program, the nation's first comprehensive growth management program, enjoys broad support though it is not without its critics. Courtesy of 1000 Friends of Oregon, Portland, Oregon.

to guarantee loans that use credits as collateral, as well as to buy credits from owners and keep a list of owners and purchasers. Over a decade, starting in 1982, nearly 10,000 acres were placed in easement, and 859 credits were granted. Over 180 development projects have been approved, making use of over 470 development credits allowing increased building densities.

. . . .

New Regional Groupings

Decades of growth and sprawl have sparked a compensating interest in regional governance. Starting in the 1960s, when transportation planning requirements hastened the formation of councils of government, the number of special districts and structures for regional governance has risen significantly. From 1972 to 1987, the number of special districts doubled, from 14,500 to 29,000.

This growth has occurred in response to increasing awareness that state and local governments are limited in their ability to manage land use and infrastructure, including road and transportation planning, water and sewer line extensions, greenway and park conservation, and environmental quality issues, such as air and water pollution, that do not conform to political boundaries. Regional agencies coordinate and manage various metropolitan area needs, including sewers, soil and water conservation, metropolitan parks, metropolitan planning, and taxes.

Regionwide entities develop in several ways—through reform of existing councils of government, establishment of special or single-purpose organizations, creation of new comprehensive regional planning and service groups—and arrive through a variety of legal instruments, including voter referendums, state edicts, and local compacts. In Florida, Dade County expanded its planning and growth management powers through a county referendum. In Minnesota, the state legislature created a new regional council, the Twin Cities Metropolitan Council, to manage a variety of metropolitan tasks, including property taxation. In Oregon, voters passed a referendum establishing the new Metropolitan Service District of Portland. And in Indiana, Marion County and the city of Indianapolis merged to form UniGov.

Metropolitan planning and land trust organizations in Chicago, New York, Philadelphia, San Francisco, and elsewhere have launched initiatives to encourage the planning of metropolitan greenspace infrastructure. This kind of planning strengthens connections between parks, greenways, and rural countryside. It often enables competing jurisdictions to recognize opportunities for working together on recreation, aesthetics, and watershed protection.

In spite of some notable successes, however, there continues to be little or no consensus and no effective political and administrative mechanisms in many parts of the country for acting responsibly on local land use initiatives having regional impacts. The obstacles to regionalism are many, for most metropolitan areas are severely fragmented. Not only do separate state, county, and municipal jurisdictions disagree on values and policies, but they also jealously guard their autonomy and view other jurisdictions with suspicion. In the regional economic sphere, the result is intergovernmental competition and conflict rather than consultation and cooperation. Jurisdictional fragmentation has created a situation in which the rules reinforce the tendency of large developers to keep deliberation and negotiation confined within the boundaries of the county or municipality where a project is to be located. The absence of regional infrastructure and land use planning, coupled with resistance to collaboration, ensures continuing waste of both public and private investments.

In such a climate, it is only logical, both for private developers and government agencies, to try to make deals in the smallest venue possible, scrutinized by the fewest number of eyes. For large developers, making a well-targeted and well-financed proposal to interested, although generally unsophisticated, parties in local government is entirely consistent with the norms and traditions of land development in the United States. Given the fragmentation of the political landscape, it is little wonder that the physical landscape is similarly disordered.

Nor has the spread of regional structures always translated into better government. Where regional agencies have been managed well, given strong enforcement authority, and been liberated from crippling opposition, success has followed—in Portland and Indianapolis, for instance. In other cases, especially where regional planning agencies lack enforcement authority, the added layer of government has not improved regional governance. To the contrary, it has exacerbated existing problems among local jurisdictions. Several years ago, voters in King County, Washington, were so frustrated that they decided to disband their ineffective metropolitan planning authority and return its responsibilities to the county government.

. . . .
Local Initiatives

Faced with haphazard development and its accompanying costs, for ward-thinking communities across the country are working to find strategies that will enable them to protect and enhance their distinctive and desirable qualities. Successful communities incorporate many elements—commercial vitality, jobs, good schools, a mix of housing types, adequate transportation systems, and a proper scale for human interaction.

Conventional wisdom holds that constructing new housing, expanding commercial developments, and generating a larger tax base are unmitigated benefits. Recent estimates of real costs and benefits are beginning to demonstrate that growth, especially residential growth, is often a mixed blessing. Traffic congestion, crime, and increased land costs accompany the transformation from rural town to suburbs. Requirements for schools, sewers, roads, and other services add burdens to local budgets. In many cases, especially for residential development, these added services often exceed the revenues from an expanding tax base. A study done for Culpeper, Virginia, showed that for every $1.00 of revenue from residential development, $1.25 was spent on additional county services. Too many local officials see only exclusionary zoning, large single-family lots, and high exaction fees as viable means for developing their communities. These practices add as much as 35 percent, however, to the cost of building a house.

Recent progress in computer simulations and database extrapolation has given local officials an opportunity to foresee and avoid some of these problems. The Institute of Urban and Regional Development of the University of California at Berkeley, for example, has developed the California Urban Futures simulation model to test the spatial impacts of land development policies. The model assembles, manipulates, and displays millions of pieces of information describing land development potential and helps planners and policy makers identify the effects of their decisions on the location, pattern, and density of new development, both in their own jurisdictions and in neighboring areas. The model also projects the demand for residential units in and around every political jurisdiction in the study region; identifies sites where projected residential growth might be allocated, given the existing environmental constraints, the zoning rules, and the carrying capacity of installed infrastructure; estimates future population growth by calculating and mapping the expected profitability from potential residential developments; and determines areas likely to be annexed by nearby cities, based on past annexation practices.

Cost of Sprawl

In Loudoun County, Virginia, officials in 1994 estimated that a new home must sell for at least $400,000 to bring in sufficient property taxes to cover the cost of all the services the county provides. By contrast, the average home sold that year for slightly less than $200,000. The fastest-selling properties in 1995 were town homes averaging between $120,000 and $160,000.

Although one question often raised in view of such scenarios is whether the property tax is the right vehicle for financing local government, another is whether typical development patterns increase the cost of providing services such as roads, sewers, water, and schools. Kevin Kasowski, director of the National Growth Management Leadership Project in Portland, Oregon, asserts, "In fact, the tax revolts that began with Proposition 13 in California, and continue to this day, are an indirect acknowledgment that current patterns and rates of development simply are not sustainable."

Since the Urban Land Institute produced *Effects of Large Lot Size on Residential Development* in 1958, a number of so-called "cost of sprawl" studies have suggested that typical strip development, coupled with large-lot, single-family detached housing built in neighborhoods with features such as culs-de-sac, increases costs in comparison to more compact development that emphasizes mixed-use urban and town center planning. Perhaps the most comprehensive of these studies was the Real Estate Research Corporation's *The Costs of Sprawl: Detailed Cost Analysis*, commissioned in 1974 by the President's Council on Environmental Quality. Others include the American Farmland Trust's *Density Related Public Costs*, in 1986, the DuPage County (Illinois) Regional Planning Commission's *Impacts of Development on DuPage County Property Taxes* in 1991, Rutgers University's *New Jersey Interim State Development and Redevelopment Plan*, in 1993, and, finally, in 1995 a joint study by the Bank of America, California Resources Agency, Greenbelt Alliance, and Low Income Housing Fund, *Beyond Sprawl: New Patterns of Growth To Fit the New California*.

From each of these studies, certain key themes emerge. The 1974 Real Estate Research Corporation study concluded that planned, higher density development not only resulted in lower economic costs and fewer demands on the environment and natural resources but that it also reduced harder to quantify personal and social costs. A 1989 study, *The Costs of Alternative Development Patterns: A Review of the Literature*, by the Urban Land Institute found that providing services to a 3-unit per acre development ten miles from employment and other centers would cost an estimated $8,000 more per house than for a 12-unit per acre development located closer to facilities and offering a mix of town houses, garden apartments, and single-family homes.

Communities that have studied their own growth patterns have reached similar conclusions. In 1988, the Piedmont Environmental Council commissioned *Fiscal Impact of Major Land Uses in Culpeper County, Virginia* and found that "for every dollar of revenue collected from residential land, $1.25 is spent on county services; for every dollar collected from industrial/commercial land, 19 cents is spent on services; similarly, for every dollar collected from farm/forest/open space, 19 cents is spent on services." The DuPage County, Illinois, study found that both residential and nonresidential development resulted in higher taxes—at odds with the common argument that growth improves a community's economy. The American Farmland Trust study of Loudoun County determined that net public costs were approximately three times greater at a density of 1 unit per 5 acres compared with a density of 4.5 units per acre. This, too, seemed to challenge the accepted practice of limiting growth through large lot, tract zoning.

Some research suggests that acquisition of greenbelts and open space, sometimes viewed by community leaders as beyond their budgetary constraints, actually saves municipalities money in the long term. A 1968 study of Closter, New Jersey, found that the town's purchase of 80 acres of open space, if acquired at $500,000, would have equaled its annual tax deficit in 10 years' time had the property been developed according to zoning regulations, which allowed for the construction of 160 homes.

The tool most frequently used in determining the "cost of sprawl" is fiscal impact analysis, which compares the added revenues new development is expected to generate with the increased expenditures required to provide public services. Helen F. Ladd in *Land and Tax Policy*, commissioned by the Lincoln Institute of Land Policy in 1993, reports, "Although widely used by planners for 50 years, fiscal impact analysis is open to many criticisms." Among those she notes are the problems of determining what would happen in the absence of development and calculating the true marginal costs. A more philosophical concern is to what degree and how the cost of providing services to new development should be borne by the entire community as opposed to those directly benefiting from that development.

Ladd also observes that the Real Estate Research Corporation's study, although reporting "significant savings from the local public sector from high-density planned development," fails to account for the fact that higher density "may require more traffic lights and more traffic control officers to achieve a given level of traffic safety or traffic flow."

Some communities charge "impact fees" for services such as roads, sewers and water systems, and schools. Jim Nicholas, a professor of urban planning at the University of Florida, estimates the average impact fee is about $10,000 per single-family home, although it goes as high as $50,000 in some regions of the country. Geographically variable fees and "marginal cost" pricing have been used in communities from Florida to California, although not without controversy. Reports Kasowski, "When officials in Lee County, Florida, proposed a $7,500 'sprawl' surcharge on outlying development, it was met with 'near riots' at a public hearing, with little support even from existing homeowners in central locations, according to Nicholas." Many of those homeowners, a poll showed, were also speculating on land in the outlying regions.

Because variable pricing is so often met with resistance and additionally does not address the environmental and social costs of sprawl, recent studies have sought to look more broadly at quality of life from an economic, environmental, and social perspective. Over a 20-year period, from 1990 to 2010, the New Jersey Interim Development and Redevelopment Plan will not only result in an estimated $1.3 billion in capital costs for infrastructure and $400 million in annual savings to municipalities and schools districts, it also will require almost 130,000 fewer acres than traditional development, in particular resulting in the conservation of productive agricultural and fragile environmental lands (see table 1). A "community life assessment" that looked at housing supply and demand, housing costs, and quality of community life found that, over time, housing costs would be slightly less under the plan due to availability of housing in centers, with the plan calling for more town house and multifamily units, although an average of five out of every eight would still be single-family detached homes.

The latest study, *Beyond Sprawl*, concludes that "unchecked sprawl has shifted from an engine of California's growth to a force that now threatens to inhibit growth and degrade the quality of our life." Observing that a study in the early 1970s concluded "in some cases, a California community would be better off financially if it used a combination of zoning and land acquisition instead of permitting development of low-density subdivisions," *Beyond Sprawl* indicates, "Today, no one in California is unaffected by the costs of sprawl." Among those cited are "hidden" costs to taxpayers of building and maintaining highways and infrastructure, dealing with

Table 1 Robert W. Burchell—New Jersey Impact Assessment: Summary of Impacts for Trend versus Planned Development

Growth/Development Impacts		Trend Development	Planned Development	Trend versus Planned Development Difference	%
I. POPULATION GROWTH	(persons)	520,012	520,012	0	0
II. HOUSEHOLD GROWTH	(households)	431,000	431,000	0	0
III. EMPLOYMENT GROWTH	(employees)	653,6000	653,6000	0	0
IV. INFRASTRUCTURE	($ millions)				
A. Roads		*			
Local		$ 2,197	$ 1,630	$ 567	25.8
State		727	595	132	18.2
Total Roads		$ 2,924	$ 2,225	$ 699	23.9
B. Utilities—Water	($ millions)	$ 634	$ 550	$ 84	13.2
C. Utilities—Sewer	($ millions)	$ 6,790	$ 6,313	$477	7.0
Total Utilities		$ 7,424	$ 6,863	$ 561	7.6
D. Schools	($ millions)	$ 5,296	$ 5,123	$ 173	3.3
E. All Infrastructure	(sum of A-D in $ millions)	$15,644	$14,211	$1,433	9.2
V. LAND CONSUMPTION					
A. Overall Land	(acres)	292,079	117,607	174,472	59.7
B. Frail Lands	(acres)	36,482	6,139	30,343	83.2
C. Agricultural Lands	(acres)	108,000	66,000	42,000	38.9
VI. HOUSE PRICE					
A. Median Cost per Unit	(1990 $)	$172,567	$162,162	$10,495	6.1
B. Housing Index	(higher if more affordable)	118	126	8	6.7

*–millions of 1990 $

Source: Burchell, Robert W., and Listokin, David, "Land, Infrastructure, Housing Costs, & Fiscal Impacts Associated with Growth: The Literature on the Impacts of Traditional versus Managed Growth" (New Brunswick, New Jersey: Center for Urban Policy Research, Rutgers–The State University, 1995. Reprinted with permission.

social problems in neglected neighborhoods, and solving environmental problems. Businesses have suffered because of the reduced quality of life and resistance to further growth and development, as well as higher direct costs and taxes, abandoned investments, and a "geographic mismatch" between workers and jobs. According to the report, the cost of buying and maintaining automobiles, time lost commuting, and the cost of new infrastructure all offset gains for residents in new, safe, and prosperous neighborhoods. By contrast, the central cities and older suburbs have lost jobs, suffered economic segregation, and contain underused investments. In addition, California has lost almost 500,000 acres of productive farmland between 1982 and 1987, 95 percent of its wetlands in the past 200 years, and many of its dramatic landscapes. The report lists the cost of air pollution in the four-county Los Angeles area at $7.4 billion annually, or $600 per resident, while it projects that by the year 2020 "the state will face a water supply deficit of between 2 million and 8 million acre-feet."

Having concluded that collegial approaches bringing together all stakeholders must be embraced to solve California's land use dilemmas and provide for planned growth, *Beyond Sprawl* nonetheless drew criticism from a number of stakeholders who took issue with its substance and the manner in which it was prepared. The California Building Industry Association called it "an effervescence of opinions with little or no basis in fact" and objected even to use of the term "sprawl" to define suburban development patterns. The association rejected the conclusion that these patterns were solely responsible for the "costs of sprawl" cited in the report and contested the assertion that suburban development is prohibitively expensive when compared to urban infill. "In many instances," said the association, "private development costs for dispersed development can be much lower than if development is compelled into urban infill areas. Additionally, if and when an existing infrastructure system is re-tooled, one can expect local antigrowthers to object strenuously to the sizing of the infrastructure to meet future growth."

A separate response by Steven Hayward, research and editorial director of Pacific Research Institute for Public Policy, observed that "there is a large and growing body of urban planning scholarship that calls into serious question most of the conventional wisdom about sprawl." According to Hayward "The most significant findings of this scholarship are that, (1) sprawl may not be as cost-inefficient as supposed; (2) sprawl may actually be more conducive to 'infill' development than deliberately phased, higher density development; and (3) sprawl may actually be reducing— not increasing—traffic congestion." In particular, Hayward says that government data reveal "only about 22 to 25 percent of all vehicle trips in urban areas are commute trips, or even work-related trips." Most of the increased urban and suburban traffic congestion is not related to work trips, raising questions about the "jobs/housing imbalance" concern cited in the report.

Determining the costs, financial and otherwise, of various development patterns clearly remains a contentious subject, loaded with interpretation and misinterpretation. Communities throughout the country are legitimately concerned about how to minimize and fairly assess the costs of growth and development. No growth pattern is without economic, environmental, and social consequences, and, most likely, a definitive "one size fits all" solution will never be found. However, taking a second look at conventional wisdom, whatever that wisdom may be, is well worth the time and expense.

Growth management ordinances and easements are among the devices cities are using to mitigate the negative impacts of development, to protect critical natural and historic resources, and to foster development that enhances local character. The successful efforts of Chattanooga, Portland, Seattle, and other communities stand as useful models.

In these places and elsewhere, a broad array of practical tools has been used to enhance the conviviality, economic well-being, and quality of life of neighborhoods and communities, including conservation easements, transfers of development rights, mixed land uses, requirements for pedestrian access and public transit, incentives for historic preservation, and community development banks. Maryland's affluent Montgomery County, for example, which contains both densely populated suburbs of Washington, D.C., and a large rural reserve, has established a transferable development rights program to channel growth and preserve its remaining rural countryside and agrarian economy. In a "preferential agriculture zone" that totals 89,000 acres, development rights can be purchased for deployment in other areas of the county. Starting in 1980, this agriculture zone was restricted to a density of one unit per 25 acres. Since 1983, more than 4,000 credit transactions have been processed and over 20,000 acres of active farmland have been placed in perpetual easements.

Chicago's Southshore Bank has become a national model for neighborhood financing. For more than two decades, this community institution has been a reliable source of funding for housing, small business, and occupational training. When the bank began in 1973, the Southshore area was looking bleak, development had come to a standstill, housing stock was deteriorating, and community spirit had ebbed. The bank helped turn Southshore around and in 1984 expanded its reach to other Chicago neighborhoods. By the end of 1991, it had financed or leveraged the renovation of 7,716 multifamily housing units in the Southshore area, over 30 percent of the entire stock.

In Texas, the San Antonio Riverwalk has become a defining characteristic, key to the city's success as a tourist center. Among the most visited places in the Lone Star State, this valuable asset was about to become a paved-over underground sewer until city residents voted to raise $30 million in bonds to restore the river's edge. Over the past two decades, historic preservation requirements for Riverwalk areas have grown increasingly stringent. The city carefully controls signs, refuse collection, new construction and renovation, and changes in drainage and gradient. In recent years, by one estimate, the Riverwalk corridor has pumped $1 billion annually into the San Antonio economy.

In Fort Collins, Colorado, after it became clear that the zoning map, adopted in 1929 and updated in 1960, failed to meet the needs of a larger city, planners abandoned traditional zoning in favor of a land use system that allows market forces to work. Instead of strictly segregating uses, the Fort Collins Land Development Guidance System aims only to control the negative effects of growth. No use is automatically ruled out.

Located at the foot of the Rocky Mountains only an hour's drive north of Denver and home to Colorado State University, Fort Collins is a city of 90,000 that retains the atmosphere of a small town. Five miles from shopping centers, fast-food restaurants, and downtown office buildings, cows graze on nearby rangelands. According to a former mayor and planners, Fort Collins is interested in managing the quantity of growth and encouraging quality.

The new development guidance system is based on five principles. First, any land use can be made compatible with any other through good design and appropriate buffering. Second, land use regulations should support private decision making. Third, the city should identify overall goals but let the private sector determine how to meet those goals. Fourth, landscape architecture should be incorporated into the process through incentives. And fifth, consumers are better judges of land uses than are government officials.

A point scheme permits developers to propose any land use on any piece of property, but the developer must meet 46 criteria covering a wide variety of impacts, such as traffic congestion, noise, shadows, pedestrian

The San Antonio Riverwalk is one of the most prominent attractions in Texas. It stands out as a dramatic example of local initiative that capitalized on a community asset to bolster the economy and revitalize downtown. Courtesy of The Conservation Fund, Arlington, Virginia.

convenience, and access to public transportation. The city assigns weights to the scores based on the nature and location of each project. The weighing is further multiplied by a set of government-defined "community goals and aspirations," such as attractive landscaping. Developers can meet the criteria in whatever way best suits their plans and marketing needs.

Most developers prefer Fort Collins' new system because of its predictability. By stressing design quality, the system has also tempered no-growth sentiments. Developers are willing to work within the system as an acceptable trade-off for increased flexibility and certainty. After more than a decade, Fort Collins has yet to be involved in a single land use lawsuit. Tax rates have remained low. Mixed use is now the rule, not the exception, and residents in newly developed sites are almost always within walking distance of retail outlets, offices, and parks or playgrounds. The time devoted to administrative review has been cut to a minimum, as little as three weeks.

· · · · · · · ·

CHAPTER THREE

New Interests Awaken, New Strategies Emerge, New Problems Arise

The land use experience of the past 25 years, as assessed by developments at the state, regional, and local levels, offers encouragement—innovations in some localities, cooperation on a regional level in several parts of the country, pioneering growth management programs in a number of bellwether states. Advances have come in integrating transportation and agricultural policies with land use. Stakeholders in the land use arena have multiplied, with some private conservation interests now having a profoundly positive impact. The strategies with which land use goals have been pursued have broadened. Some of the most noteworthy and innovative strategies, greenway and historic preservation, for example, succeed in part because, when combined in various ways, they result in a synergy that effectively addresses several concerns simultaneously. The news is by no means all positive. Yet there have been some genuine achievements on which to build a better future.

· · · · · · · · ·
New Stakeholders

The dramatic emergence of new stakeholders over the past 25 years, in both the nonprofit and for-profit sectors, has introduced an unusual degree of flexibility and responsiveness to an increasingly complex set of land use issues. In particular, the grassroots expansion of land trust organizations has been extraordinary. Foundations and corporations have increased their involvement in productive efforts, too.

Community by community across America, local land trusts represent a new direction for land conservation. They pull together citizens working to develop common agendas for community land use. The explosion of these local initiatives, with the help of the national umbrella organization, the Land Trust Alliance, is one of the most exciting prospects for the 21st

century. Today, more than 1,100 private land trusts purchase, place ease-
ments on, and manage tracts of land locally for conservation purposes.
This is double the number of a decade earlier, putting land trusts among
the fastest-growing segments of the American conservation movement.
National land trusts and related organizations that work at the local level
include The Nature Conservancy, The Conservation Fund, the Rails-to-
Trails Conservancy, the American Farmland Trust, and The Trust for
Public Land.

Many businesses, recognizing that investments in goodwill have economic consequences, have increased their cooperative efforts with local
government and community organizations to conserve open space, create
recreation opportunities, and protect wildlife habitat, while generating
economic value. DuPont, Tenneco, USX, and Weyerhaeuser, for example,
have begun habitat programs. Since 1983, DuPont has run a wildlife enhancement program on properties that cover 160,000 acres. International
Paper donated 20,200 acres of land in the Adirondacks to New York State
and The Conservation Fund for recreation and wildlife management. This
donation, valued at more than $5 million, represents the largest single gift
of private land in the northern forests. The donated property surrounds

The Jackson Hole Land Trust is one of more than 1,100 land trusts nationwide,
double the number a decade ago, working locally to acquire, protect, and manage
tracts of land for conservation and recreational purposes. Courtesy of Jackson
Hole Land Trust, Jackson, Wyoming.

the Raquette River, a prime waterway for kayaking, canoeing, and fishing.

Corporations support wildlife in other ways as well. DuPont helps underwrite the bald eagle propagation project of the Patuxent Wildlife Research Center. Miller Brewing supports the "Save the Eagle" program. Shell and Mobil have contributed toward the recovery of the Ridley's Sea Turtle in the Gulf of Mexico. Dow Chemical donated $3 million over four years for federal wetland and habitat acquisitions as part of the North American Waterfowl Management Program.

To promote more such voluntary initiatives, The Wildlife Habitat Council, a collaboration between conservationists and corporations, was established in 1987. The council helps corporations enhance their undeveloped lands for the benefit of wildlife, fish, and plant life. This kind of support for conservation is critical because of the vast acreage involved. Of the 2.2 billion acres of land in the United States, more than 1.3 billion are owned privately by 34 million owners, with 5 percent of these landowners, including corporations, owning 40 percent of the acreage. Much of the land held by private owners is well suited for multiple uses, including wildlife conservation, recreation, and other quasi-public purposes.

Transportation

No country in the world rivals America's dependence on automobiles and highways; thus, transportation policy plays a pivotal role in shaping land use. The passage of the Intermodal Surface Transportation Efficiency Act (ISTEA) of 1991 was a seminal achievement, with the promise of enormous benefits for improving the way land is used.

A quarter century ago, transportation was a catalyzing factor in the creation of modern American environmentalism. Activists watched with increasing dismay as interstate highways shattered urban neighborhoods and parks, carved up rural landscapes, obliterated wetlands and scenic vistas, fostered air pollution, and promoted wasteful energy use.

These concerns arrived relatively late in the history of the United States. For many years, the nation's transportation infrastructure was comparatively primitive, having little impact on landforms and watersheds. This situation changed rapidly, however, with the arrival of the locomotive, automobile, airplane, pipeline, and supertanker and their supporting structures, services, and fuels. As the infrastructure for moving

More and more, companies are managing their landholdings with wildlife habitat values in mind. The Wildlife Habitat Council, a collaboration between conservationists and corporate leaders, was created in 1987 to promote this concept. Courtesy of Bob Moore, Thunder Basin Coal Company, Wright, Wyoming.

more and more people and goods grew complex and pervasive, costly, dangerous, and visible polluting by-products accompanied the growth.

With the passage of ISTEA, Congress affirmed for the first time the linkages between transportation and land use planning. Public participation and environmental concerns, including attainment of the Clean Air Act's standards for automobile emissions, have gained much stronger standing. The impact of new transportation facilities on wildlife habitat, wetlands, and other natural resources must be mitigated. Substantial funds are provided for these purposes and for such projects as landscaping and bicycle and pedestrian pathways as well as infrastructure improvements to support new development around urban and town centers and thus preserve open space.

Suburban sprawl and inefficient land use planning are now issues specifically tied into transportation planning. Historic buildings and cultural landscapes must be respected. Compact, transit-oriented design for

Compared to 25 years ago, 85 million more cars are on the road driving twice as many miles. Automobiles, the network of highways and roads on which they travel, and relatively inexpensive gasoline afford Americans unprecedented mobility, which they value highly. Yet the predominantly low-density, auto-dependent developments characteristic of the past 25 years also exact a toll, including time-consuming traffic jams and an unending tug on scarce public dollars to finance costly road extensions and repairs. Courtesy of U.S. Environmental Protection Agency, Washington, D.C.

human settlements is encouraged, as are visual preference surveys that ground aesthetic choice in objective findings.

ISTEA requires state and local governments, through metropolitan planning organizations, to develop comprehensive plans for any transportation projects receiving federal funding. It also encourages coordinated solutions to traffic congestion and gridlock, and requires that the public be afforded opportunities to take part in planning transportation and improvement programs.

In the San Francisco region, the Bay Area Metropolitan Transportation Commission's 1993 Surface Transportation and Congestion Mitigation Project has been cited as a model for planning and public involvement. The $864-million program, which includes $214 million in ISTEA funds, has sparked 225 projects ranging from alternative-fuel buses, bicycle lanes, and park-and-ride lots to freeway service patrols, renovation of a trans-Bay transit tube, intermodal container transfer facilities at ports, system management improvements, and even a day-care facility at a rail transit station. Reaching consensus involved working with stakeholders that included federal, state, regional, and local agencies, regional commuter groups, and representatives from 9 congestion management areas, 9 counties, 100 cities, 24 transit operators, 6 seaport authorities, 11 airports, and an array of groups representing rail, trucking, and community and neighborhood interests, the transportation disadvantaged, and environmental concerns. A large and seemingly unwieldy array—but the results have been effective.

ISTEA authorized $155 billion in funding through fiscal year 1997 for highways and mass transit, including $45 billion for new highways and repairs and $24 billion in the Surface Transportation Program for safety and enhancements. A minimum of 10 percent of state matching funds for the Surface Transportation Program must be dedicated to projects involving historic, environmental, or aesthetic improvements. Although ISTEA has not been fully funded at authorized levels, it has received substantial support and been lauded for its ability to spur comprehensive planning and for the flexibility it grants states and localities in tailoring projects to meet their needs. It stands as one of the most important sources of funding for land-related projects.

How completely the opportunities afforded by ISTEA will be realized depends on how well states and regions embrace the legislation, according to land use expert John DeGrove. He notes that ISTEA is making a considerable difference in South Florida's ability to try to provide for more compact urban growth while protecting and restoring the Everglades and has also helped fund a set of linked greenways throughout the state. Florida has passed its own ISTEA to further strengthen the link between transportation planning and comprehensive planning.

Embracing an open process that fully involves all stakeholders is clearly a key to maximizing ISTEA's potential. As the Bay Area process revealed, success requires a willingness on the part of transportation agencies to change the way they do business by allowing citizens to participate fully in decision making.

. . . .

Greenways

The arrival of the greenway concept is a welcome, bold new planning tool for giving structure to urban growth: It encourages communities to set design standards for development that incorporate linear corridors linking open spaces across the landscape. Greenways were virtually unknown 25 years ago, but gained a big boost in 1987 when the President's Commission on Americans Outdoors called for the creation of a national system of linear greenways for recreation, water quality, and habitat. A related benefit was seen: to give structure to future urban growth.

Greenways are an increasingly popular answer to the growing demand for more natural areas close to home, particularly within and around urban and suburban neighborhoods. They provide recreational opportunities—for walking, biking, jogging, fishing, canoeing, even cross-country skiing and horseback riding. Because they are close to home, they offer a respite from the everyday pressures of urban life. At the same time, they give shelter to native plants and wildlife, protect habitats that might otherwise be lost to development, provide a buffer against soil erosion and runoff, and offer opportunities for humans to interact with the nature around them.

"Greenways can provide a multitude of benefits for people, wildlife, and the economy," says Edward T. McMahon of the Conservation Fund. "They can be publicly owned or established on private land, with the understanding that they are limited to a trail easement, or to protecting a stream or a scenic vista. Greenways are now being built into the design of many new communities, linking homes with recreational facilities, schools, and nearby commercial and office buildings."

Many national conservation organizations are working to create an "emerald necklace" of greenways that crisscross the United States, linking cities, suburbs, and rural areas. For example, The Conservation Fund's American Greenways Program provides technical assistance to states seeking to create networks of green space and small grants to local groups working on greenways projects. The Rails-to-Trails Conservancy has already helped local communities convert more than 7,000 miles of abandoned railway corridors into multipurpose public paths.

Perhaps one reason greenways have become one of the most rapidly growing conservation initiatives is that they also stimulate the economy by providing an array of economic benefits. Numerous studies demonstrate that parks and greenways can increase nearby property values, which in turn increases local tax revenues. Greenways also generate spending by local residents on activities such as bicycling and fishing. Greenways are often major tourist attractions. For example, the San Antonio Riverwalk is one of the leading tourist destinations in Texas. Greenways even provide locations for new business opportunities and figure in corporate relocation decisions.

Hudson River Greenway:
A Regional Success Story

David S. Sampson, Hudson River Valley Greenway Communities Council

The Hudson River Valley Greenway Act of 1991 created a legal structure designed to promote regional connections and cooperation within New York's 10-county, 3-million-acre Hudson River Valley. The act took two existing organizations—the Hudson River Valley Greenway Council and the Heritage Task Force for the Hudson River Valley—and joined them under a new umbrella called the Hudson River Valley Greenway. Both of the existing organizations—now called the Greenway Communities Council and the Greenway Conservancy, respectively—were given a new focus and a new mandate. The Hudson River Valley Greenway is relentlessly bipartisan and has received excellent cooperation from both sides of the aisle in Albany, and from mayors, supervisors, and city managers regardless of political affiliation.

The original Hudson River Valley Greenway Council was created in 1988 to study environmental and economic trends in the Hudson River Valley. After intensive public hearings, it was restructured within the state's executive branch to work with local and county governments to foster a voluntary, regional planning "compact" in the valley. Under the compact, communities are encouraged to design a process for regional decision making about land use, using common planning ideas and criteria. If they do so, they receive financial and procedural incentives unavailable elsewhere in New York State.

At the same time, the state's legislature created the Greenway Conservancy to replace the Heritage Task Force and to assist the valley's communities and organizations in implementing the ideas and projects that arise out of the council-sponsored planning process. The conservancy's main legislative directives are to assist the council in establishing the compact; work with local governments to create a Hudson River Trail system east and west of the river; develop a strategy for the Hudson River Valley to promote itself as a single tourism destination; and work with the agricultural community to promote and protect the industry of agriculture in the Hudson River Valley.

The symbiosis of the council and the conservancy justifies the initial recommendation of the Greenway Study Council, whose efforts guided the enactment of the legislation, to create one organization for planning and the other for project implementation. The two organizations, although separately budgeted and structured, have established a close working relationship and have become integral to the success of each other's programs. The study council chose this path after visiting the California Coastal Conservancy and Coastal Commission and seeing the efficacy of separating planning—and the political questions it sometimes raises—from specific projects such as trails, dockage, and waterways.

To date, the conservancy has assisted the council in initiating a "Model Community" program—a step that will lead to the regional compact envisioned in the legislation. Likewise, the council has participated in the conservancy's development of a strategic plan to help the communities and organizations in the greenway area implement the visions and goals they have identified. What controversy there has been—and it has been centered largely in one community—has involved the greenway idea as a whole and has not been specifically focused on the council or the conservancy.

Both organizations believe that the combination of planning and projects—of visions and the means to attain these visions—has led to early successes within the Hudson River Valley Greenway region. Currently, the council has 10 model community projects under way in the Hudson River Valley involving 23 communities. Several projects embrace more than one community, highlighting the greenway's premise that local political boundaries should not prohibit regional thinking and planning. The greenway's planning process *requires* the creation of a local committee, development of a community planning profile, and subsequent formation of a vision based on several public meetings. One of the keys to the success of the program has been the idea that, as a broad community vision is developed, small, doable physical projects should be identified and implemented to give substance to the planning process.

The model community program has not been without mistakes, leading the Hudson River Valley Greenway's staff to note, "That's why we call them 'model' communities." Initially, for example, too many staff members were sent to local committee meetings, thereby inhibiting each local committee's efforts to assume a life of its own. The greenway also concentrated too much initially on zoning, master plans, and other traditional mechanisms. The local committees, however, wanted to talk about visions for their communities and how specific projects could help achieve them. Thus, zoning issues were moved to the last part of the discussion, not the first.

The Hudson River Valley Greenway also learned early on that, no matter how well intentioned its membership was, there were significant groups—such as the sports and recreation community—who felt they needed direct representation on the council and conservancy.

To date, the greenway council's model community planning process has led, for example, to the total revision of a town master plan (Stuyvesant), development of a specific waterfront strategy (Troy), and creation of a common trail and tourism strategy (Croton and Ossining). Two of the model community cities, Newburgh and Beacon, have developed a cross-river partnership that has incorporated planning, a cross-river "Trail of Two Cities," and proposed reinstitution of ferry service.

As the greenway council's model community planning process has progressed throughout the valley, the Hudson River Greenways Trail, fostered by the conservancy, has reached more than 85 miles and will probably double that amount by the end of 1995. A voluntary, participatory approach similar to that of the model community program is used in each community for trail development. A regional tourism strategy that will seek to take advantage of one of the most historically important areas of the United States is also nearly completed, and includes the establishment of a coalition of 58 historic sites that exist within the greenway area. Many of the representatives of these historic sites had never even met one another before.

Following are three illustrations of the Hudson River Valley Greenway experience:

Catskill (Town and Village, Greene County)

The village and the town of Catskill, adjacent municipalities in Greene County, were designated as one of the model communities in the early part of 1994. Their goal is cooperatively to plan and implement projects that physically and economically improve the area.

The rural outskirts of the town, which ascend into the rugged Catskill Mountains, surround the bustling urbanized village. The combined waterfront of the two municipalities is over nine miles long and culminates at Catskill Point, adjacent to Catskill Creek and the Hudson River in the heart of the village.

A local committee combining citizens from both communities began planning at a public meeting in late 1994. Elements of the committee's draft work plan include reclamation of Catskill Point for recreational uses, adaptive reuse of a large vacant department store, development of a canoe/hiking trail tour, construction of new pocket parks, unification of Main Street, and redevelopment of a deepwater port.

The history of the village and the town of Catskill is of prime importance to local citizens. A preliminary work plan calls for promoting the historical importance of the area, with emphasis on artists and writers such as Thomas Cole and Washington Irving. The two municipalities were set to begin implementation of several projects in the summer and fall of 1995.

Hudson (City, Columbia County)

Hudson, the only city in Columbia County, has over a mile of urban waterfront that citizens want to reclaim for recreation and tourism and tie in with

The economic potential of tourism in the historic Hudson River corridor has sparked cooperation among neighboring communities eager to capitalize on this region's heritage. Courtesy of The Hudson River Valley Greenway Council

Main Street. Toward this goal, a group of over 25 citizens, with support from the local government, initiated the Hudson Vision Plan Task Force in August 1994. The greenway has assisted the task force, now with more than 80 participants, in creating a vision for the revitalization of Hudson's downtown.

The greenway facilitated a series of public meetings, some with over 100 participants, to brainstorm and prioritize planning and project ideas and draft a work plan. Greenway staff also assisted Hudson's task force in successfully securing a grant for $26,000 to fund this process. The work plan calls for retaining existing business and enticing new tourism business opportunities, creating new cultural programs, adding and improving community gardens and pocket parks, and linking these elements together with a system of public parks, trails, and signage.

Hudson's Vision Plan Task Force is now beginning work with a consultant to study potential markets, develop design criteria, and implement projects that will help to realize the collective downtown and waterfront vision. It expects to have a completed vision and implementation plan before 1996.

Stuyvesant (Town, Columbia County)

The town of Stuyvesant is the first rural community to participate in the model community planning program. Stuyvesant has over nine miles of riverfront. Agriculture is the primary land use in the area, accounting for much of the town's natural character.

Through a 16-member volunteer committee, the town has used

$30,000 of greenway council funds to inventory and analyze its natural and cultural resources and develop a comprehensive land use plan based on retention of agriculture as the chief goal. The planning process drew intense public participation through a series of townwide meetings, workshops, and surveys, culminating in the public support necessary for official adoption and implementation of the plan.

As a direct result of the greenway's technical assistance, Stuyvesant received a $3,000 award from the Rural New York Planning Program and has been chosen to receive over $200,000 from the federally funded ISTEA Enhancement Program (see discussion elsewhere in this book) to rehabilitate the historic Stuyvesant Railroad Station. The Greenway Conservancy also has facilitated meetings—and accomplished a settlement—between the town and state agencies to give local residents a voice on proposals to increase public access to the Hudson River over active railways and across state land. This outcome led the Columbia County *Independent* to write: "[I]t was the local Greenway Waterfront Committee and the (Hudson River) Greenway that were there every step of the way over the past few years toward a solution. The Greenway's unique status gave it the standing needed to bring the state agencies into line with local objectives." Stuyvesant Town Supervisor Granci made the following simple, but supportive, assessment: "They've done a tremendous job living up to their legislation."

Among the country's notable greenways is the Cuyahoga Valley National Recreation Area, which follows the route of the historic Ohio and Erie canals from Lake Erie to Zoar, Ohio. The Ohio and Erie Canal Corridor Coalition has built a greenway that extends 22 miles down the Cuyahoga River Valley from the national recreation area to Cleveland, Akron, and Canton, Ohio. The C & O Canal Greenway stretches nearly 200 miles along the historic canal abutting the Potomac River, from Washington, D.C., to Cumberland, Maryland, providing resource conservation and outdoor recreation.

Greenways are about connectivity. In recent years, as the landscape has become increasingly fragmented, the importance of creating and protecting linear corridors through public-private partnerships has become more important for conservation and recreation purposes. Greenways often follow rivers, streams, and other natural features and link nature reserves, parks, cultural features, and historic sites with each other and with populated areas. Some greenways are open to visitors; others are not. Some appeal to people; others attract wildlife. Few conservation initia-

Virtually unknown 25 years ago, today greenways are an increasingly important part of the community planner's toolkit. Lafayette Moraga Trail in California and similar linear corridors provide Americans with growing access to open spaces and wildlands for a variety of purposes, while at the same time helping define the boundaries of urban areas. Courtesy of East Bay Regional Park District, California.

tives can match the ecological, economic, and quality-of-life benefits that flow from greenways. They provide Americans with access to open spaces and wildlands for the widest possible variety of outdoor activities.

In cities and suburbs, greenways encompass natural or built features that can be managed primarily for resource conservation, recreation, or nonmotorized transportation. In the country, greenways are planned natural corridors linking large natural areas such as state parks, forests, or wildlife refuges. Rural greenways preserve habitats and wildlife migration routes and often provide impetus to restore environmentally valuable landscapes. In conjunction with existing and proposed recreational trails, such as the National Scenic Trail System, rural greenways will form the heart of America's green infrastructure in years to come.

. . . .
Historic Preservation

Historic preservation safeguards physical links to the past. It is through these links that memory of the enduring community is preserved and passed on to succeeding generations. Modern life tends to subvert

memory. The bulldozer relentlessly obliterates points of reference in both
cities and rural landscapes. Without anchors for memory, retention of the
past becomes difficult. Congress recognized this principle in the National
Historic Preservation Act of 1966: "The historical and cultural foundations of the nation should be preserved as a living part of our community
life and development in order to give a sense of orientation to the American people." Over the past 25 years, historic preservation has made good
on this mission, helping to improve the use of land and the quality of life
Americans enjoy.

Jacksonville, Florida, is home to a project that may become a national
model for rejuvenating a depressed neighborhood without destroying the
existing urban fabric. The area now designated as the Springfield Historic
District is plagued by vacant lots, crime, drugs, deteriorating infrastructure, prostitution, and the problems associated with a high ratio of ab-
sentee landlords. There are nearly 200 vacant buildings in the 140-block
neighborhood. Most of the occupied housing is in disrepair. The area is a
microcosm of the problems that have vexed the nation's cities for decades.
It is also a collection of underused assets.

Fortunately, Springfield still has abundant housing stock worthy of rehabilitation; its surprisingly gracious, tree-lined streets are close to the
downtown core. In its heart, one can still trace the outlines of another age,
where climate, old social and economic arrangements, and the terrain itself combined to determine the pace of life and the shape of buildings and
communities.

The Springfield Historic District Revitalization Strategy, announced in
1991, seeks to reinvigorate Florida's largest designated historic neighborhood with housing and employment opportunities and, at the same time,
avoid gentrification and the dispersal of current residents. A five-year plan
called for $6.6 million in public and private funding during the first two
years, over half as loans from Jacksonville's banking, insurance, and other
financial sectors. Some of the leaders of business and civic organizations
lived in Springfield as children, and their memories of those times are still
vivid.

Jacksonville is working in partnership with the National Trust for Historic Preservation. Chartered in 1949, the National Trust, with more than
240,000 individual and 4,500 organizational members, is the largest historic preservation organization in the United States. It is the umbrella, the
switchboard, the attorney, the advisor, the library, and the coordinating
body for thousands of state and local groups in all 50 states. In just 15

years, these preservation groups have reclaimed more than 21,000 historic buildings and spurred a private sector investment of nearly $14 billion. Since passage of the 1986 Tax Reform Act and its rules on passive activity that limit investor benefits, however, the pace of rehabilitation has slowed considerably.

The National Trust sees Springfield as a model for reviving attractive neighborhoods and retaining their multiracial, multi-income character. The Springfield story reveals a strategy at work—seeking out a wide diversity of partners, brokering the many interests that converge on such an effort, and using unique position and prestige to tackle tough problems. In this process, the most important leverage is bringing isolated and sometimes hostile groups and individuals together to build a community. The whole becomes far more than the sum of its parts. The Springfield experience also exemplifies the broadened perspective of historic preservation, which has shifted from a focus solely on protecting architectural gems to a concern for context, settings, and neighborhoods.

The National Trust's involvement with land use issues dates to the 1970s when it developed its Main Street Program to work with small communities in revitalizing downtowns that were losing business to suburban malls. Despite the program's success—commercial districts in more than 1,000 communities have been revived—leaders of the preservation movement decided that an even larger effort was needed to get at the root of the problem. Thus, the National Trust placed the entire state of Vermont on its 1993 list of "America's 11 Most Endangered Historic Places." Suburban sprawl has been testing that state's commitment to the preservation of its cohesive small towns and countryside. The leadership of the National Trust has gradually expanded horizons to encompass as well the preservation of historic landscapes—Civil War battlefields, for example.

The historic preservation movement has shown that memory—particularly local memory—can serve as both a common ground and a catalyst for the rebuilding of communities. Common interest in the past becomes common ground for the present.

· · · · · · · ·

New Designs for Communities and Neighborhoods

America's small towns are more than charming anachronisms. They are a model for how American communities and neighborhoods, even to some extent in the cores of metropolitan areas, could grow in the future. Across

In the Springfield Historic District, of Jacksonville, Florida, old historic homes serve as an anchor for neighborhood rejuvenation, which stresses housing and employment opportunities for the people who live there. Photo by Judy Davis and David Vedas. Courtesy of Planning and Development Department, Jacksonville, Florida.

America, small towns built to human scale with homes and shops and schools in close proximity still rest like jewels in their pastoral setting.

Originally settled in 1733, the tightly knit village of Waterford, Virginia, along with its encircling 1,420 acres, is now a National Historic Landmark that shelters some 300 residents. Visitors speak of a timeless sense of well-being as they stroll along narrow streets or gaze at working farms on neighboring ridges. By retaining the integrity of its scale and setting, Waterford has become an important anchorage for understanding the American experience.

Nevertheless, Waterford is hardly ripe for retirement. As a model, Waterford's true value derives from the simple fact that it is still a real community whose residents work hard, raise children, trade gossip, argue politics, and enjoy a strong sense of place. With its roots firmly grounded in the traditional patterns of American life, Waterford embodies the continuing presence of the past—and the importance of keeping it.

Metropolitan Growth Patterns—A Homebuilder's Perspective

W. Joseph Duckworth, President, Realen Homes, Ambler, Pennsylvania

Since the end of World War II, new housing in America has been almost entirely suburban in character, consuming more ground per home than ever in our history, resulting in what many refer to as "sprawl." There are economic, political, and technological reasons that made this sprawl possible, even inevitable. The following discussion looks at the role of the entrepreneurial developer—the implementer of change that in turn has driven many more fundamental changes in America.

In the 1950s rising incomes supported by federal policy (for example, the Federal Housing Administration, the interstate highway system, cheap gasoline) permitted, even encouraged, middle class Americans to leave the cities and establish new lives on the surrounding farmlands. These people were moving in pursuit of the American dream: each family's right to its own home on its own lot. Homebuilders, exemplified by Levitt and Sons, developed highly efficient methods of production to meet this market demand. They worked within local jurisdictions that encouraged this activity as "progress"—a central theme of the era.

Homebuilders then and now are "change agents," working within the rules of the system with a goal of creating profits while minimizing risk. They are above all responsible to their financial investors to survive in a business of an extraordinary cyclical nature; the homebuilding cycle of boom and bust is often characterized by 50 percent declines from peak to trough nationally, with local markets often being even more severe. This compares to the general economy, where a 5 percent decline in GNP is considered a severe recession. As a result, builders must minimize all risks to maintain their businesses. Even so, many fail. Each recession causes failure among builders in numbers just below those of restaurateurs.

As profit-oriented entrepreneurs, homebuilders seek opportunities to meet market needs in the shortest time, with the least capital commitment possible. This orientation leads them to exist within the rules of zoning and other codes of local municipalities rather than attempting to change those codes. Most suburban codes favor single-family homes on large lots, which points an arrow toward the easiest and most profitable course to follow. A builder who attempts something different (for example, a "traditional neighborhood design," or "open space subdivision") risks extensive time delays and substantial expense, which may never be recovered in the marketplace. As a result, builders tend to do the conventional type of subdivisions all of us know, ones that have little market risk and are the easiest to get approved.

The public sector writes these rules of land use. Builders create their subdivisions within these rules. Each operates within its own limited, often short-term, self-interests. If our current land use patterns do not please us, we as citizens must change the rules. But this is not an easy process, because local land use controls are the outgrowth of the short-term vision of existing residents and property owners. Existing residents at the developing edge of suburbia often encourage planning for large-lot single-family homes with several thoughts in mind.

First, large lots are rural in nature and thus are in keeping with the area's historical character.

Second, large lots are expensive to develop. This assures that expensive housing will be built and improve the property value of existing homes. It also ensures economic segregation at a finely grained level—the $150,000 homes are separated from the $200,000 ones.

Third, because large lots are expensive to develop, the immediate pressure to develop in the area may be delayed until less expensive areas are exhausted. This delay is considered a victory by many residents who are trying to avoid all growth. However, when growth does occur, it will be of the most land-consumptive nature because large lots have been codified into law.

Large landowners also encourage large-lot single-family zoning, because there is a proved market for the resulting lots. Open space protection is anathema to these owners if there is no compensation for the value they would otherwise have with large-lot conventional zoning.

To achieve a better growth pattern, a longer view is necessary. Civic leaders must project the future of their communities with at least a 20- to 30-year horizon. They must decide what they wish their communities to be in the future, not just allow them to grow piecemeal under codes developed to protect short-term interests. This takes political wisdom and courage, because the future has no active constituency.

Consumers in the United States, enamored of the American dream of owning a single-family home, have displayed their consistent desire for detached homes. Planners' efforts often have ignored this fundamental desire. The Utopian cities of Mies Van de Rohe and Frank Lloyd Wright included visions of residents living in high-rise towers on common plazas. With rare exceptions in a few urban areas, American consumers have rejected this model when given the choice. Those without choice have demonstrated the failure of these models in public housing towers. We must therefore understand what consumers will choose when offering alternatives. Planners are irrelevant if the market won't support their ideas.

Two alternatives to conventional large-lot zoning have been proposed to reduce the impact of sprawl: "traditional neighborhood design" and "open space subdivisions" (sometimes known as cluster development). These are interesting concepts. They are principally single family in nature, thus having potential market acceptability, yet offer social and/or environmental advantages over conventional zoning. They are not new concepts; planners have offered them for years. But they comprise a statistically insignificant part of new development.

A developer who wishes to create something nonconventional must overcome regulatory and institutional barriers. Traditional zoning codes typically prohibit nonconventional development patterns, and, if allowed as an alternate use, they are only permitted after a costly and problematic conditional use process. Lengthy and numerous hearings result in delay and expense not found in conventional large-lot approvals. Local codes, for example, are replete with traffic engineering requirements for wide expensive streets and turnarounds that only a fire chief could love. These requirements are antithetical to either traditional neighborhood design or open space subdivisions, which seek less heavy-handed improvements (roads, curbs, and sewers are known in the trade as "improvements" to the land). But few builders have the stomach or the resources to try to convince local authorities to overrule "experts" who are trained to create roads friendly to cars and trucks but unfriendly to people. Before World War II, streets were designed for walking and living; since then, they have been designed only to move traffic. Those delightful small towns and villages that many of us cherish, with their mixed housing types and small shops responsive to residents' needs, are outlawed by modern zoning. They were often built before zoning existed at all. It is noteworthy that the most heralded new community of the last decade, Seaside, was built in a jurisdiction without a municipal zoning code.

Developers of nonconventional communities face another hurdle—that of the financial sector. Ordinary subdivisions are proved in the marketplace and thus win the favor of lenders. Any unusual project must raise more equity and pay higher borrowing rates because the presumed risk of failure is higher. Thus, most rational builders will favor the conventional route.

Local authorities unsatisfied with the current pattern of development should proactively change their codes to permit the types of development they wish to see in the future. If traditional neighborhood design or open space subdivisions are desired, they must be encouraged with a stream-lined process of approval that provides an advantage over conventional subdivision. The codes must be in place before the developer appears. If the codes are created only when a developer is on the horizon, delay and poor codes are the most likely outcome. Only the most public-spirited and/or foolish of developers will enter into that process. The prudent developer will check the existing rules of the municipality and then build accordingly. The result? The sprawl that many of us detest.

In the housing market, many people speak about the need to preserve open space and community character. But little is done to effect change where it must originate, with zoning codes. My company recently pur-chased a large site in the path of development with hopes of building an open space subdivision, conserving over 50 percent of the land. However, the tract is zoned for one-acre lots. After several months of discussion, we are making little progress toward a new code. My proposal for an open space subdivision is greeted with skepticism: Is this a better plan for the community, or just a way to make more money for the developer? Sadly, we are likely to take the only legal route permitted and build the one-acre sub-division. We are in the business of building. If sprawl is the only building pattern feasible, then we will be a part of it.

As a citizen, I sit on my county's planning commission and attempt to create zoning codes that I hope will result in a better pattern of growth. Only if all of us as citizens actively participate will the pattern improve. It is not the responsibility of the homebuilders of America to change the rules of development. That is the job of the civic leaders of each community. Builders will create what the market and the codes demand. We will all be affected by the result.

The new urbanists, a school of architects and planners who first ap-peared in the early 1980s, believe that the conviviality and efficiency of traditional communities like Waterford are both accessible to the design professions and portable to new locations. Also known as the neotradi-tionalists, this school borrows the evolutionary logic of vernacular settle-ments to undergird their designs for intentional communities. Their ideas echo the work of William H. Whyte, who followed his classic treatise on 1950s suburban America, *The Organization Man*, with the visionary, *Cluster Development* (1964), which promoted the concept embodied in the title: Put the same number of houses on a portion of the tract but leave the bulk of the land for open space and recreation. The new urbanists are finding a niche amidst mounting discontent with the suburban development of the post-World War II era. In essence, they advocate a return to tradition by building new developments in compact, close-knit patterns to foster walking and social interaction.

The first commandment of the new urbanism is that human settlements should be designed to fit the pace and scale of the human being, not the appetites of the automobile. Communities should be compact and convenient, oriented toward the requirements of pedestrians and public transportation.

Open space should primarily be common space, arranged in squares, parks, and playgrounds—the places where neighbors can gather for casual conversation, idle leisure, and public events. This dictum leads to what one urban designer describes as "space-making" rather than "space-occupying" development. In other words, the buildings of a viable community should have, in addition to their central functions, the ancillary purpose of helping to frame its public spaces.

The new urbanists believe the best land use is a mosaic of mixed uses. In their designs, the venues of work, play, sleep, commerce, and civic life are closely juxtaposed and interwoven. Large front lawns are discouraged. Front porches are celebrated. Energy efficiency is imperative. Housing is diverse: detached homes, town houses, multifamily dwellings, and even single rooms perched atop garages on back alleyways, also called granny flats, are encouraged.

Wherever possible, the natural terrain, drainage, and vegetation are preserved. Streets are narrow and usually arrayed in grids, with on-street parking to discourage high-speed traffic. Trees planted between streets and sidewalks provide shade and beauty.

These design preferences of the new urbanists have been supported by visual preference surveys, which are slide presentations that can be used as part of the planning process to elicit public responses to various design options. Visual preference surveys of over 100,000 people in 80 different communities have found that most people do not like "cookie cutter" subdivisions, front yards dominated by driveways, house fronts dominated by garage doors, wide streets, conventional multifamily projects, strip commercial development, and boxlike, off-the-shelf commercial architecture. Most people prefer human- and pedestrian-scale development, narrow streets with sidewalks and shade trees, community greenspace, corner stores and "Main Street" commercial areas, and front porches. Most people will accept higher density development (if designed properly) closer setbacks than most suburban zoning allows, narrower lots than most suburban zoning allows, rear garage doors with access from alleys, and a mix of housing types in close proximity.

The visual preference survey has become a highly effective tool to achieve agreement on how a community wishes to develop its land and has demonstrated that a considerable amount of consensus exists on a vision for the future. Walter Cudnohufsky, a landscape architect and planner, observes, "As participants and sometime organizers of planning activity, we must more fully account for, and discover, the often hidden community of needs, intents, desires, values, perceptions, and places. Without succeeding at this important task, citizens will continue to be disenfranchised from their true authority and power as community decision-makers."

George and Vicky Ranney, a bold planning team based in the Midwest, understand this principle. Prairie Crossing, an innovative housing project now under construction in Grayslake, Illinois, demonstrates how real estate developments can be designed to conserve land and nurture environmental values. Growing out of the vision of the late business executive Gaylord Donnelly and his wife Dorothy, this 317-unit project, located on a 667-acre site 45 miles from Chicago, is expected to prove itself in the market by quickly recovering its original investment.

A conservation easement donated to The Conservation Fund protects 60 percent of the site as permanent open space. A large farm will supply fresh food to residents and tie down a scenic vista. Each home, designed to cut energy consumption by 50 percent from the typical house, based on the traditions of regional farmhouses, and priced from $189,900 to $399,900, will have easy access to more than 10 miles of trails connected to nearby schools, stores, restaurants, and commuter stations. Native prairies and wetlands will be restored. Historic buildings will provide a sense of place.

As a general rule, it is still difficult to replicate towns like Waterford in all of their detailed splendor or to construct new communities like Prairie Crossing. Ironically, the American system of land use controls has gradually become so complex that it is now prohibitively expensive and cumbersome to develop old and new sites in the image of the traditional American community. Equally important, traditional approaches to financing development often discourage innovation in community design. The path of least resistance leads directly to the kind of bland suburb that has spread throughout the country.

There may be better times ahead, however. The concepts of the new urbanists are just now being tested in the marketplace. It is still too early to say whether the appeal of neotraditionalism will remain a small niche

A relatively new technique, visual preference surveys suggest what people like and do not like about community design. They have been used in 80 communities and with more than 100,000 people. Results indicate that most people prefer a pedestrian scale, narrow streets with sidewalks and shade trees, community greenspace, and front porches, among other features, and do not especially like front yards dominated by driveways or garage doors and strip commercial development. Photo by Joseph Molinaro. Courtesy of National Association of Homebuilders, Washington, D.C.

Prairie Crossing, in Grayslake, Illinois, is one of a new breed of housing developments that promotes compact neighborhood design, land conservation, energy efficiency, and other environmental values. Courtesy of Prairie Holdings Corporation.

serving a limited market or whether it will eventually flower as a populist revolt against the prevailing patterns of postwar development. Nevertheless, the new concepts are beginning to capture the enthusiasm of an energetic vanguard of developers and local land use officials.

. . . .

Farmlands

Despite mounting evidence showing clear economic benefits to farmland protection, many local and regional governments continue to encourage development and investment patterns that consume these productive lands (see figure 5). Encroachments that threaten farmland also threaten other values: open space and the culture of rural life, air quality, employment opportunities, and equitable taxes.

One of the most fertile agricultural areas in America, the Central Valley of California, is also one of the most threatened. Increasingly, California farmers are feeling severe growth pressures because of population increases and urban expansion. Over the next 50 years, California's population will double to 60 million, with much of that growth taking place in the Central Valley, currently the source of more than 250 agricultural commodities, including year-round supplies of fruits and vegetables, poultry, dairy products, and many specialty items. The economy of the

Billions of Acres

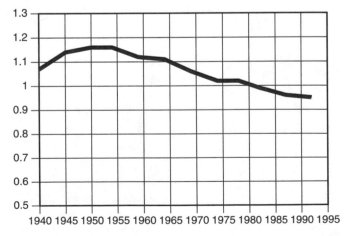

FIGURE 5 Farmlands in the United States, 1940 to 1992. *Source:* U.S. Bureau of the Census, *Historical Statistics of the United States: Colonial Times to 1970 (1976); Census of Agriculture for 1992* (1994); and earlier census reports.

valley revolves around agriculture: For every dollar earned on the farm, four to six dollars of related goods or services are produced.

In recent years, favorable location, climate, and cost of living have attracted increasing numbers of urban dwellers to the Central Valley. During the 1980s, population increased by 33 percent, or three times the national average. Low land prices, existing agricultural infrastructure, open space amenities, and housing prices as much as 50 percent lower than in the San Francisco Bay area contribute to a constant stream of development. Banks, government and insurance agencies, and high-tech firms have relocated to the valley.

Residential and commercial growth diminished the amount of Central Valley land in farm production by 616,000 acres during the 1980s. This loss to suburbanization has contributed to a reduction in agricultural services in the region and a corresponding increase in the costs of land, taxes, and such residential services as schools and police. The farmers who still cultivate the urban fringe suffer rising business costs and increasing incentives to sell land for development.

Urban development has intensified air, water, and soil pollution in the valley, thus further degrading crop production and enlarging the

One of the most fertile agricultural areas in the United States, California's Central Valley is also one of the most threatened by population growth—a one-third increase during the past decade, three times the national average. With more growth projected, California is struggling to protect agriculture in the valley. Courtesy of the Department of Water Resources, California Resources Agency, Sacramento, California.

competition for scarce water resources. On an average day, over 1,000 tons of nitrogen oxide and hydrocarbons are emitted, contributing to a projected loss of over $333 million in valuable agricultural crops annually. Increasing urbanization will exacerbate these problems by increasing the number of automobiles and thus the amount of auto emissions. Urban water use is projected to increase 1.6 million acre-feet between 1985 and 2010, and, with viable sources at a premium, this demand will be met at the expense of agricultural users.

The American Farmland Trust recently estimated that in 12 critical farming districts—areas of significant production that confront intense growth pressures—some 3 million acres of farmland were converted to other uses during the 1980s. These data contradict conventional wisdom, which insists that the rural land lost to metropolitan development is of marginal utility to the farm economy. The U.S. Department of Agriculture's (USDA's) latest Census of Agriculture shows that urban edge agriculture generates 56 percent of gross U.S. agricultural sales, including more than 86 percent of the country's fruit and vegetables, 80 percent of its dairy production, and 45 percent of its meat and poultry. Suburban sprawl poses serious threats to this rich, specialized farm belt.

The American Farmland Trust also estimates that the United States converts to other uses about 2 million acres of farmland annually, much of it on the edge of urban America. The USDA National Resources Inventory found that developed land increased by 14 million acres between 1982 and 1992. This increase came from conversion of about 6 million acres of pastureland, 10 million acres of rangeland, and nearly 40 million acres of cropland. In 1992, developed land totaled 92.4 million acres, nearly 5 percent of the U.S. land base.

Agricultural policy is shifting, albeit gradually, to meet concerns evident in the Central Valley and other farm communities. In the past, agricultural subsidies, amounting to federal outlays of $30 million per day, encouraged farmers to maximize short-term yields at the expense of a long-term commitment to the land. Farmers were induced to excessive use of pesticides and fertilizers. Rational crop rotations and other erosion control practices were not encouraged. As a result, farming is the leading cause of soil and groundwater pollution and is responsible for over 75 percent of wetlands losses. Today, old subsidy programs are being replaced by programs that are better adapted to the environment.

The 1985 Farm Bill established the Swampbuster Program to restrict farming in wetland areas. It also called on farmers to develop erosion control plans. By 1992, some 1.5 million farmers had submitted conservation

The U.S. Department of Agriculture's National Resources Inventory found that, between 1982 and 1992, 14 million acres of crop, forest, range, and pasture lands were developed in the United States. Many of these acres lay at the edge of expanding urban America. To preserve these productive lands, new strategies, programs, and partnerships will be needed. Courtesy of American Farmland Trust, Washington, D.C.

plans to the Soil Conservation Service. When these plans, covering 132 million acres of farmland (about 30 percent of total U.S. acreage in cultivation), are fully implemented, they should reduce erosion by an estimated 700 million tons per year.

The 1990 Farm Bill added a Wetland Reserve Program that provided easements and financial incentives for farmers willing to preserve and restore wetlands. (This program is modeled on the Conservation Reserve Program, which has enrolled more than 800,000 acres of degraded or converted wetlands.) Also under the 1990 Farm Bill, the Farmers Home Administration (FmHA) became responsible for reviewing lands obtained through foreclosure and placing easements on lands deemed valuable for conservation. FmHA had placed 110,000 acres into easement as of 1993, authorized the transfer of 95,000 acres of land in fee title to the U.S. Fish and Wildlife Service and other federal and state agencies, and recommended another 200,000 be placed in easement.

Virtually all states have programs aimed at preserving farmland, typically involving some form of preferential tax treatment. Yet according to the USDA, property taxes nationwide now cost farmers as much as seed, fuel, or pesticides. In 1992, USDA's most recent survey, agricultural property taxes nationwide climbed an additional 3 percent.

In the early 1990s, Omaha, Nebraska, attempted to relieve this problem by shifting the cost of local government services from the property tax to an income tax. But *Top Producer* magazine in 1995 quoted one Nebraska farmer as saying that his property taxes "have already crept back up to what they were—and now we have higher income taxes as well." In Wisconsin, with an average tax of $2.15 per $100 of market value for farm real estate (second only to Michigan), one farmer who also happens to be a former state agriculture secretary pays $20,500 in property taxes for his 543-acre farm, an equivalent of $37.75 per acre, about $20 per acre more than farmers in the adjoining states of Minnesota and Iowa.

In sum, although state programs do provide some incentive for continued farming, none seems to insure permanent protection, and a broader mix of tools and incentives is necessary to keep productive farmlands in agricultural use.

•   •   •   •   •   •   •   •

Affordable Housing

Still poorly understood by the general public is the significant influence of growth patterns over the last 25 years on the availability of affordable housing and jobs, on the widening social divisions between inner cities and suburbs, and on the weakening physical quality and integrity of communities. Charles C. Geisler, professor of rural sociology at Cornell University, contends that "the omission of land from discussions of poverty is a serious oversight." Both public and private land use policies, he argues, have significant implications for lower-income households.

Home ownership continues to be an elusive goal for many Americans. In 1995, the U.S. Department of Housing and Urban Development (HUD) launched a national campaign with the goal of raising the proportion of American households owning their home. Home ownership rates, which grew from 44 percent of all households in the late 1940s to 65 percent in 1980, have remained steady over the past decade. The HUD campaign is designed particularly to increase home ownership among lower-income populations and people of color. Just over 40 percent of African-American and Latino households own their homes, according to a 1995 HUD task force, which prepared the National Homeownership Strategy. The task force identified 100 actions to boost home ownership, among them encouraging construction of small starter homes and overcoming resistance to mobile homes.

Why has affordable housing remained such an elusive goal for so many Americans? Why have home ownership rates stabilized? Opinions vary. Some experts say that the major obstacle to home ownership is the widening gap between income and housing prices, with the average price of a residential lot having increased 813 percent, from $5,200 in 1969 to $42,300 in 1989. Incomes have hardly kept pace. State and local governments, say some experts, can help reduce the cost of new housing by eliminating so-called "snob zoning" laws that require large lot sizes for homes in suburban enclaves. Another factor contributing to housing costs is residential road standards that require wide widths in new subdivisions, in some cases adding as much as $9,000 to the price of a new home.

Most experts agree that public sector initiatives alone cannot solve the housing dilemma. Instead, a vigorous public-private partnership offers the most promising solution. In 1993, the Neighborhood Reinvestment Corporation launched a five-year campaign to develop 10,000 homes for low- and moderate-income families through a network of more than 180 nonprofit organizations in 150 cities. The campaign is based on three principles: First, a sound home ownership program must address an entire neighborhood or block. Second, counseling potential home buyers results in much greater success. Third, partnerships—among lenders, local businesses, government agencies, and nonprofits—are required to get a program off the ground and provide flexible yet secure loans. Having spurred approximately $200 million in local reinvestment in 1992, the network set a goal to triple its assistance over the course of the campaign.

The city of Louisville, Kentucky, offers one example of how a partnership of government, business, community organizations, and higher education institutions is working to revitalize one of the nation's poorest neighborhoods. In the Russell district, 79 percent of the 10,000 residents had incomes below the poverty level in 1990; 90 percent were female-headed; yearly household income averaged $4,800. In addition, half the population was on public assistance of some kind, while about 65 percent were unemployed. Under the new partnership, 350 affordable housing units will be built or renovated, creating 400 jobs and bringing in about $18 million in new investment to the neighborhood. One in ten Russell residents will benefit from the project.

The mayor of Louisville and the director of the Housing and Neighborhood Development Strategies program at the University of Louisville credit "unique team effort" as the source of the project's success. Already, they say, the neighborhood is "undergoing a dramatic rebirth" and point out that the crime rate has been cut almost in half.

The Russell neighborhood of Louisville offers an example of how government, business, community organizations, and the University of Louisville are working in partnership on a broad-based strategy—involving jobs, education, crime reduction, and community services—to revitalize one of the city's poorest sections for the benefit of people living there. Photo by Melissa Barry. Courtesy of the Russell Urban Renewal Project, Louisville, Kentucky.

Moreover, the team approach focuses on a broad range of issues—case management, job training, education, home ownership, community leadership, and community design services. Locally driven, the effort is funded by HUD and the U.S. Department of Education with matching local support. The city government has provided millions in infrastructure improvements; the private sector is providing affordable housing loans; and developers have agreed to build single-family, cottage-style homes. The university is providing planning and design services, and a broad array of community groups has offered leadership and training expertise. Indeed, the Louisville experience underscores an important point: It may not be home ownership per se but overall neighborhood improvement that is essential to breaking the cycle of poverty and despair.

•   •   •   •   •   •   •   •

Assessing Environmental Impacts

Recognizing the effects of pollution on human and overall ecological health, the nation's lawmakers in the late 1960s and early 1970s embarked on an aggressive program. Over the next two decades, starting with passage of the National Environmental Policy Act of 1969 and continuing with the Clean Air Act, Clean Water Act, Endangered Species Act, Surface Mining Control and Reclamation Act, Coastal Zone Management Act, Superfund, and other laws, the federal government has acquired the means to force municipalities and private industries to reduce and treat pollution discharges, assess the environmental impact of industrial development, restore lands degraded by mining and oil drilling, and dispose of hazardous waste.

The country has much to show for the hundreds of billions of dollars spent to improve the environment. The air in American cities is significantly cleaner than it was 25 years ago; important bodies of water show signs of improvement—advances that have come even as the nation's economy has grown substantially during the same period. Today, the U.S. economy is unquestionably greener than it was a quarter century ago. The most energetic, successful, and competitive enterprises now increasingly try to prevent pollution before it causes problems and to improve energy efficiency.

One of the linchpins of these dramatic achievements has been the National Environmental Policy Act (NEPA). Although not directly linked to land use planning, NEPA has considerable influence on the way that federal agencies and federally funded or approved projects deal with land. Before the act was passed, agencies focused largely on the costs and technical feasibility of proposed projects, from highway construction and nuclear testing to timber harvesting and cattle grazing. Since NEPA's passage, agencies must also consider significant environmental impacts of their actions. These actions cover a variety of programs that directly affect the development of urban areas—community development block grants, Economic Development Administration grants, transportation projects, and the like. Although the act does not require the selection of less environmentally damaging alternatives, it does result in more informed decision making through the preparation of an environmental impact statement.

After 25 years and some 30,000 draft and final environmental impact statements, how well has NEPA fulfilled its purpose and expectations? The President's Council on Environmental Quality (CEQ), created by NEPA to ensure federal agencies' compliance with the act, conducted a study of NEPA's effectiveness, canvasing the law's authors, federal and state officials, Native American tribes, academicians, and businesses, to assess its success. Their consensus was that NEPA's most important contribution has been opening up federal decision making to the public in a manner unlike any other environmental statute. Through scoping meetings, public hearings, and other vehicles, the process has given states and localities, nonprofit organizations, and developers and private citizens the opportunity to comment formally on proposed projects.

Some critics disparage NEPA for being procedural rather than substantive. Others point to a need to coordinate the environmental impact statement process with requirements of other laws such as the Endangered Species Act. Still others say that public input comes too late in the process or that the federal government fails to publicize hearings through channels that reach the average citizen. Overall, though, NEPA is considered to have brought "sunshine" to a previously closed process. Because few citizens have ready access to the *Federal Register* or other publications in which federal agencies file notices and statements, CEQ is planning to set up a "NEPA NET" and place such documents and information on the Internet, the global computer network, in an attempt to reach more citizens earlier in the process.

Since NEPA's passage, 16 state legislatures have adopted their own "little NEPAs," while 19 states (including 5 that have little NEPAs) have some level of environmental review requirements established by statute, executive order, or administrative directives. Eight states and political jurisdictions—California, Hawaii, Minnesota, New York, North Carolina, Puerto Rico, Washington, and the District of Columbia—require environmental impact reviews at the local level.

At both the state and national levels, recent criticism has focused on the costly, cumbersome, and sometimes duplicative requirements of the process as well as on the lack of coordination among federal, state, and local agencies. California and New York also are looking at linking socioeconomic concerns with the environmental review process, and seeking better coordination with federal agencies at the same time.

The state of Washington took action to correct deficiencies in its laws in May 1995. Based on the recommendations of the Governor's Task Force on Regulatory Reform, the State Environmental Policy Act is now aligned more closely with the state's Growth Management Act. Supported by a bipartisan coalition of business, environmental, labor, and local governments, the legislation requires local governments to combine land use planning and environmental review and provides funding to back up this requirement. The legislation also broadens public participation during the planning and decision-making process, requires local governments to rely on scientific evidence, consolidates development reviews, and mandates decisions within 120 days.

A joint statement signed by the diverse coalition that supported the new law suggests that, although difficult, it is possible to resolve the many environmental, economic, and social concerns expressed by disparate groups. "You don't often see our names on the same sheet of paper supporting amendments to the state's key land use laws," the statement begins. "Two years ago, when the Governor convened this bipartisan Regulatory Reform Task Force, we could not have guessed we would get to this point. This law is the result of years of hard work, shuttle diplomacy, and willingness by many people to come up with solutions, rather than slogans."

·   ·   ·   ·   ·   ·   ·   ·   ·

Further Environmental Progress

Notwithstanding the successes of the past 20 years, there is obviously much more to do to provide a healthy environment for this and future generations. With smokestacks and industrial discharges already heavily regulated, and the prospect that tighter controls may yield marginal reductions at significant costs, the country needs new strategies, including attention to the relationship between environmental problems and the land.

Some of America's most pressing unsolved environmental problems relate to the way land is used. Water pollution offers a good illustration of the changing nature of the pollution problem. A quarter century ago, water quality problems were clearly dominated by gross pollution coming out of discharge pipes. These pipes were the primary target of opportunity. For more than two decades, government regulators did what seemed reasonable and straightforward, requiring increasingly stringent controls, down to parts per billion for some pollutants, on the effluents from industry and municipal sewer systems. Today, however, most water pollution is attributed to nonpoint source runoff from parking lots, city streets, roofs, farmland, lawns, and similar sources dispersed across the landscape. Because so many different people bear responsibility, progress in reducing nonpoint source water pollution requires strategies that provide market-based solutions and foster a greater degree of stewardship in the way land is used, rather than more federal regulation.

Air pollution provides another illustration of the changing agenda. Twenty-five years ago the worst air pollution came from refineries, manufacturing facilities, and utilities. Today, most plants are in compliance with or well on their way to meeting air quality standards. Now the challenge comes from vehicles. Car engines today burn 98 percent cleaner than those in 1970—an impressive engineering feat—but there are 85 million more cars on the road driving twice as many miles. In 20 years, the trend toward clean air in most metropolitan areas could be offset by more people driving even more miles. The number of automobiles that families require and the number of miles people drive to get to their jobs and fill other needs—shopping, recreation, and so on—is a direct function of land use and development patterns (see figure 6).

Some of the most vexing natural resource controversies also revolve around how land is used. In the Northwest, the Endangered Species Act was invoked to save the spotted owl from extinction, but the owl really has been a surrogate for saving the last stands of old-growth forests, which are also home to other threatened species. In a highly polarized climate, forest managers in the region must balance the short-term needs of loggers with those of such other economic interests as fisheries, outdoor recreation, and tourism, while also protecting water quality and wildlife habitat. In Chesapeake Bay, shellfish beds are degraded by pollution associated with shoreline development, threatening the economic livelihood of watermen. Along the Mississippi River, wetlands once filled for development no longer perform their natural functions of buffering riverside communities from floods and purifying water. Protecting New York City's drinking water already requires limits on land development in upstate communities, and may require more. How land is developed and used lies at the center of these and many more natural resource controversies around the country.

As a matter of federal policy, land use has been a stepchild, relegated to the background, a reflection, perhaps, of the fierce, abiding aversion to federal control of land. As evidenced in the emotionally charged debates over logging, wetlands protection, and safeguarding the habitat of endangered wildlife, there is strong and vocal opposition to the notion of federal bureaucrats dictating to communities or private landowners what they may or may not do with their land. Further progress on environmental problems, because they are so closely linked to the use of land, will require new formulations—new ways of thinking, new strategies, and new partnerships, especially between the public and private sectors.

Most water pollution today is attributed to runoff from parking lots, city streets, farmland, lawns, and similar diffuse sources dispersed across the landscape. Further progress in improving water quality requires strategies—here wetlands created to capture stormwater runoff—that foster a greater degree of stewardship in the way land is used. Courtesy of Natural Resources Department, City of Fort Collins, Colorado.

Vehicle Miles Driven Annually
by Passenger Cars and Taxis (in millions)

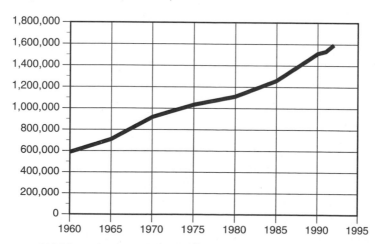

FIGURE 6   Vehicle Miles Traveled, Passenger Cars and Taxis, 1960 to 1992.
Source: National Transportation Statistics, 1995.

The Land and Water Nexus

The mere fact that most of the water used by humans falls first on the land is sufficient to knot the two elements in a tangle of overlapping relationships. Nowhere is this nexus more complex and visible than in the perennial debates that affect the watershed from which New York City's water supply comes.

New York is the only American city with a population of more than a million that does not filter its water. Until recently, the city's water was famously clean. Now, however, leaking septic fields from proliferating vacation homes and nonpoint runoff from new suburban developments and agricultural lands threaten the purity of the water.

Responding to these threats and acting under authority granted by the Safe Drinking Water Act, the U.S. Environmental Protection Agency has issued an ultimatum. As a result, New York City can avoid building a huge filtration plant—at costs ranging from $4 billion to $8 billion for construction, $365 million annually for debt servicing, and $145 million for yearly maintenance and operations—only by limiting development and protecting its vast watersheds in Westchester, Putnam, and Dutchess counties and in the Delaware Valley and Catskill Mountains. Covering 2,000 square miles and incorporating 19 reservoirs and a maze of aqueducts and tunnels, the watersheds supply 9 million urban and upstate residents with drinking water.

Already squeezed by fiscal constraints on all of its city services, New York prefers to exercise land use controls and other techniques to sustain its water supply. To this end, city officials—already skeptical about the effectiveness of filtration, especially against cryptosporidium and other waterborne pathogens—are willing to spend $750 million in dedicated funds to upgrade sewage and septic systems, pay farmers to reduce agricultural pollution, and acquire 80,000 acres of land at market prices from willing sellers.

Opposition to this strategy is strong, particularly among landowners, developers, public officials, and farmers in the Delaware and Catskill watersheds. They fear that limits on development will consign their region to economic oblivion. A recent shift in the state's political balance from urban to suburban jurisdictions may soon jeopardize New York City's long-standing special powers to regulate land use in its upstate, and increasingly suburbanized, watersheds.

. . . .
Backlash

Twenty-five years of environmental activism, a period that witnessed mounting regulatory controls, stiffer penalties, and more land purchases, especially during the last decade, has fueled an organized opposition. Federal rules governing wetlands, water rights, and endangered species, in particular, have helped energize a segment of private landowners and users into a political movement. Some members of this movement are concerned about the future use of resource lands, including public lands, they rely on for their livelihood. Some represent extractive industries seeking to reduce government fetters and boost profits. Some lack confidence that government can regulate or manage land effectively for the public good. Some fundamentally question the validity of government landownership and resource management.

Coalitions of property owners, loggers, mining companies, and other private development interests are frustrated by rules and processes that limit profits, narrow development options, and subject every alteration in plans to lengthy and expensive review. Their frustrations are further aggravated by a growing public distrust of government and cynicism over the motives behind government policies.

Today, the property rights movement has a momentum not unlike the environmental movement of 25 years ago. The champions are full of passion. Money is flowing. Legal arguments are finding a responsive judiciary. The movement is capturing public attention and driving a political agenda favoring less government and fewer regulations.

Backlash over government land policies is not new. The Sagebrush Rebels of the early 1980s, the National Wetlands Coalition, National Inholders Association, Wise Use Coalition, and other recently created property rights organizations who are enraged over government regulations follow in the footsteps of the industrialists, bankers, and developers of earlier decades. Today's organizations, however, bring a new savvy to grassroots organizing and the targeting of state legislatures. Two types of legislation have been proposed at the state level: assessment bills that require state agencies to evaluate virtually all government actions to determine whether such actions could result in a taking of private property, and compensation bills that require the state to pay property owners when regulations decrease a property's fair market value by a certain percentage. To date, legislatures in nearly a score of the states have passed laws requiring takings assessments or compensation. In 1994, at least two dozen states considered takings legislation, and four others considered commissions or ballot initiatives. State legislatures in the future can expect to see waves of renewed pressure.

Where takings bills have been rejected, it has been largely out of fiscal concerns voiced by state legislators, governors, attorneys general, and local officials. During the 1994 legislative sessions, state legislatures rejected 80 out of 86 takings proposals. On November 8, 1994, Arizona citizens, entrusted with the nation's first popular vote on a takings proposal, soundly rejected the measure, Proposition 300, by a margin of 60 percent to 40 percent.

Environmental advocates are concerned that a rewriting of the rules on compensation and accounting of costs and benefits could have a chilling effect on conservation and environmental protection. As a result, they have mounted strong opposition to takings and assessment efforts across the country, and argue that government activity must be viewed in proper perspective. Government action is as likely to increase the value of private property as it is to decrease it, through infrastructure investments, agricultural subsidies, flood insurance, home mortgages, zoning ordinances, or other mechanisms. Government "takings" and government "givings" both need to be considered when suggesting ways to rationalize federal activities that affect land use.

Critics also say the assessment and compensation proposals could force the government to pay polluters to stop polluting and require potentially huge outlays of public funds. Another criticism arises from the difficulty in determining whether and how much government action actually reduces land values, a problem that could lead to dueling appraisers and cumbersome, bureaucratic procedures to establish, process, and appeal claims.

Review requirements for takings are only one of the many avenues that opposition groups are following to reduce the scope of environmental activism and land use controls. Other efforts include attempts to force agencies to take cost into account when establishing regulatory requirements and make regulations binding only if funding is provided to states and localities to carry them out. Who will pay has always been at issue when environmental laws are considered. Now, however, the heat of the debate has increased as the complexity and cost of environmental protection collides with mounting obligations in state and federal budgets. With more requirements at greater cost and with fewer federal dollars available, state and local governments, along with the private sector, shoulder an increasing proportion of the expense of complying with federal mandates. Direct attacks on the budgets of the agencies charged with enforcing these programs are also gaining strength.

Whose Property Is It Anyway?

John C. Shanahan, The Heritage Foundation

Adapted from "A Guide to Wetlands Policy and Reauthorization of the Clean Water Act" (printed with permission).

The *de facto* taking of property through regulation, known popularly as "regulatory takings," now occurs under regulation of wetlands and other property. One of the most unfair and burdensome hardships inflicted by regulatory takings is that wetlands owners are not reimbursed for their loss. For instance, if an elderly couple spends a large portion of their retirement savings to buy property on which to build a dream home and that property is subsequently designated a wetland, the value of their property—and their savings—is gone. Unfortunately, tales of financial hardship caused by government designation of lands as wetlands have become commonplace.

When he was director of the Office of Management and Budget, Leon Panetta said it would be "an unnecessary and unwise use of taxpayer dollars" and a drain on the federal budget to pay landowners whose property is designated a wetland. Landowners counter that regulatory takings are a drain on the family budget. Wetlands regulation has evolved into a question of whether constitutionally guaranteed property rights are being infringed; since the courts have been of limited help, landowners are in need of legislative protection.

To understand why legislative protection for landowners is appropriate, it is necessary to understand the broader issue of governmental taking of property. The Fifth Amendment to the U.S. Constitution implicitly recognized that the federal government may take private property for public use. This power, known as eminent domain, was recognized by the Supreme Court as early as 1795 in *Vanhorne's Lessee v. Dorrance* when the court found that "the despotic power, as it has been aptly called by some writers, of taking private property, when state necessity requires it, exists in every government . . . government could not subsist without it."

The Fifth Amendment explicitly mandates, however, that government must pay the property owner for the land confiscated. This concept, embodied in the clause "nor shall private property be taken for public use, without just compensation," ensures that property taken for public use is paid for by those who benefit—the public—and not by the citizen unfortunate to own land the government wants. In its most basic sense, this is a fairness issue: Why should one American bear the entire burden of the government's pursuit of a national good?

The Founders well understood the positive economic consequences of protecting owners' investments in their property. If property is to be put to its best and most highly valued use, ownership must reside in the hands of those who value it for as much or more than the fair market value. If government had a free hand to take property without payment, its incentive to confiscate property that conferred only a small benefit on the public would be large; after all, even small benefits outweigh a zero cost. The problem is that costs are nonexistent only to the government. The actual costs, borne by someone else, are often substantial.

Another positive result of requiring just compensation is increased security. The Founders well understood that protection of property restrained usurpation of other rights recognized by the Constitution. It is this relationship to which Supreme Court Justice Potter Stewart referred in *Lynch v. Household Finance Co. Inc.* when he stated that there is a "fundamental interdependence . . . between the personal right to liberty and the personal right to property."

Practically speaking, governments can control a wide spectrum of individual activities if they can control whether individuals remain financially secure or must surrender their property. The majority truly can tyrannize a disfavored minority if property rights are uncertain. As James Madison characterized the problem of individual rights in *Federalists Paper No. 10*, "it is that [pure] democracies have ever been spectacles of turbulence and contention; have ever been incompatible with personal security or the rights of property." It was to restrict just such tyranny over individuals that the Framers put severe limits, such as the requirement of just compensation, on the unchecked will of the majority.

The Supreme Court has been clear in requiring federal, state, and local governments to pay just compensation if governmental bodies physically take or occupy land or real estate. Essentially, the Court has held that if only a small amount of real property is involved, a taking has occurred and just compensation is required. Unfortunately, however, the Court's decisions regarding regulatory takings have been less clear and consistent. One landmark case, *Penn Central Transportation Co. v. New York City,* essentially found that if any compensation was provided, whether a just level or not, a taking had not occurred. This reasoning was faulty because the question of whether a property right has been taken is independent of the issue of compensation, which by definition can take place only if property has been taken or lost. If a small payment negates the finding of a taking, it also would negate the requirement of "just" compensation.

The Supreme Court in recent years has begun slowly to move back toward protection of property owners. In its most recent regulatory taking case, *Lucas v. South Carolina Coastal Council,* the Court in 1992 found that a regulation prohibiting property use that also destroyed 100 percent of the property's value was a taking requiring just compensation. The Court, however, specifically declined to address the issue of whether anything less than a complete devaluation was a taking. Thus, it is uncertain whether the government must compensate owners when the property retains, say, 20 percent of its previous fair market value.

If the government infringes any property right by denying an owner use of his own land, the affected landowner should be given the full fair market value of any reduction in the value of his property. While any devaluation should be compensated, legislation should specify that a 25 percent devaluation of real property after an infringing governmental action is a presumptive taking requiring full compensation for the value of the land taken. The owner also should be allowed to elect payment for the entire value of the regulated land—rather than just the reduction in value—if he forfeits title to the government. These provisions will constrain judicial latitude and thus minimize the possibility of misguided judicial interpretation limiting protection to property owners.

Most Americans recognize that government has an important role to play in encouraging common sense land use management. At the same time, many believe that the government's authority stops at the property line. Proponents of rational land use policies and practices argue that the regulatory programs under attack protect a wide array of individual rights. They also maintain that many environmental regulations actually protect property. To highlight only one example, the law that protects wetlands also, in effect, protects nearby houses from periodic flooding.

Of late, there seems to be a preoccupation with the clash between two deeply held viewpoints starkly and vociferously expressed by a relatively small number of people and interest groups. Their rhetoric, which in large measure has framed the political debate about land use at the national and state levels, is often heated, divisive, and counterproductive. Left out of the equation are the views of the vast number of Americans who, according to every opinion poll on the subject, clearly want environmental progress to continue, with greater cooperation between regulators and the regulated community and greater flexibility in methods. It would not be surprising to find that most Americans, expressing a fair-minded, middle-of-the-road point of view, similarly would like to see the more efficient use of land pursued in a way that respects the rights of landowners. Nor would it be surprising to find that Americans expect their leaders to develop that consensus.

CHAPTER   FOUR

· · · · · · · ·

More Growth and Change Are Coming

Since 1960, the population of the United States has increased from 179 to 255 million. In a single generation, the number of Americans has grown by 76 million, a figure equal to almost 150 percent of the entire population of France. Each year another Paris, some 2.2 million citizens, joins the American population. These newcomers require resources. They must be sheltered, clothed, fed, educated, and allowed to roam, and they must be accommodated without adding a single acre to the nation's land base.

The future looks even more crowded. Although birth rates are declining or holding steady in many regions, the U.S. Census Bureau projects a 50 percent increase in population—to 383 million by the year 2050 (see figure 7). According to a recent study cosponsored by the Bank of America, the population of California continues to grow at astounding rates—adding as many as 6 million new faces in boom years and never less than half a million during recession cycles.

While the number of people has been growing, household characteristics have been changing as well. The raw numbers on household formation are telling: In 1930, there were 29 million households in the United States. In 1985, more than 86 million. By the year 2000, there will be an estimated 105 million households (see figure 8). Significantly, the average number of people in each household has fallen from 3.28 in 1940, to 2.63 in 1990, to a projected 2.48 in the year 2000 (see figure 9). Many households have only one parent. Living alone is far more common, as is living longer.

These trends partly reflect the relative sizes of various demographic cohorts as they move through their life cycles. For example, more households were formed as the children of the baby-boom generation, the largest in the nation's history, matured and started their own families. In the not too distant future, it will be time for another great bulge in the population, the grandchildren of this post-World War II generation, to start their own households.

The distribution of population growth is as critical as absolute

In millions

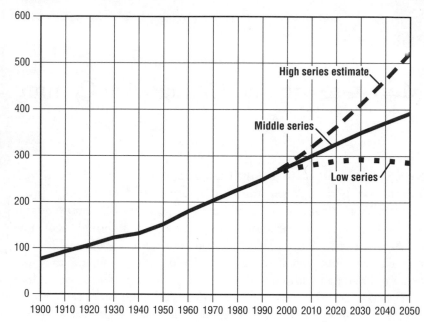

FIGURE 7   Total U.S. Population, 1900 to 2050. *Source:* U.S. Bureau of the Census, *Current Population Reports,* "Population Projections for States, by Age, Sex, Race, and Hispanic Origin: 1993 to 2020," Series P-25, Nos. 311 (1965), 519 (1974), 917 (1982), 1111 (1994).

Estimated number of households (in thousands)

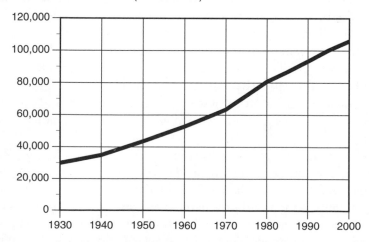

FIGURE 8   Number of U.S. Households, 1930 to 2000. *Source:* U.S. Bureau of the Census, *Current Population Reports,* "Projections of the Number of Households and Families: 1986–2000," Series P-25, No. 986 (1986).

numbers. Every dwelling unit constructed to accommodate new house-holds requires land. If prevailing settlement patterns persist, at least 80 percent of the new people—and their jobs—are likely to locate in edge cities and suburbs that disperse development on the far fringes of metro-politan areas, further extending roadways and encroaching onto farm and other resource lands (see figure 10).

Coastal states, especially in the South and West, have experienced es-pecially intense development since World War II. In 1960, 80 million people lived in the 451 coastal counties of the United States, which to-gether account for 20 percent of the U.S. land area (11 percent if Alaska is included). The population of these coastal areas grew by 17 percent during the 1960s, and by 9 to 11 percent in the 1970s and 1980s. Since 1960, roughly 35 million more people have become coastal residents, making coastal areas the most densely populated in the country (see figure 11). In 1988, coastal counties averaged 341 persons per square mile, more than four times the national average.

California, the bellwether of the coastal migrations, has already become the most urbanized state in the union. California's population increased by 40 percent over the past two decades, while vehicle miles dri-ven rose by 200 percent, a result of the postwar move to distant suburbs. More than 80 percent of all 32 million Californians live in metropolitan areas of one million or more, with 30 percent living in Los Angeles

Average number of persons

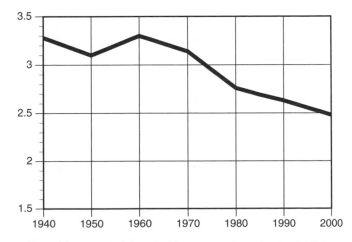

FIGURE 9   Average Size of U.S. Household, 1940 to 2000. *Source:* U.S. Bureau of the Census, *Current Population Reports,* "Projections of the Number of House-holds and Families: 1986–2000," Series P-25, No. 986 (1986).

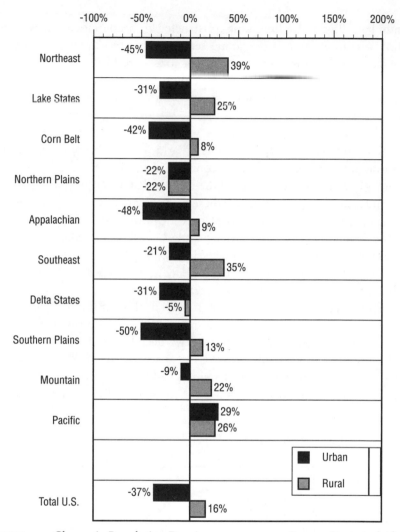

FIGURE 10   Change in Population Density, 1950 to 1990. *Source: Statistical Abstract of the United States, 1953, 1992.*

County alone. While Greater Los Angeles increased its population by 45 percent between 1970 and 1990, its geographical reach expanded by nearly 300 percent, with the metropolitan region now occupying space equal to the size of Connecticut.

Meanwhile, Metropolitan Cleveland lost 8 percent of its population during this period—and yet increased the size of its urbanized outskirts by a third. The May 15, 1995, *Newsweek* notes that the New York City area now stretches into eastern Pennsylvania, across 100 miles of northern New Jersey, and that Phoenix gobbles the Arizona desert at the rate of an

Persons per square mile

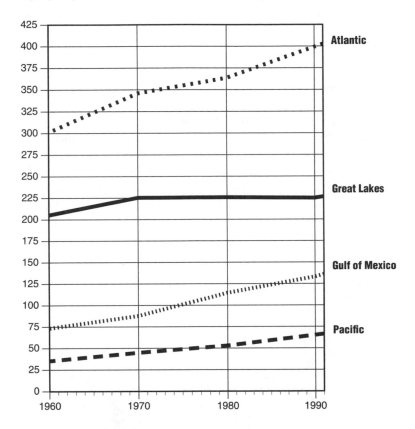

FIGURE 11   Population Density in Coastal Areas, 1960 to 1991. *Source:* U.S. Bureau of the Census, *Statistical Abstract of the United States: 1993; Census of Population and Housing, 1990.*

acre an hour. Aerial photographs taken three months apart in 1995 reveal 5,000 new houses around Phoenix, a city that began the 1950s with a population of only 107,000 and a territory of only 17 square miles. A former mayor says that Phoenix is rapidly approaching "the marginal disutility of suburban sprawl," the point at which each new subdivision subtracts more from the quality of life than the new inhabitants will contribute to the economy. A prime reason for Phoenix's wobbly behavior is the spillover effect of middle-aged couples fleeing California.

Affluence, combined with ease of movement, is generating yet another population trend in the 1990s. Urban migration to small, rural communities, often adjacent to national parks and other scenic areas, is increasing. These moves—often from Los Angeles and other California cities to smaller places like Boise, Idaho; Santa Fe, New Mexico; Jackson, Wyoming; Aspen, Colorado; and Park City, Utah—are driven by a quest for an easier pace of life, beautiful scenery, a favorable climate, or a lower cost of living (see figure 12).

In part, this phenomenon is a function of an aging population (see figure 13). In 1950, there were about 12 million people over the age of 65 in the entire country, about 8 percent of the total population. In 1990, there were more than 31 million, or almost 13 percent. By 2030, the number will reach 58 million, or 20 percent. The generation born immediately after World War II fueled school expansion in the 1950s and strained job and housing markets in the 1970s and beyond. Now, as this same generation approaches retirement age, many of its members are looking for a safe and scenic haven for their remaining years and will no doubt contribute to the run on rural America.

In Bozeman, Montana, the swarm of newcomers, many from California,

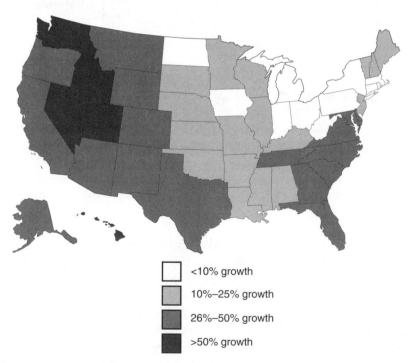

    □   <10% growth

    ▢   10%–25% growth

    ▣   26%–50% growth

    ■   >50% growth

FIGURE 12   Projected Percentage Growth by State, 1990 to 2010. *Source:* U.S. Bureau of the Census, *Current Population Reports,* "Population Projections for States, by Age, Sex, Race, and Hispanic Origin: 1993 to 2020," Series P-25, No. 1111 (1994).

has become so thick that many oldtimers are trying to protect their small city (population 23,000) and its traditional way of life. Fast-food outlets are proliferating. New houses are springing up along the banks of every watercourse. Old fishing streams are being depleted. Even hunting is threatened by the effects of land division, which disrupts the habitats and migration routes of wildlife and compresses the amount of land where hunters are still welcome.

Many other towns located in some of America's most scenic areas are also, reluctantly, in the vanguard of new settlement pressures. The fastest-growing counties in Colorado, Montana, and Wyoming are adjacent to Yellowstone and Grand Teton national parks. This growth, in tandem with rising park visitations, severely taxes the managerial talents of the U.S. National Park Service and the carrying capacities of the communities and the ecosystems surrounding some of the nation's most scenic areas.

Even in the sluggish Midwest and Northeast, commercial development has followed the residential suburbs to the outer fringes. The incentives for middle-class residents and commercial businesses to occupy the nation's center cities have largely disappeared. The Urban Land Institute

Scenic areas in Colorado, Montana, Wyoming, and elsewhere—pictured is Estes Park, Colorado—rank among the fastest-growing places in the United States. Rapid growth is taxing the capacities and capabilities of these attractive settings. Courtesy of Land Ethics, Annapolis, Maryland.

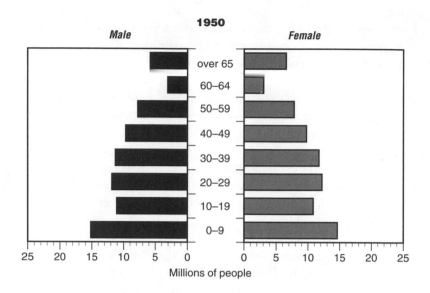

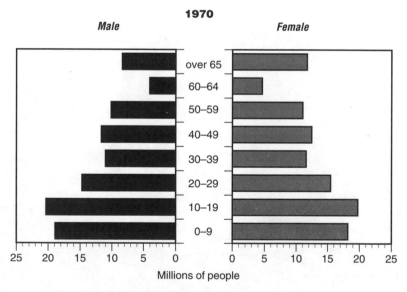

FIGURE 13   Age Distribution Profiles, 1950 to 2010

(*Continued on next page*)

FIGURE 13 *(continued)*

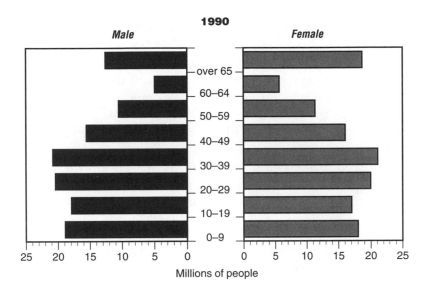

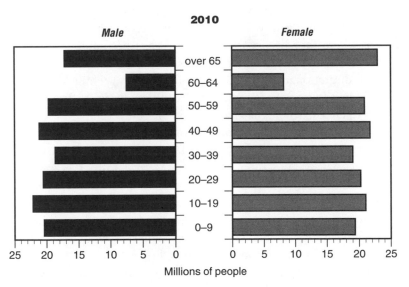

Source: U.S. Bureau of the Census, *Current Population Reports,* "U.S. Population Estimates by Age, Sex, Race, and Hispanic Origin, 1990–1994," Series PPL-21, No. 90 (1995); *Population Estimates and Projections,* Series P-25, No. 917 (1970); Population Projections of U.S., by Age, Sex, Race, and Hispanic Origin, 1993–2050," Series P-25, No. 1104 (1992); "Population Estimates," Series P-25, No. 311 (1965).

puts it bluntly in a 1993 report entitled *Land Use in Transition*: "With a growing urban underclass that is prone to periodic violence and is generating fear and avoidance on the part of businesses and the middle class, the distant suburbs will remain the most likely locations for residential and commercial real estate growth throughout the 1990s. Suburban infill may play an important role, especially considering the lack of sufficient infrastructure in many outer suburban areas, and the resulting traffic congestion."

In short, the land area covered by new development has greatly expanded since the early 1970s, and suburban communities are now the dominant residential, retail, and commercial centers of growth and political muscle. These trends, and especially their replicating patterns, place enormous pressure on land, water, and other resources.

. . . .

The Changing Economy Also Means More Pressures on the Land

Profound shifts in the nation's economic profile are also reshaping the landscape. The diverse ways in which Americans occupy their land—what they do, where they live, work, and play—has become extraordinarily sensitive to recent changes in employment and technology. The accumulation of discretionary wealth, the ability to travel quickly, and the changing distribution of economic opportunities give more Americans the freedom to choose where they live.

The leap from a manufacturing economy to one grounded in information and services is the dominant trend. The latest economic census shows that, between 1967 and 1987, the city of Detroit lost 51 percent of its manufacturing jobs; New York City, 58 percent; Chicago, 60 percent; and Philadelphia, 64 percent. Even Sun Belt cities like Atlanta and Los Angeles lost manufacturing jobs during this same period. These changes have significant implications for land use. The new centers of white-collar growth are increasingly on the metropolitan fringe. Enticed by lower taxes, lower costs, increased safety, proximity to an educated workforce and economic incentives provided by suburban jurisdictions, businesses have flocked to the suburbs. During the 1980s, over 95 percent of the growth in office jobs occurred in low density, auto-dominated suburbs. Office employment accounted for 15 million of the 18 million new jobs created during the decade.

These relocations are made possible by advances in transportation and telecommunications that free many companies from the logic of being located near population centers on the coasts. New technologies have arrived to shape land use patterns at the very moment when access to deepwater ports or major suppliers has become less essential to many businesses and industries. Citibank, for example, now runs credit card services out of Sioux Falls, South Dakota. Other communities—Douglas, Colorado; Delaware, Ohio; Fayette, Georgia; Shelby, Alabama—that were once rural crossroads on the outskirts of urban centers now count themselves among the fastest-growing, wealthiest, and best-educated jurisdictions in the country.

Silicon Valley in California is the most famous of the high-tech regions to emerge over the past 25 years, but other places are experiencing this kind of growth as well. Knight-Ridder, for example, situated its Information Design Laboratory in Boulder, Colorado, far from its headquarters in Miami, Florida. Even in a traditional port city like Seattle, software giant Microsoft surpasses fishing and airplane manufacturing as the city's preferred symbol for the entrepreneurial spirit of the times.

The implications of new industry for the use of land are already materializing, and they suggest that regions of the country that were immune to population explosions in the past may quickly have to upgrade their capacity for land use planning, or succumb to overwhelming growth pressures.

In 1994, an estimated 7.6 million people across the country participated in telecommuting arrangements with their private sector employers. Telecommuting and other innovations, such as flexible work hours, are being promoted in areas like Greater Washington, D.C., to solve traffic problems and meet Clean Air Act requirements. A number of Washington, D.C., area governments are experimenting with new working arrangements; government officials in Loudoun County, Virginia, hope that up to 40 percent of their 1,200 employees may work at home at least part of the time. Although the impact of new technologies still seems small compared with birth rates and other demographic and economic factors, it appears to be accelerating.

. . . .

Social Values in Transition Are Changing How Land Is Used

Beneath the hard data of demography and economy lies a substratum of values. Gone is the archetype of the nuclear family as a dominant model.

The norm may persist, but reality no longer accords with it. The stable and cohesive family in which dad earns the paycheck and mom runs the home is no longer a convincing picture of American life. Unwed motherhood is increasingly common, rising from under 10 percent of all births in 1965 to almost 30 percent today. Divorce is equally familiar, affecting about half of all marriages. Inevitably, living arrangements are increasingly elastic.

Even in two-parent households, women carry a greater variety of responsibilities. A survey released in May 1995 found that half of employed married women now contribute half or more to their family's income. The expense of educating children for success in the modern economy is itself sufficient motivation for doubling a household's income. Rising costs for other essentials and amenities intensify financial pressures. In search of cash to pay for the greater needs of children and the longer care of parents, women are leaving farm, town, and neighborhood on a daily basis and for extended periods.

The typical American expects to dwell in at least 10 different houses during a lifetime. With this expectation in mind, a homeowner seeks resale value in each purchase, a practice that hardly encourages departures from the conventional designs of the real estate market. And, given where housing is increasingly located, and the need to get to key destinations, not just to jobs, but to shopping, recreation, school, and the like, the three-car family has spread across the country.

Amidst the changing landscape of the United States, the desire for open space and outdoor recreation, especially in the vicinity of home, continues to grow in popularity—especially hiking, bicycling, bird watching, and other sports that put people in touch with the natural world (see figure 14). A 1995 study found that bike paths, hiking trails, and open space top the list of what American home buyers want in most new communities. By contrast, in the mid-1980s, top draws were tennis courts, swimming pools, and golf courses. In the 1995 study, 77 percent of respondents ranked "lots of natural, open space" as a top priority, second only to quiet and low traffic density, and followed by walking and biking paths.

The trend toward a desire for open space and outdoor recreation is seen in visitation rates to the National Park System as well. A report by the National Parks and Conservation Association revealed that so many Americans are visiting the parks that "we risk loving some to death." In 1994, almost 270 million people visited the national parks. By the year

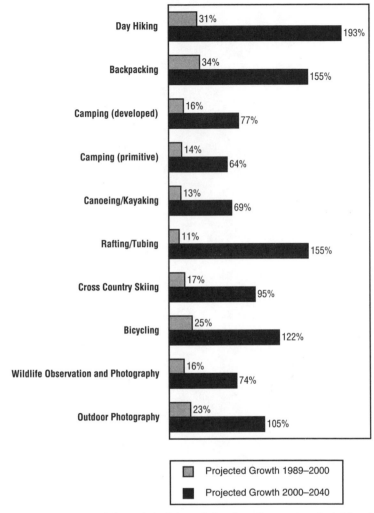

FIGURE 14   Projected Growth in Selected Outdoor Recreation Activities through 2040. *Source:* U.S. Forest Service, *An Analysis of the Outdoor Recreation and Wilderness Situation in the U.S.: 1989–2040* (1989).

2000, that number is expected to reach nearly 310 million, a 15 percent increase.

In light of these inexorable trends in demographics, economy, and values, it is apparent that only a more efficient use of the land can strengthen the basic social and economic underpinnings for the American way of life.

• • • • • • • •

CHAPTER FIVE

A Land Use Agenda
for 21st Century America

America must do better by its land. Using land well is a key to improving the quality of life in communities everywhere. Otherwise—in light of significant projected growth in population and the number of households—the countryside will be chewed up, ugliness will prevail, urban cores will continue to decline, public service costs will be unnecessarily high, and water, air pollution, and waste problems will get worse.

Land is central to the well-being of the United States. Assuring a healthy, productive land base, making efficient use of the land, protecting landmarks and resource lands, and meeting other land use needs are requisites for continued economic growth, environmental improvement, and a better quality of life for all Americans. Central to achieving these goals is a land ethic. Whether one cares about wilderness or neighborhood playgrounds, treating the land with respect is a responsibility of American citizenship.

It may seem odd, given America's recent political mood, to call for reinvigorated land use planning. It may seem out of step to petition the federal government to pay more explicit attention to the manifold land use implications of its policies. A conservative majority was swept into Congress and many state legislatures in the November 1994 elections. A vigorous property rights movement has appropriated not only some of the vocabulary central to conservation thinking but also some of its political momentum.

Yet good land use is not radical doctrine. It follows from rational decision making. It is neither of the left nor the right politically. Conservatives should be every bit as concerned as liberals about good land use decisions. Good land use saves public money by avoiding wasteful and expensive sprawl. Good land use adds predictability to the planning process, takes into account economic and environmental factors, and avoids divisive controversy and time-consuming litigation.

. . . .
The Agenda

The following agenda reflects the importance of achieving good land use and the urgency of addressing the many obstacles to attaining it.

AGENDA ITEM #1
Local governments must take the lead role in securing good land use. Initiatives in land use planning and growth management need to be anchored in a community-based process that develops a vision for the future.

The question confronting most communities is not whether, but how, they will grow and change. That requires a vision for the future. What do Americans want their cities, towns, and countryside to look like in 25 years? Land use decisions ultimately will reflect the value people attach to specific places and the desire to shape a common destiny. The community itself must be the driving force. Public officials today must help ordinary citizens understand how effective community planning can improve their lives by supplying public services efficiently, fostering economic growth, preserving open space for recreation, minimizing the havoc of natural disasters, and protecting critical natural resources.

A community must take the initiative, inventory its resources, consider what it values, determine its preferences, and formulate plans that respect local circumstances and traditions. The community must find a proper balance between common needs and the needs of the individuals, including developers and landowners, who make it thrive. In other words, communities must do what they have been doing for years but do it better, faster, smarter, more comprehensively, and more flexibly. They are going to have to craft and employ new appropriate tools—easements, incentives, performance standards, mitigation banks, greenways, and growth boundaries, to name a few.

Land use and growth management initiatives must be rooted in the community if they are to succeed and endure. There is no alternative to a bottom-up, grassroots, community-by-community approach to improving land use across the United States. No shortcut, no mandate from Washington or a state capital will work. The willingness of community leaders and citizens to engage in a planning process cannot be imposed from outside. Although encouragement can come from elsewhere, leadership must come from within the community. Even the best plans are doomed unless citizens understand them and participate in their preparation. No community can retain its character, its open spaces, its natural and cultural assets by accident. Nor can it accommodate growth or build a constituency to realize a community dream by remaining passive.

Sustainable Communities

As quality of life becomes an increasingly important requisite for a community's economic health, local officials and citizens across the country are trying to define what a "sustainable" community is and in some cases track progress using quantifiable measures. Although as diverse as the communities exploring them, these attempts in general take an integrated look at the social, economic, and ecological aspects of their community.

A number of places have developed indicators to assess quality of life and sustainability. Others are participating in extensive "visioning" exercises to build consensus on what the community should look like. Some initiatives address a range of issues that relate to community sustainability. Others focus on particular aspects of development such as energy, affordable housing, or the environment. Following are some examples of what is being done in a few places across the country.

A Sustainable City Plan for Berkeley (Berkeley, California, 1992)

The Berkeley city plan, sponsored by Urban Ecology, includes 71 specific recommendations for action in 7 broad areas: land use; open space, greening, and agriculture; transportation; housing; energy, resources, and pollution; social justice; and sustainable economics. The plan does not contain specific indicators; rather, it lists key principles for responding to environmental problems and creating a better city. The principles include: encouraging mixed-use development around transit and neighborhood centers; restoring damaged natural features of the urban environment; revising transportation priorities to favor foot, bicycle, and mass transit over the automobile; creating decent, affordable, safe, convenient, and racially and economically mixed housing; nurturing social justice; supporting local agriculture; promoting recycling; supporting ecologically sound economic activity; promoting voluntary simplicity; and increasing environmental awareness through education.

Sustainable Cambridge Coalition (Cambridge, Massachusetts, 1992)

The Cambridge project seeks to determine the city's impact on the surrounding environment and to minimize undesirable effects. Data for a sustainability profile have been compiled for the following factors: energy (including the use of oil, natural gas, gasoline, and electricity at the residential, commercial, institutional, industrial, and municipal levels); waste generation (solid waste, sewage, hazardous waste, and recycling); water usage

(residential, commercial, institutional, and industrial); transportation (including car, bus, and subway use); population (age distribution and eth-
nicity); agriculture (including quantities of homegrown goods, inflow of
out-of state goods); local employment (in industry, local business, services,
education).

Chattanooga Venture (Chattanooga, Tennessee, 1984)

Chattanooga is embracing a new civic attitude founded on government,
business, and citizens uniting to achieve economic growth while respecting
the resources that make this growth possible. In 1984, Chattanooga Ven-
ture launched "Visions 2000," bringing together thousands of Chat-
tanoogans to seek consensus about what the city should be like in the future. After 20 weeks of "visioning" sessions, the participants agreed on 34
goals. Participants then recruited investors who were interested in turning
the goals into reality. Two hundred and twenty-three separate projects resulted from the visioning exercise. The Chattanooga Area Regional Transit
Authority, for example, is replacing diesel buses with electric shuttles manufactured in Chattanooga. Multipurpose terminals and transfer facilities,
strategically located, are being designed to conserve time and energy by
decreasing dependence on automobiles. A partnership between the city of
Chattanooga and Orange Grove runs the Recovery Facility (a nonprofit
workshop for people with disabilities), which recovers materials from the
community waste stream and returns them to the manufacturing sector.
Chattanooga Neighborhood Enterprise has completed more than 4,000
low-and moderate-income housing units. And the city has added miles of
park and green space to its environs with a riverfront park in an area that
had previously housed abandoned factories.

Jacksonville Community Council Indicators (Jacksonville, Florida, 1985)

In 1985, the Jacksonville Chamber of Commerce and the Jacksonville Community Council Inc. came together to discuss their shared concern for the
quality of life in their city. Volunteers formed committees, drew up targets,
and completed a vision for the city for the year 2000. Seventy-four indicators were chosen to reflect trends in nine areas: education, economy, public
safety, natural environment, health, social environment, government/poli-
tics, culture/recreation, and mobility.

Since then, data have been collected and compiled for each of these 74
areas on an annual basis. After 10 years of data collection, both positive and
negative trends are emerging. Nonprofit groups and government officials

use the information as a tool for planning and decision making. The project is beginning to have an impact on the way that citizens see and assess their community's well-being. For example, the economy is increasingly recognized as only one of the many components of a healthy community.

The Sustainable Seattle Indicators Project (Seattle, Washington, 1993)

Volunteer committees in Seattle have selected 40 indicators for data development and grouped these indicators into four broad areas: environment; population and resources; economy; and culture and society. The indicators, which serve as a report card for the city's health and help guide long-term planning, include both qualitative and quantitative measures, from water quality to community involvement in the arts. Some indicators are based on readily verifiable data; others involve testing public opinions and attitudes. Some deal just with Seattle, others with King County, and still others refer to Seattle in a regional, national, or global context.

Measures of environmental trends in the Seattle area from 1980 to 1992 showed a 70 percent decline in salmon runs, an increase in good air quality days, and a decrease in per capita water consumption. Population and resource trends for that same period include an increase in population, a rise in solid waste per capita, and an increase in vehicle miles traveled per person. Economic data showed an increase in children living in poverty and a rise in per capita health expenditures. These findings are used as the basis for local planning programs to develop tools and projects to transform negative trends into positive ones, and to improve the overall quality of life in Seattle.

Plenty of land use guidebooks, manuals, and references exist to aid community leaders and citizens in seizing the initiative, defining a vision, developing an agenda and suitable programs, mobilizing resources, and building consensus. It is not the "how to" that is in short supply. Rather, communities throughout the country must gather the will and leadership essential to meet the challenge.

AGENDA ITEM #2
State governments must help local governments by establishing reasonable ground rules and planning requirements, assisting small and rural areas, and providing leadership on matters that affect more than one local jurisdiction.

If community leadership and initiative are crucial, there is an equally compelling role for the states. They cannot expect local governments to assume the entire responsibility for land use planning. States have a crucial role in setting ground rules and enabling communities to deal with complex land use problems. What happens in one town can affect neighboring towns. The effects of growth often cross jurisdictions. Protecting large natural systems like watersheds, for example, requires a broad geographical perspective to avoid development that encroaches on floodplains and other critical natural systems. Shopping malls, airports, highways, and other projects may well have consequences that stretch over large areas. These types of development have provided impetus in the past for statewide land use planning initiatives.

Moreover, management of some problems may require cooperation among many states and local jurisdictions. States are in the best position to assure a broad view for planning and investments and to foster cooperation when needed.

State help is also necessary to assist smaller communities and rural areas before growth pressures become overwhelming. Many communities are unable to plan for growth, to protect agricultural lands, provide safe drinking water, or stimulate new employment opportunities.

How states meet their responsibilities will vary, reflecting the variety of circumstances and traditions found across the country. Each state has its own political traditions. Each starts with its own geography, natural history, cultural traditions, growth patterns, economic base, and so on. No formula works everywhere. Although about a dozen states have some sort of statewide growth management program, and others may decide to start one, not all states will want to do so. Some states will choose to tackle specific issues, like farmland preservation, because a political consensus exists, whereas there is no consensus for a comprehensive program. Each state will have to devise its own approach.

States considering a comprehensive growth management program should learn from the experience of others. At a minimum:

- Localities should be required to develop a planning program that is consistent with such statewide goals as preserving agricultural lands, establishing greenways, protecting the integrity of river systems and underground aquifers, providing a base for future economic growth, and so forth.

- State actions should be consistent with these plans, and state agencies should be required to coordinate their activities better in light of them.

- There should be a mechanism that assures consideration of the impacts development will have beyond a local jurisdiction, either a comprehensive regional planning process or a project-specific environmental impact review.

- There should be firm links between state investments in infrastructure, including transportation, and local land use plans.

- There should be a plan and wherewithal for acquiring and managing an appropriate amount of open space to meet community conservation and recreation needs.

State programs to influence growth should be linked to other programs. Education, transportation, and other forms of aid, for example, could be used as incentives to ensure that local land use decisions are congruent with state planning goals.

In any consideration of the state role, fiscal questions loom large. To improve land use practices, states must free localities from the burden of raising all revenue through property taxes. Excessive reliance on the property tax results in competition among communities for major development projects, typically commercial or industrial development, to generate local revenues. This system produces glaring disparities among communities in funding for schools, services, and facilities. In his paper in the following section, Vermont's Governor Howard Dean argues that by far the greatest disincentive to good land use planning in his state is reliance on the property tax. Contributor John Georges argues that typical property tax assessments, which are pegged at the highest and best use of land, usually for development, can be a serious disincentive to retaining forest cover and managing forestlands for productive and sustainable use. Contributor Charles Jordan writes of the disparities among communities in the Portland metropolitan region, where working-class areas are straining under limits to property tax increases and inner city transportation is underfunded, yet wealthier suburban areas enjoy lower property tax rates and receive the bulk of available money for implementing the 50-year growth management plan. The weakness of the property tax system has been understood for years. Only states can intervene to correct inequities, distribute burdens across metropolitan regions, and provide ground rules to encourage retention of resource lands.

Should the property tax system be tossed out or revamped? To date, the consequences and alternatives have not been fully explored or adequately laid out. The state of Michigan has been searching for alternatives. To reduce inequities in funding education across the state, Michigan shifted school financing from the property tax to the sales tax. A task force created to consider ways to preserve dwindling agricultural land recommended that property be taxed at its present use instead of at its potential for development, as is now the case. Clearly, there are lessons to be learned as various options are explored. At a minimum, states should consider sharing part of the revenues from property taxes regionwide to discourage land use decisions that are made merely to increase the local tax base.

AGENDA ITEM #3
The rules governing land development need to be overhauled. They need to be more efficient and more flexible, encouraging—not hindering— new approaches to land development and conservation.

Traditional land use tools—zoning, subdivision ordinances, impact reviews—have preserved some community assets and set minimum standards for new development. But too often these tools are outdated and inflexible, thus discouraging innovative designs that cluster buildings, conserve open space, or integrate land uses. Development today too often must conform to standard setbacks, yard requirements, curb cuts, and street widths. With few exceptions, low density development—detached, single-family homes on large lots—predominates, not only consuming more land directly, but of necessity requiring more roads, which consume even more land.

Ordinances routinely allow only what has been tried before. On one hand, developers, investors, and homebuyers may find this reassuring. After all, predictable earnings are the developer's key to securing capital, risk-averse financiers prefer market-tested configurations, and homebuyers want to be sure their houses can be resold. But the net effect has stifled creativity. Some of the most praiseworthy new residential developments would not be allowed under most existing zoning ordinances. In one case, Kentlands in suburban Washington, D.C., the code had to be revised completely before the developer could proceed with a neighborhood-oriented site plan that clustered development and linked open space.

Revisions, reforms, and new approaches to local land use regulation are a must. Prompted by concerns over waste, duplication, confusion, and uncertainty in regulations, regulatory reform has taken root in many states. As part of this process, a review of local regulatory aims and procedures offers a chance to engage a spectrum of stakeholders in the community and build consensus for appropriate ways to guide decisions about land use and growth.

Zoning, subdivision ordinances, environmental impact reviews, and other traditional land use tools have helped preserve some community assets and set minimum standards for new development—street widths, curb cuts, setbacks, and the like. But they have not proved sufficient by themselves to create quality communities.

The participation of the business sector and the real estate development industry is essential for a land use strategy to succeed. Their cooperation in designing an efficient review and approval process might be secured by offering something in return. Developers want certainty and expedited approvals because they have funds tied up in projects and can ill afford a process subject to unpredictable delays and extensions. Knowing when a decision will be made often is as important as learning what that decision will be. Securing certainty and expeditious decisions might be a good trade-off for steering their projects to areas designated by the community for growth.

A broad-based community review will likely reveal that many requirements are worth keeping because they protect land and property values. Other long-accepted standards, for street widths or setbacks, say, may be too rigid. Greater flexibility may be warranted. Moreover, opportunities should be sought not only to streamline existing processes—through, for example, "one-stop shopping" for permit seekers—but to integrate the variety of environmental, economic, and land use reviews that precede development.

In some communities, greater flexibility is being introduced into zoning by rewarding projects that incorporate additional amenities, conserve open space, include moderate-income housing, and so on. The rewards either allow increased density (more units or more square footage) or waive certain requirements (height limits, setbacks, parking stipulations). Additional experimentation of this sort is in order.

Improvements in the current regulatory system can only go so far, however. More tools are required. As Jean Hocker indicates in her paper, land exchanges and transfer of development rights are two that have proved useful in an ever-increasing number of places. Requirements for offsetting, or mitigating, the adverse effects of development are being tried as well. Through wetlands banking, for example, public agencies or developers permanently protect high-quality wetlands ahead of time in exchange for expedited reviews and permission to fill other wetlands on a project site as the need arises. California has just established new statewide guidelines for mitigation banking, which offer landowners an option for land conservation. The Bank of America, one of the first to sign up, is selling mitigation credits to others who need them and helping protect contiguous tracts of threatened habitat. Mitigation banking potentially has broad applicability to provide not only flexibility in land use decision making but certainty for developers as they pursue expedited permit reviews.

Of all tools, however, none has been more effective than the conservation easement, a partial interest in property transferred to an appropriate nonprofit or governmental entity either by gift or purchase. Easements restrict the development, management, or use of land. They are applied to retain land in a natural condition, provide recreational access, or to protect historic, scenic, or other values. Little known 25 years ago, their status has been validated by the Internal Revenue Service as a charitable contribution. Today, easements are widely used by land trusts, conservation groups, developers, and others. They can affirm or restrict the rights to timber, hunting or fishing, or development. In some cases, they provide public access. Easements have proved themselves a flexible instrument in fulfilling conservation goals while meeting the specific needs of individual landowners.

Contributor John Baden argues for harnessing the market to encourage innovation through incentives and voluntary arrangements. By creating economic value in pollution reduction, federal regulators have already reduced the cost of compliance with environmental goals. A similar approach could be applied at the state and local levels to the difficult

One of the most flexible, effective tools for private land conservation, conservation easements are a partial interest in property that stops short of outright ownership. They are used by land trusts, conservation groups, developers, and others to protect or restrict public access; rights to timber, hunting, or fishing; development; scenic vistas; and other important values. Courtesy of Maryland Environmental Trust, Annapolis, Maryland.

problem of nonpoint source pollution. Perhaps a whole new system based on incentives and trading among landowners, municipalities, and so on can be devised, as envisioned in William Reilly's paper.

All of this is a complicated business. Entrenched points of view and insufficient funds limit the potential of some ideas. Some approaches entail extensive cooperation among levels of government and between public and private interests. The consequences of one or another initiative must be considered from different perspectives. Transfer of development rights, for example, may be opposed by areas of the community that are slated to receive the higher densities. Some methods may be challenged in court. Smaller communities may not have an adequate planning capability, nor the funds to create one.

None of these reasons should deter the needed experimentation. In the best situations, communities are learning from others, drawing on a menu of techniques that introduce flexibility into planning efforts.

AGENDA ITEM #4
Landowners must be treated fairly and oppressive regulations fixed. But making government pay in order to apply environmental safeguards for the common good is a bad idea.

Polarization over environmental and land use issues is reducing chances to improve communities and manage growth. As Reilly says, a primary reason for the failure to manage land rationally is lack of consensus among people about the proper reach of government and public authority in constraining the use of the land.

As noted elsewhere in this book, a lot of angry private landowners and land users have become visible. Their concerns cannot be dismissed, ignored, or pushed aside. They are a growing political force throughout the nation. At the state level, their influence may spill over to local affairs insofar as legislation establishes the ground rules for local land use planning and growth management. The concerns driving the property rights movement must be addressed. If not, with two-thirds of the land in this country in private ownership, including almost all the land in the shadow of growing communities, the politics of private property can thwart even the best laid plans.

Achieving community land use goals must be done in a way that treats private landowners and those who derive their livelihood from the land fairly. There is nothing trivial about private property and the rights associated with it. They are tenets of a free society. The rights of landowners cannot be ignored as communities address land use and growth issues.

Communities rely on regulation to constrain landowners' decisions. In general, landowners can use their land as they want to, illicit activities excepted, as long as the activities meet minimum standards established by relevant codes and do not create a public nuisance or harm a neighbor's property. The challenge for public officials is to protect and restore natural systems, to foster quality development, and to manage growth without treating property owners unfairly or arbitrarily denying them the use of their land.

For decades, the United States has largely relied on the judiciary to protect the rights of landowners, as contributor Jerold Kayden relates. The courts weigh the public benefits, the private costs, and the particular circumstances and render a judgment about whether government action treats a landowner fairly. No one disagrees, for instance, that compensation is warranted when the government directly appropriates private land to build a highway. The debate increasingly centers on the extent to which government regulation that *limits* the use of private land, especially with respect to protecting wetlands and wildlife habitat, should also be defined as a taking and compensated.

The courts have been moving in recent years to refine the takings threshold, according to Kayden. In so doing, they are recognizing some of the concerns expressed by private landowners. Altering the balance the courts have crafted over the years through legislative action at the federal or state level, however, promises to open a Pandora's box of unintended consequences. The rush to pass takings compensation measures to satisfy political constituencies could undercut the ability of local jurisdictions to deal with community growth pressures and make state and national environmental programs so expensive as to be useless.

Although the basic rule set by the courts over several decades should not be changed, there are many ways to eliminate excessive unfairness and reduce the resentment it generates. Careful review of regulatory impacts on a case by case basis can help avoid inequities. Addressing egregious situations for small landowners, assuring timely decisions on permit applications, and providing expeditious routes for appeal are important objectives irrespective of one's views on property rights and compensation. Bureaucratic arrogance wherever it rears its head must be eliminated.

But going to automatic compensation on the basis of a hypothetical, formula-based assessment of reduction in land value does not constitute a practical approach to reconciling the many and varied objectives and responsibilities with which landowners, land users, community officials, and government regulators must contend. Rather, it raises the specter of more litigation and greater uncertainty. Instead, such techniques as dispute resolution and expedited administrative reviews, tax abatements, mitigation banking, and transfer of development rights should ease the interactions between government regulators and property owners.

AGENDA ITEM #5
Many government policies and actions—agricultural, highway, and environmental programs—impact land use. If they are not better coordinated, they will continue to result in land use policy by accident.

The sum of actions by all levels of government on transportation, housing, banking and credit, environmental cleanup, military base closures, agriculture, and other issues creates an implicit, *de facto* land use policy. These activities influence the use of land in subtle, indirect, and sometimes unanticipated ways. Without an explicit land use policy, decisions affecting land turn on narrowly focused laws and regulations, on court decisions, on the actions of diverse agencies and special interests, and on uncoordinated public investments in highways, sewers, and other undertakings.

In responding to growth pressures at the community level, planners face a serious obstacle. Federal policies that have implications for local land use, and state policies as well, are often beyond the reach of those local officials with responsibility for land use planning. Both federal and state agencies offer up a patchwork of uncoordinated or poorly coordinated policies with unintended consequences that too often drive land use decisions.

Coordinating government policies and programs is hard work. There are multiple layers of government with overlapping responsibilities and no clear accountability, a mind-numbing array of agencies administering narrowly focused laws that sometimes work at cross-purposes, inadequate resources, insufficient flexibility in approach, and so on. Contributor Doug Wheeler describes how a lack of coordination has complicated California's efforts to restore the San Francisco Bay Delta.

The policies and actions of the federal government, states, counties, regional authorities, and municipalities all have a strong role to play in influencing the direction and pace of development. Few jurisdictions today are adequately prepared to coordinate policies and programs to meet the growth challenge. At the local level, neighborhood groups may protect their own backyard, for example, pushing unwanted activities and traffic elsewhere with no concern for the larger trade-offs that the community as a whole may have to consider. Contributor James Lighthizer recounts the adverse consequences he witnessed, as a local and then a state official, as a result of the failure to link major transportation investments with local land use plans. He also notes the enormous potential for integrating transportation policy with environmental and land use goals through the Intermodal Surface Transportation Efficiency Act (ISTEA).

As a means of harmonizing the competing and conflicting objectives that inevitably plague a complicated system of governance, the Coastal Zone Management Act embodies a principle that may be worth emulating: For states enrolled in the program, the federal government requires coastal planning at the state level and agrees that federal actions will be consistent with the resulting plans. Similarly, the plans, policies, and activities of various levels of government should strive for conformance and consistency once state or local land use plans are formally adopted.

AGENDA ITEM #6
In selective situations, public land acquisition is needed, and a reliable source of funds must be available to pay for it.

Public ownership of some places makes sense under any circumstances. Therefore, some funding for public land purchases is still essential. There are places where full public access is warranted: beaches and parks and significant historic monuments like Independence Hall in Philadelphia. At these places and elsewhere, government serves as caretaker and manager of land in trust for the entire community. Each generation of Americans adds to the inventory of parks, wilderness areas, historic sites, protected trails and rivers, and other public lands. In California, where nearly half the state is publicly owned, public lands meet important wildlife habitat needs, thereby lessening the burden on private landowners.

Successful planning efforts should use land acquisition selectively and strategically. Public land acquisition cannot by itself fulfill conservation or land use goals. Some people oppose public ownership of more land. They believe that government owns too much already. They point to the ineffectiveness of government management. Far from preserving and efficiently managing resources, contributor Baden argues, government agencies have engaged in and even encouraged ecological degradation and economic waste.

Public ownership of land is constrained by lack of funding. There will never be enough money to purchase all the sensitive and important lands—even if this made sense, which it does not. The backlog of authorized but unfunded federal parkland acquisitions and maintenance projects, for example, has stood for years at several billion dollars.

Management of the San Francisco Bay Delta has been complicated by the fact that numerous federal, state, and local government agencies have overlapping authority, duplicative procedures, and little direct accountability. Nonetheless, the state is pressing ahead in a partnership involving all the stakeholders to safeguard this important natural resource. Courtesy of Department of Water Resources, California Resources Agency, Sacramento, California.

Moreover, government decision-making processes for land purchases are lengthy and cumbersome. Detailed procedural safeguards govern the expenditure of public funds. Legal challenges over appraisals or procedures can take years to resolve. These difficulties affect public land purchases at the federal, state, and local levels.

Nonetheless, there is still a strong justification for public acquisition. This is especially true for smaller parcels—steep slopes prone to landslides, land over an aquifer that is the source of community drinking water, land highly susceptible to flooding, critical wildlife habitat—that form part of a larger mosaic linking sensitive lands or are critical in implementing a community development plan. Increasingly, it is public-private partnerships, rather than outright public ownership, that offer the most practical, flexible approach to creating this network. Protection strategies can be tailored to the nature of the resource and the community. Public funding remains essential to catalyze broad partnerships.

The Land and Water Conservation Fund (LWCF), administered by the U.S. Department of the Interior, once played a pivotal role in helping federal agencies and states purchase parklands and wildlife habitat. Some 30,000 useful projects spread through all 50 states testify to the program's efficiency. The fund has been starved in recent years, however, and may be cut back even more severely as Congress seeks to reduce the federal deficit.

In the past, state and local bond issues earmarked for open space acquisition often augmented monies available from the LWCF. More recently, states and localities have tried to compensate as best they can as appropriations for the fund were reduced. Portland, Oregon, approved $200 million for open space and greenway acquisition; Michigan and Arkansas passed statewide funding measures in 1994. Bond issues are one means by which states and localities can assure themselves of a continuing source of funds for land acquisition. Real estate transfer fees dedicated to a land acquisition program are another.

The Intermodal Surface Transportation Efficiency Act also has helped. ISTEA provides enhancement funds for a broad array of purposes tied to transportation projects, emphasizing land conservation. Some states, Florida for one, have passed their own versions of ISTEA. Within a couple of years, ISTEA is going to be considered for reauthorization by Congress. No doubt there will be arguments that it is a luxury the country can ill afford in a time of budget cutbacks and that regulations and procedures must be streamlined to get on with the job of building and repairing highways and putting people to work. But the recognition that transportation projects have considerable impact on the land and that transportation funds can be used to minimize and mitigate that impact is a welcome, long-overdue development. Somewhat ironically, ISTEA is currently among the most important sources of funding for land conservation. Therefore, ISTEA should be reauthorized as an important land use resource, as well as on its merits as transportation policy.

Something more, however, is needed at the national level to support public land acquisition. Congress should either fund the LWCF at a decent rate or create a new mechanism—a permanent trust fund, for instance, that is not subject to annual appropriations. States and localities need to know that some federal funds will be available over time to meet land conservation objectives established within an overall land use and growth management plan.

In this budget-conscious era, where does the money come from? There is a principle that still makes sense: Resource depletion should help pay for resource protection. LWCF monies came from royalties on offshore oil and gas production. For example, if there is drilling in the Arctic National

Wildlife Refuge, as undesirable as that may be for many, the revenues generated ought to pay for a greenway in every county in America.

AGENDA ITEM #7
*Older areas in cities and suburbs must become a focus for renewal. Gov-
ernment policies should help fill in vacant land in already built-up areas
and renew older properties rather than promote unplanned expansion at
the urban fringe.*

Improving land use decisions will not only protect open space and the
countryside and build better suburbs, it will also improve the quality of
life in older cities and the inner ring of older suburbs. The problems in
these areas are familiar and severe. Populations are declining. Employers
are leaving. Roads, bridges, and other public facilities are decaying. The
costs of city services, especially social services, are mounting, while the tax
base erodes. Renewal is hard for cities and older suburbs.

Richard Kahan, president of the Urban Assembly in New York City,
cites the need for integrating the inner city into the economic mainstream
by emphasizing, as Harvard University business school professor Michael
Porter calls it, "the competitive advantage of inner cities," the untapped
economic potential to generate profitable, unsubsidized businesses that
can serve not only the local community but export outside it. Kahan's priorities for urban areas include investments in education to assure a skilled
labor force, as well as investments in communications, transportation,
financing, research and development, and quality of life—the ingredients
that enable enterprises to grow, provide jobs, pay taxes, and attract a
skilled workforce. A favorable tax and regulatory environment alone
cannot do the job.

Contributor Chris Leinberger's paper reflects on the movement away
from city centers toward new development on the urban fringe or outlying
sites as a response to market demand. Often, it is easier and cheaper to assemble land at the urban fringe. The regulatory thicket of plans, reviews,
and permits, as well as improvements required of project sponsors, is less
onerous on the urban fringe than in city centers and older suburbs.

Accommodating growth in older cities and suburbs involves redeveloping already built-up areas and infilling vacant sites. Existing neighborhoods and commercial districts should be able to capitalize on their
greatest asset, a sense of place and history that is typically lacking in new
developments. Yet a good deal of law and regulation works against using
sites in older areas.

Knoxville Center City Business Park Brownfields Redevelopment Project

Mayor Victor Ashe, Knoxville, Tennessee, past Chairman of the U.S. Conference of Mayors

Like many cities in the United States today, Knoxville, Tennessee, has been frustrated by the lack of national policies and programs to assist in recycling abandoned and contaminated inner-city industrial properties called "brownfields." These sites sit idle, generating no revenue for the local tax rolls, because the private sector is understandably wary of investing in their redevelopment, given the high cleanup costs and potential liability for prior contamination. Lenders are equally wary of financing such redevelopment because of possible liability for expensive cleanup in the event of foreclosure. Moreover, federal and state cleanup requirements are often overly rigid and unwarranted for most proposed uses.

The result is a crisis for both our cities and surrounding communities. Businesses seek out clean lands and open space in surrounding suburbs and rural areas because the permitting process is less cumbersome and time consuming, and these lands are cheaper to develop, with no threat of liability. As a result, development sometimes consumes tracts that might well be conserved for other uses at the same time blighted areas continue to languish and deteriorate.

In Knoxville, we are taking a different approach. In 1992, the city of Knoxville, with the assistance of the Tennessee Valley Authority, completed a feasibility study of alternatives for comprehensive, rather than piecemeal, development of a Knoxville Center City Business Park. We looked at 566 center city acres, strategically located west of the central business district, and concluded that about 150 acres are potentially suitable for development as commercial or industrial sites. A wide range of possible uses include service, commercial, retail, office, light industrial, or wholesale and distribution firms that could bring an estimated 1,800 new manufacturing jobs to the community, in close proximity to neighborhoods where unemployment is high and the demand for blue-collar work is great.

The plan will encourage "green" business and industry compatible with its location bordering three residential neighborhoods. We plan not only to take an old inner-city industrial area and convert it to a vibrant business park but also to attract manufacturing enterprises that use recycled materials and recycle used products themselves. Incorporating greenways and open spaces, the park will enhance the physical environment and help transform a "community" of islands, no-man's-lands, physical walls, and barriers into a place that instills identity, pride, and ownership in the community. Involving community neighborhoods is essential to our plan. Through such entities as the Center City Business Park Advisory Council, Partnership for Neighborhood Improvement, and local neighborhood groups and associations, we are incorporating the ideas and goals of local residents at every step.

From the start, the proposed business park has had the strong support of both the public and private sectors—and, indeed, such collaboration is essential. However, if substantial, planned economic development is to occur in this area, the public sector must spark the action. The city is seeking a grant from the U.S. Environmental Protection Agency's (EPA's) Brownfields Economic Redevelopment Initiative to conduct further assessments of 27 sites that were identified as requiring further environmental review and cleanup. Several of the sites are listed as federal or state Superfund sites. While we have designed the park so that it can be developed in phases, we estimate that projected costs for the entire park, including property acquisition, relocation and clearance, site preparation and infrastructure, and related costs, will range from $17.8 to $18.4 million, an average of about $121,000 per acre. The EPA funds, if awarded, would be used to identify and rank hazardous waste sites and sources for funding for cleanup and to form partnerships at the federal, state, and local levels to implement a cleanup program.

We do not, however, plan to rely on EPA money alone. In Knoxville, we are fortunate to have a number of local sources of technical support, including the Waste Management and Remedial Action Group at Oak Ridge National Laboratory and the Energy, Environment, and Resources Center at the University of Tennessee. In addition to a mix of other federal, state, and local aid, we anticipate securing assistance from the Knoxville Community Investment Bank, launched in late 1994 thanks to the leadership and $1 million in seed money provided by National Football League pro Reggie White, who lives in the Knoxville area and attended the University of Tennessee in Knoxville. The bank, managed by the Inner City Community Development Corporation, is set up to provide financing for microenterprises and businesses that will locate in the feasibility study area and will provide jobs for residents in surrounding neighborhoods.

Clearly, the park is an ambitious and expensive endeavor and one that will take time to develop. However, we believe that the potential return, in jobs, quality of life, community pride, and revenues, is substantial. Calculating financial return only, we estimate that, based on a target market price of $60,000 per acre for a full-service industrial site and assuming a modest growth rate in manufacturing, the project could directly recover about $8.5 million, or about 46 percent of total costs, over a 9-year period. Over a 30-year period, the remaining investment could be recovered through revenues generated by the creation of new manufacturing jobs, increased personal income and spending, and private sector investment resulting in significant sales and property tax income.

Projects like Knoxville's could easily be replicated throughout the nation. However, they cannot succeed without a recognition that federal and state policies must do the following: incorporate standards for acceptable levels of cleanup based on intended use, encourage voluntary cleanup, require cleanup before an industry can relocate, exempt purchasers from liability if they do not contribute to the pollution, provide clear site titles, create a brownfields revolving loan fund, expedite the permitting process, and provide tax incentives for the redevelopment of brownfields.

The potential for private investment in and collaborative development of such sites is great—again, if government, and particularly EPA, undertakes the necessary steps to jump-start the process. There is so much more to be done. Locally, we are trying to do as much as we can to renovate these sites and return them to productive use, but, until EPA undertakes the necessary regulatory changes, we are severely limited in how much we can accomplish. With the very vitality of our communities at stake, EPA must establish programs and policies that harness the resources of both the public and private sectors to restore these once-vigorous commercial and industrial areas. The resulting success will mean not only jobs and revenues but also environmentally robust and aesthetically appealing commercial centers in the very neighborhoods that need them most.

Some urban and older suburban sites unfortunately carry a legacy of hazardous waste. In older areas, under Superfund, the federal program to clean up abandoned hazardous waste sites, and related state programs, there are often significant cleanup costs. In outlying areas, cleanup costs are rare. Developers, lenders, and investors are wary of cleaning up past contamination at "brownfield" sites. Even if they are willing to pay for expensive groundwater remediation or other long-term solutions, they fear uncalculated liabilities that may last for decades. The result? Developers and investors look for easier to develop "greenfield" sites in comparatively pristine outlying areas. Development leapfrogs to the urban fringe, pushing settlement farther out. Urban areas and older suburbs decline apace.

Public policy and investment should aggressively encourage redevelopment, giving older cities and suburbs a fair chance at renewal. At the very least, disincentives to redeveloping sites should be removed. One way to do this is to circumscribe cleanup standards and liability under Superfund. Lenders and investors who hold title but do not engage in substantial management of a property should be exempted from liability. Realistic, pragmatic goals for land use and redevelopment should set the cleanup standards for each site. Former industrial sites need not be cleaned up to be playgrounds. Once the cleanup is carried out, future liability should be limited. These steps alone may not induce urban redevelopment, but they can help level the field.

On the other hand, liability reforms should not undermine the intent of the Superfund law by providing unequal health protection for the nation's inner cities. Where residential areas are threatened by Superfund sites, wherever these sites may lie, cleanup standards must be sufficiently stringent to provide reasonable protection of neighbors' health.

Beyond removing unnecessary impediments, what is the public role in fostering the renewal of older cities and suburbs? Government alone, whether federal, state, or local, cannot restore declining urban areas. Private capital and entrepreneurship, lured by incentives, will make the significant difference. The 1976 tax law, for example, included incentives for the rehabilitation of historic structures, which proved to be a boon to urban revitalization. Community residents and groups must also be involved actively, for little worthwhile or lasting will happen without local citizen involvement.

Government can serve as a catalyst in a variety of ways. New public buildings, for example, can anchor downtown redevelopment. Public and private universities, hospitals, museums, and other institutions, which are committed to a specific location, can foster neighborhood restoration. Redevelopment plans can be fashioned around historic buildings, parks, greenways, waterfronts, and other distinctive community features. New cultural and sports facilities can be sited to spark renewal. Failed high-rise public housing projects must give way to modestly scaled housing that works for families.

Physical improvements, incentives for businesses seeking to expand downtown, or special efforts to recruit or create new businesses are essential. Assembling land into sites suitable for development, including clarifying title to abandoned properties, can help attract private invest-

Pittsburgh and other cities, as well as older suburbs, know that neighborhood renewal is hard work. Successful strategies to redevelop these areas and infill vacant
lands require partnerships involving citizens, neighborhood groups, government
agencies, and private investment. Courtesy of Western Pennsylvania Conservancy's Pittsburgh Park and Playground Fund, Pittsburgh, Pennsylvania.

ment. Anticrime efforts and school improvements are critical to maintaining the long-term economic viability of an area. Simplifying and ex-
pediting regulatory reviews can provide an incentive to developers to
build in predesignated places according to plan.

All these strategies—and many more—are already familiar to city officials, urban planners, and community activists who are seeking to renew
older areas. But they must be put into practice widely and vigorously if
older areas are to contribute positively to the metropolitan region's role as
the engine of economic growth in the United States and the global
economy.

AGENDA ITEM #8
As most land is privately held, private landowners must be galvanized to
assure a healthy land base. Corporate and individual stewardship must
be encouraged by providing education, tax incentives, and other benefits.

What the private sector does in advocating and exercising land stewardship is going to have enormous impact. One of the most significant
positive developments in land use over the past 20 years has been the out-
burst of private activity to improve the management of land resources.

More private landowners and developers must join this effort. For government, galvanizing private sector initiative means creating the incentives to stimulate private land conservation and stewardship by individuals and corporations.

Private involvement is key to assuring continuing productivity of the land and building communities that satisfy human needs. As noted earlier, private landowners own the majority of this nation's land, and most of the land that influences the quality of community development—farmland on the fringe of a growing metropolitan area, for example—is privately held. The future of the land in this country largely rests in the hands of private owners.

It is therefore especially significant that the most promising models of land conservation and sustainable resource use are the result of private initiative. A growing number of corporations and individuals, including timber companies and ranchers, for example, are managing their extensive holdings for wildlife habitat and other resource values, although their chief purpose is realizing a profit from the commodity value of the land. Environmentalists and business leaders do have common ground. Environmentalists are searching for new, nonregulatory means to achieve their goals, and businesses can often help them while benefiting both community relations and land productivity. Contributor Georges elaborates on the reasons that his company, for one, has chosen to manage its forestlands for sustainable use.

In 1994, the American Forest & Paper Association adopted principles and implementation guidelines for sustainable forestry. These guidelines are beginning to change the way member companies meet the need for wood and paper products while improving the management of forestlands. Among other objectives, members are encouraged to employ scientifically, environmentally, and economically sound management practices; protect water quality through riparian protection measures; promote wildlife habitat and diversity; and ensure the most efficient use of forest resources.

The Urban Land Institute (ULI), which represents 13,000 land use and real estate development professionals, is beginning to promote environmentally responsible development on a voluntary basis. Through conferences and publications, ULI communicates new options about site planning and building design, energy efficiency, and progressive lending practices that not only improve environmental quality but make money.

Voluntary initiatives like those of the American Forest & Paper Association and the Urban Land Institute, as well as initiatives by other

Progress in curbing water and other pollution problems increasingly depends on individuals exercising stewardship in how they use the land and other natural resources. Courtesy of Chesapeake Bay Foundation, Annapolis, Maryland.

trade associations, corporations, and private landowners must be recognized and encouraged by government agencies, community officials, and citizens groups. Government must also provide incentives—tax assessments that encourage the retention of forest cover, simplified procedures for swaps to consolidate resource lands fragmented in checkerboard ownership patterns, among others—to retain forestlands and the many benefits they provide, including fiber for consumer use, water quality, recreation, wildlife habitat, and more. In the absence of sufficient incentive, Georges fears, forestlands and agricultural lands could be rapidly converted to ranchettes or second homes, shopping malls, or classic suburban subdivisions.

As pointed out by contributor Hocker, a variety of tax policies can provide incentives for land stewardship. An income tax deduction may serve as an incentive to donate or sell land or grant an easement for conservation purposes. Exemptions from estate or inheritance taxes, or reductions of those taxes, as well as reduced local property assessments or taxes, offer other means for encouraging long-term stewardship of the land.

Another good idea is a "safe harbor." A safe harbor offers protection from liability, as well as from further restrictions or penalties that could be imposed by government agencies, provided the landowner enters into an

Some of the most promising models of land management for conservation of forestlands, wildlife habitat, and other open space are the result of private initiative. Community officials and citizen groups should encourage more cooperative, nonregulatory, and voluntary approaches to land conservation. Courtesy of International Paper Company, Purchase, New York.

agreement to improve habitat or restore damaged lands, for example, even while the land remains in agricultural or another use. According to contributor Wheeler, California has made use of safe harbors and is including this incentive in proposed revisions to the state's Endangered Species Act. Landowners are offered relief from regulation in exchange for agreements to manage habitat.

Cost-sharing arrangements between government agencies and private landowners to encourage stewardship of farmlands, wetlands, forestlands, open space, and other resource lands have proved fruitful, as has the expanding use of practices like the transfer of development rights to compensate landowners without resorting to public appropriations.

Federal, state, and local governments are experimenting with these incentives and others. They are indispensable to spurring land stewardship in the private sector. And that stewardship is indispensable to the future of land and life in this country.

AGENDA ITEM #9
A constituency for better land use is needed based on new partnerships that reach beyond traditional alliances to bring together conservation-

ists, social justice advocates, and economic development interests. These partnerships can be mobilized around natural and cultural resources that people value.

Without a strong constituency, few land use initiatives will succeed or endure. Strategies that draw on well-loved, broadly popular features of the landscape, both natural and cultural, mobilize constituencies. Abstract laws and prescriptive regulations do not.

A constituency is only part of the equation. A new spirit is needed among all involved individuals to achieve land use goals and build quality communities. Collaborative projects foster understanding and cooperation "across the barricades," as contributor Reilly notes. Businesses come to embrace an environmental ethic. Environmental groups come to understand business's point of view.

Contributor Georges recounts the experience of the regional Northern Forest Lands Council, created in 1990 by the governors of four northeastern states. Composed of representatives from government, the forest industry, environmental groups, and community leaders, the council was tasked with examining policies and programs to secure the future of forests in the economic and community life of the region. Everyone collaborated. In its final report, the council recognized that a working forest landscape, aside from wilderness protection, imposes the least impact of any human use on the land, and recommended ways to maintain private forestlands.

At the state level, new umbrella groups modeled after 1,000 Friends of Oregon are promoting citizen involvement in land use and community planning. Florida and Colorado have launched such groups, which offer extraordinary potential to foster collaborations and partnerships among diverse constituencies.

Every community needs a forum, a neutral meeting ground, where residents can seek consensus about land use and growth issues. Broad-based panels of local citizens and elected officials can craft a growth management plan, introduce performance zoning, and pursue other progressive measures.

Other local partnerships are needed to pursue specific goals. Contributor Jordan calls for multi-interest alliances that transcend traditional boundaries and can thereby gain the political strength to address community problems. He describes the Portland, Oregon, Coalition for a Livable Future, an organization that draws together environmentalists, church leaders, transportation and land use reformers, and social justice advocates. The group's purpose is to encourage a vibrant urban core and prevent suburban sprawl. Contributor Ken Buelt explains why he and other farmers are part of the constituency for Oregon's land use law: It assures that fertile farmland remains in agricultural production.

It has been the vision and tenacity of neighborhood groups that have made the difference in the South Bronx, once America's foremost symbol of urban decay, where pockets are now showing signs of bouncing back because of programs that rebuild housing for families, reclaim streets, and improve community services.

Communities can benefit from citizen-run land trusts that work in tandem with other interests. Land trusts provide an attractive, workable adjunct to public sector programs to conserve land. Contributor Hocker reports that they succeed because they encourage voluntary citizen action and use a variety of tools and funding mechanisms suited to local situations. Offering home-grown solutions tailored to local needs, land trusts typically are small and flexible, leveraging limited financial resources with voluntary involvement at the community level. They stress problem solving and cooperation rather than confrontation to achieve consensus solutions. A local land trust may be particularly well positioned to stimulate an initiative that goes beyond its specific conservation agenda to address local land use and community growth issues.

Private sector forums and task forces convened to consider a particular issue or accomplish a particular objective also are a staple of American life. The National Geographic Society and The Conservation Fund, for example, launched the National Forum on Nonpoint Source Pollution in 1994 to identify and demonstrate innovative, nonregulatory solutions for nonpoint source pollution, including education, voluntary initiatives, and economic incentives.

Some of the past decade's most successful experiences in building constituencies and forming partnerships among diverse groups have drawn on the unifying force of specific features of the landscape—natural and cultural resources treasured by people. These landscape-oriented initiatives usefully reverse the traditional approach to environmental management. Instead of trying to incorporate separate, fragmented, complicated regulatory regimes for land, air, water, and other resources into a single strategy, planning that employs geography as the organizing principle starts with a particular resource or place, identifies the issues and problems, and devises strategies to address them. This kind of approach certainly makes sense ecologically. The watershed, for example, is increasingly recognized as a critical element in smart and effective land use planning, as scientist and contributing author Norman Christensen explains. Contributor Reilly explains how this approach can unify a community, mobilizing support, energizing citizens and organizations, and leading to creative solutions. People more readily grasp a connection between how their actions affect the health of a resource they know and treasure than between resources in general and a set of constraints imposed by distant regulators.

Geographic initiatives thus offer opportunities to public officials and citizens groups to recast issues, refocus attention, and build new alliances. The concept works on both a small scale—a local creek or neighborhood, for instance—and larger ones, like watersheds or greenways. It works, too, at the scale of the Great Plains, the Great Lakes, the Gulf of Mexico, Chesapeake Bay, and the Everglades. It works for natural or built features of the landscape. The Hudson River Greenway, the Illinois-Michigan Canal National Heritage Corridor, the Tahoe Regional Planning Agency are all examples of initiatives that build a vision for the future by motivating people to protect what they value. A geographic approach can also focus attention on the restoration of degraded lands or special places.

Land trusts, conservation groups, community organizations, and other coalitions working in partnership with local businesses, large corporations, private landowners, and others represent a new grassroots way of doing business that is beginning to change the way land is used in community after community. These partnerships, along with new community forums and statewide organizations, represent one of the most significant forces for better land use and growth management yet to emerge. They reach beyond traditional alliances. They are targeting specific community resources and mobilizing people to protect or restore them. This is a fast-growing movement that is forming a constituency to which political leaders are increasingly responsive.

AGENDA ITEM #10
New tools can help meet the new challenges of land use. Land use disputes should be solved through negotiation or mediation rather than through confrontation and litigation. Geographic Information Systems (GIS) and other advances in technology also offer new opportunities for improving land use decision making.

Conflicts over land use are inevitable. Reconciling differences, finding common ground, and building consensus among diverse groups are never easy. Although litigation and confrontation have become commonplace in the land use field, there are workable alternatives to resolve differences cooperatively. Formal, organized dispute resolution processes are an accepted, effective method for making complex decisions that involve multiple stakeholders and diverse points of view. They have proved their worth in reaching a common understanding about the facts underlying a dispute and in examining consequences and trade-offs. They have led to novel and innovative solutions that accommodate multiple objectives. And they help explore compromises and build consensus.

The formal use of cooperative approaches to problem solving for environmental decision making, including negotiation, mediation, and arbitration, was unknown until the mid-1970s. A labor mediator first applied mediation to an environmental issue, successfully breaking a stalemate over a proposed dam. Disputes settled through mediation have involved highway projects, ferry terminals, power plants, shopping centers, landfills, and parks. In all these cases, parties to a dispute agreed to try a cooperative approach when they finally recognized that each side could block the other yet neither could achieve its own aims.

This kind of approach requires a change in government's role, away from that of regulator toward that of convener, facilitator, and implementer of consensus-based planning and land use decisions. To take one example, the U.S. Environmental Protection Agency through a formal procedure called negotiated rule making was able to put forth a plan to reduce air pollution affecting the Grand Canyon that achieved greater protection at less cost than the original agency proposal. The breakthrough, ending 10 years of litigation, occurred when stakeholders, including representatives from the responsible utility, environmental groups, and the U.S. Department of the Interior, were convened in one place and during their discussion came to understand the real objectives and concerns of the others.

Given the chance, Americans can be quite creative and resourceful in devising commonsense solutions to land use problems. Under more circumstances than now applied, with the right information and a good mix of leadership, motivations, and participants, formal and informal processes can help reconcile competing objectives and multiple interests, preempting lengthy, costly litigation.

Technology can help out. Since the early 1970s, such sophisticated tools as satellite imaging, computer simulations, and Geographic Information Systems (GIS), have greatly enhanced the ability to determine which areas are suitable for which types of land uses. Computer simulations, for example, are increasingly used to suggest the consequences of various development alternatives. Should zoning density be increased on a particular parcel? If so, what would the mass of buildings look like? How much additional traffic would be added? Now, both public officials and citizens find it easier to visualize the changes accompanying a specific proposal.

Loxahatchee Greenways Project

Elizabeth Shields and Matthew Sexton, The Conservation Fund

In an effort to create consensus-based solutions to regional environmental challenges, The Conservation Fund, 1,000 Friends of Florida, and the John D. and Catherine T. MacArthur Foundation embarked on the Loxahatchee Greenways Project in July 1992, with the vision of establishing a green infrastructure that will protect the resource base around which the economy and communities in the Loxahatchee River watershed can continue to grow.

The Loxahatchee River is one of the last remaining free-flowing subtropical rivers in the nation and one of the most natural, unaltered riverine ecosystems left in southern Florida. In recognition of its unique features as both an ecosystem and the source of water supply for the region, the river has been designated an Outstanding Florida Water, an Aquatic Preserve, a Manatee Protection Area, and, within its upper reaches, a National Wild and Scenic River, the only river in Florida with this designation. Yet, despite its recognition as an outstanding resource, the river system's overall health remains threatened.

Population growth leading to urban sprawl and accompanying hydrologic alterations are the most serious threats to the long-term preservation of the region's native ecosystems. Since World War II, urban and agricultural development have dramatically fragmented and reduced the amount of native uplands, wetlands, and wildlife habitat. Construction of canals and drainage systems has lowered groundwater tables and diverted surface flows. Projections indicate that population will double over the next 25 years making this one of the fastest-growing regions in the United States. Unchecked patterns of growth would result in further fragmentation of natural systems, place an additional strain on physical infrastructure, and replace existing agricultural and undeveloped lands currently serving as buffers to the region's natural resources with residential, commercial, and industrial developments.

Until the Loxahatchee Project began, the 18 different natural resource public agencies working in the Loxahatchee River watershed had never developed a plan for the protection of the bioregion. The main challenge for the Loxahatchee Greenways Project was to develop working relationships among these 18 separate local, regional, state, and federal agencies, which focus on a host of matters from biological phenomena to drinking water supply, to identify regional greenway linkages. To accomplish this, project participants used Geographic Information Systems (GIS) technology to build consensus on the location of regional greenway corridors that would connect the remaining undisturbed natural resource lands.

The project paired natural resource professionals with computer experts. As the first step, the team used traditional GIS technology to determine the historic natural conditions of the Loxahatchee Study region, to compile current natural resource information on hydrology, wetlands, wildlife habitat, and vegetative communities, and to identify existing land use patterns.

The consensus-building process occurred during the second step: identifying potential greenway design alternatives. There were as many different requirements for the greenways network as there were agencies participating. For example, the Florida Fish and Game Commission and the U.S. Fish and Wildlife Service were primarily concerned with wildlife habitat and movement, while the water management agencies were primarily concerned with water quality and quantity. To accommodate these diverse objectives, the team's computer experts developed a new user-friendly computer application that allowed natural resource professionals to engage in complex operations, testing various design alternatives. By facilitating this experimentation, the software identified common requirements for greenways among the participating agencies, thereby building consensus. The process allowed participants to weight the appropriateness of existing conditions in the watershed, specifying the best types of hydrological, vegetative, and land use conditions necessary to accommodate each agency's objectives for the greenways network. Then these weightings were used to calculate the optimal greenways corridors to link the remaining core natural areas. All of this resulted in the proposed Loxahatchee Greenways Network, which team members are actively working to implement by helping local governments to incorporate the design into their communities' comprehensive plans.

The Loxahatchee Greenways Project has had two phases. Phase I, ended in 1994 when the Natural Resource Task Force completed the work described above. In Phase II, the Greenways Advisory Committee began in February 1994 to establish "human connections to nature" in the region. The "human connections to nature" include environmental education centers, bikeways, and trails, as well as the design of land use patterns that are compatible with sustaining the greenway network while accommodating future community growth. The committee is creating connections by assisting a number of greenway prototypes—the Limestone Creek Greenway Project, the Juno Beach Bike Trail, the West Palm Beach Environmental Education

Center and Nature Trail, the Lake Okeechobee Greenway, and the Abacoa new town. Hundreds of citizens are participating in a visual preference survey to help identify desirable design characteristics for these projects.

By developing a partnership with the public and private sectors, community residents, and schools, the Loxahatchee Greenways Project has begun to create win-win, consensus-based solutions reconciling natural resource preservation with regional growth and development. The regional greenways network will provide the green infrastructure necessary to ensure the preservation of the river, its wildlife, vegetation, and wetland systems while protecting the water supply, providing recreational and educational opportunities for regional residents and visitors, reducing the future cost of public services, raising property values, and providing an overall higher quality of life. The Loxahatchee Greenways Project provides a productive model for sustainable development in both Florida and the nation.

Advances in computer technology also have made it possible to amass vast amounts of data and organize information clearinghouses and exchanges. GIS can be used to identify, map, monitor, and evaluate the health of groundwater aquifers, floodplains, estuaries, soils, wetlands, forests, agricultural lands, and other natural resources. And help answer questions: Where are natural systems vulnerable if development proceeds? Where is land suitable for a variety of uses, or a particular use?

In the years ahead, water will be of paramount importance for land use and growth management. It will shape and determine how people use much of the landscape. Geographic Information Systems make the task of incorporating essential information about water quantity and quality much easier to assemble, use, and communicate. Knowledge of this sort is essential in setting priorities for the conservation of natural systems and in devising effective strategies to guide development toward suitable locations.

The day is near when the computer and GIS, with databases, maps, inventories, and the like, will transform the planning process. California's Environmental Resources Evaluation System is now assembling fragmented data and making the information accessible to local land use decision makers. Every state should be readying the best possible up-to-date blueprint of natural resources, transportation networks, population and employment centers, and other critical information to help make better decisions about land use and growth.

Every community will need access to this information to engage average citizens on land use issues and to make informed decisions. For small communities and rural areas facing growth, state governments should provide assistance. GIS and other technology are not yet affordable for the wide spectrum of communities that could even now put them to good use. But programs explaining how natural systems work already exist. Maps identifying fragile and sensitive lands are becoming more available. One day, every citizen may know his or her watershed address and be able to see the consequences of development patterns on a computer screen.

·　·　·　·　·　·　·

Conclusion

The preceding agenda challenges everyone involved with land use issues. Accommodating growth and new development, renewing older cities and suburbs, protecting critical natural resources, securing further progress on environmental problems—these are real issues that confront communities across the nation. They do not lend themselves to simple solutions. The traditional toolbox, as useful as it is, does not provide enough to accommodate the variety of conditions and aspirations found around this diverse country. Thus, innovation and experimentation—trying novel approaches, forming alliances that cross traditional barriers, rewarding successful programs, in short, breaking the mold—are the watchwords for the day.

This book is a call to action. Its rallying cry is a new commitment to land stewardship, quality development, and environmental progress. These are the goals that the American people must embrace, and public officials and community leaders must speak to constructively, consistently, and frequently. Across the nation, community by community, Americans must make a commitment to good land use practices and pursue an agenda for the 21st century that will improve land use much as the environmental agenda of the past quarter-century challenged every segment of society to accomplish extraordinary environmental goals. With change comes opportunity, and the future guarantees abundant occasions for citizens, elected officials, community organizations, corporations, and others to take the initiative in developing a shared vision and collaborative approach that will guide growth in the 21st century.

Contributed Papers

•   •   •   •   •   •   •   •   •   •   •   •   •

This second part of the book offers a variety of perspectives about the use of land. The contributors are not planners in a professional sense, although they do represent diverse interests that directly affect how land is used and how land use decisions are made. Several contributors hold or recently held positions in federal, state, or local government. Others come from business or nonprofit groups. Drawing on their practical experiences over many years, the contributors of these papers consider the opportunities and constraints associated with the land use field today. Most importantly, they point out new and exciting possibilities for making land use more rational, efficient, and responsive to human needs.

Growth Management Plans

. . . .

Howard Dean

Howard Dean is Governor of the State of Vermont
and past Chairman of the National Governors' Association.

. . . .

In the summer of 1993, for two weeks following the annual meeting of the National Governors' Association in Tulsa, Oklahoma, my family and I traveled northward through several Plains states and into the Rockies. Like anyone who has been to those parts of our nation, I marveled at the beauty of the countryside. The sudden eruption of the Rockies out of the great expanse of grasslands is a scenic wonder second only—I'm biased— to the panorama of Vermont's undulating foothills set against the ragged peaks of the Green Mountains.

What surprised me about the countryside, however, was the sprawl. Not that the primarily rural counties of the western Plains can be compared to the megalopolis of the eastern seaboard, but as a visitor to the region I expected to find well-defined downtowns serving as the hub of commerce and society, thriving centers of activity where people shopped, worshipped, picked up their mail, and shared a cup of coffee with neighbors. Although I saw those places, more often the strip had taken over. Driving to new dots on the map along the linear, blue highways, we repeatedly discovered corridors of plastic signs in front of big box retailers, malls, and fast food eateries all afloat in seas of pavement. Housing tracts sprang up in the strangest places, often, it seemed, with no thought of how the new homes would affect an area's traffic, infrastructure, and scenic beauty.

I fear more and more of our country looks like this now, and that we are reaching a point where, except for the backdrop of distant hills, the main road into every town of any size will have the same impersonal appearance: colorful signs for Taco Bell, McDonalds', car dealerships, K-Mart, Wal-Mart, and the latest, greatest mall—all structures sprinkled helter-skelter across the landscape, sometimes looking as if they had just fallen out of the sky without any thought for what was already on the ground.

I rarely meet people who like this sort of growth. I know plenty of people who tolerate it, who shop and eat in this environment because it's there, just off the highway and handy. Many of them would gladly spend their money in a more human-scale environment if it were available. And from what I've heard in my years of talking to people about what sort of landscape they like, most folks would prefer to live in housing developments that were more community-oriented, where houses were clustered closer together amidst substantial open space—but still allowing for some elbow room between homes—rather than in a cookie-cutter row on one-acre lots.

And yet, for all that I've heard about the need to keep our downtowns vibrant, to direct new growth in a way that will have the least impact on our land and highways, to build homes in a way that will keep plenty of fields and forest undeveloped—for all that, if you begin talking about land use planning, people recoil in distrust or confusion.

The challenge to us who see the great value in good land use planning is to strip it of its jargon and make it simpler, to help people understand that land use planning is an integral part of making communities livable, along with quality schools, protection against crime, and other factors. This challenge falls first and foremost to the states, who are the obvious level of government to provide leadership. Nobody advocates a role for the federal government in this matter; planning based purely on local ordinances would lead to a hodgepodge of confusion and animosity. Only the states are positioned to coordinate the policy objectives of their environmental regulations with local and regional plans.

In Vermont, we have accepted the challenge, and we have a mixed record. On the regulation side, we have the nation's premier land use law, Act 250. Now nearly 25 years old and still our principal bulwark against unchecked growth, Act 250 relies on citizen panels to review individual projects. On the proactive planning side, we are still struggling, as are many other states.

Act 250 and, to a lesser extent, Act 200, its planning cousin, are working because of the strong environmental ethic of Vermonters. In many other parts of the country, this ethic is not as deeply embedded in the consciousness of the citizenry. To help people appreciate the value of good land use planning, state leaders need to articulate its benefits more clearly and repeatedly. These are the themes to visit again and again:

- We must protect our natural resources not only for the sake of the diversity of wildlife but for our benefit as well: We need aquifer recharge areas, wetlands to minimize the threat of flooding, and undeveloped land purely for the healthful and spiritual benefits of being in the outdoors. As a physician, I know that an increase in outdoor recreation opportunities has a direct impact on reducing health care costs. In addition, hunting and fishing are important parts of my state's heritage, and they generate more than $200 million in economic activity.

- We must make better use of our public investments. If we allow housing tracts, suburban shopping centers, and business parks to sprawl willy-nilly across our countryside, we all pay. In the wake of such growth, schools need to expand, highways need more lanes and interchanges, sewer lines must be run more miles—at a much greater cost than if we thoughtfully had planned development.

- Moreover, planned growth can make for more affordable housing, meaning people with more moderate incomes would not be forced to live farther away from their jobs, schools, and parks.

- Good planning goes hand in hand with intelligent economic development. The common misconception is that growth management equals no growth. Hardly. Economic development has been a focus of my administration, but not at the expense of Vermont's quality of life. With good land use planning, economic growth can be encouraged in designated growth areas, which will reduce infrastructure costs and save developers money in the regulatory process.

- Good planning protects the quality of our life and enhances our sense of community. In Vermont, we cherish our towns—from town meeting, democracy in its purest form, to our small elementary schools, where the personal touch is an important part of our children's education. Without good planning, our shared sense of community erodes, lost to sprawl, far-flung and impersonal housing tracts, and increased anxiety over how we, the residents of small political subdivisions, will pay for more municipal and school services.

Now I will attempt to explain why land use planning does not drag down a state's economic growth, then outline the various approaches to growth management used by some states, discuss common problems that arise when a state adopts a growth management law, using Vermont as the example, and note how land use planning is one part of the puzzle to keep our communities intact.

. . . .
Planning and Economic Growth

Doesn't land use planning throw a wrench into the economic engine of our nation? Don't towns that plan for growth wither economically, seeing jobs move to areas where laissez-faire mentality rules? Don't all states that devote time and energy to protecting their natural resources and quality of life lose when it comes to fostering a healthy economy?

Hardly. As governor I've heard those arguments often enough to have them memorized. There certainly are occasional glitches in land use regulatory processes. These processes are administered by humans, and humans make mistakes. But those who say land use laws drag down economic growth base their opinion on anecdotal information, not sound research.

A 1992 study by Stephen M. Meyer, professor at the Massachusetts Institute of Technology, conclusively discredits the belief that environmental protection statutes hinder economic well-being. The report did not look exclusively at land use planning laws, but its results are applicable. There is no correlation between strong environmentalism and weak economies, Meyer concludes:

> States with stronger environmental policies and programs did not exhibit hobbled economic growth or development compared to those with weaker environmental records. Moreover, rather than detect the absence of a systematic relationship between pursuit of environmental quality and economic growth and development—which would have been sufficient to dismiss the environmental impact hypothesis—the data revealed a clear and consistent positive relationship between the states' environmental effort and their economic performance. States with higher environmental rankings outperformed states with lower environmental rankings on four of the five economic growth indicators. This surprising yet solid finding allows us to dismiss the environmental impact hypothesis with even greater confidence.

Meyer states that while "these results may tempt the reader to infer that environmentalism stimulates economic prosperity, any such conclusion at this point would be speculation." States with strong environmental records may have also invested heavily in education, health, transportation, and communications infrastructure, which would stimulate their economies. But Meyer notes:

> There are, of course, some plausible arguments for accepting the positive association between environmentalism and economic growth as an indicator of a partial cause and effect relationship. Highly skilled and well educated workers tend to be attracted to regions that offer a better quality of life.

The Institute for Southern Studies sounded the same theme in its 1994 "Green and Gold" report. Using 20 economic indicators and 20 environmental measures, the report found that 9 states ranked among the top 12 on both scales, while 12 other states were among the worst 14 on both.

Vermont's growth management law, Act 200, is too new—we are still a year away from full implementation—to measure its impacts. Our regulatory land use law, Act 250, has existed for a quarter of a century. Although Act 250 occasionally says no to specific projects, which fuels animosity in a vocal minority opposed to the law, its overall impact on the Vermont economy has hardly been detrimental. Vermont's economic performance compared to the U.S. average during the past 25 years shows steady improvement. A 1992 report by the Vermont Natural Resources Council noted these economic benefits directly associated with Act 250:

- Act 250 will save Vermont ratepayers approximately $500 million during the life of the buildings affected by the act due to stronger insulation standards.

- Vermont banks performed better than their counterparts in every other New England state during the recent recession, in large part because Act 250 curbs the drive for speculative real estate ventures. In short, Act 250 levels out the peaks and valleys.

For a direct comparison, 16 New Hampshire banks, including 5 of the state's largest, failed during the recent recession. In Vermont, only 2 banks failed.

The intangible benefits are virtually impossible to measure. More than 8 million people visit Vermont annually, and tourism trade generates approximately $1.5 billion for our state annually. We know a large percentage of these visitors come to Vermont to enjoy our rural countryside

and small villages. Likewise, I know many business owners who were attracted to Vermont because of our state's quality of life.

Finally, what about the impact on individual towns? Don't towns have
to pursue development to make ends meet? No. A 1992 study by the
American Farmland Trust (AFT) looked at the economic impact of different types of development in three Massachusetts towns and concluded
that farms and open land:

> required very little in the way of public services. They may not
> have raised much in terms of gross revenue, but neither were
> they a drain on town resources. Although they may not have in-
> creased the towns' affluence, their net contribution was notable.
> This information should help towns resist the pressure to de-
> velop simply to increase their ratables, especially if they are ex-
> panding the residential base.

An October 1994 report produced by the Bennington [Vermont] Regional Commission reached the same conclusion:

> On average, municipalities with higher property values (aggre-
> gate as well as total residential and total commercial/industrial
> fair market value) have higher property taxes than those with
> lower levels of total property value. This fact indicates that
> towns with extensive development do not necessarily benefit, in
> terms of residential property tax burden, from a large tax base.
> To the contrary, towns with high property taxes tend to be those
> with high levels of development—due most likely to the associ-
> ated demand for public facilities and services.

The evidence collected in these reports refutes any notion that planning
to protect open space, consolidate growth in designated areas, and promote affordable housing stifles economic growth. On the contrary, every
state growth management plan has an economic development component. No governor is going to sign into law a growth management plan
that would stop growth. Planning for economic growth, orderly economic
growth, is an essential element. We welcome growth in Vermont, but on
our terms.

.   .   .   .

Some States' Approaches to Growth Management

Ten states now have growth management designs of some kind: Florida,
Georgia, Hawaii, Maine, Maryland, New Jersey, Oregon, Rhode Island,

Vermont, and Washington. The common thread among these states and plans is *coordination,* finding that elusive balance among municipalities, regions, and the state, with all three levels of government working toward the same goals.[1]

There is no magic formula that will work for every state. Each has its own traditions, political structure, and level of tolerance for new forms of governance, and its growth management plan must fit within those confines. In some states, there will be more emphasis placed on planning at the local level, because that's what the citizenry expects and will ultimately demand. Consider the difference between Vermont and Hawaii. Although the two states are roughly the same in terms of land mass, and both have small populations, they are virtually worlds apart in terms of governance. One good example: Hawaii has a single school board; Vermont has more than 300. Hawaii's approach to land use planning consolidates more—in fact, almost all—power at the state level, whereas in Vermont more authority is vested with the municipalities.

In sifting through the subtleties among the 10 states' growth management efforts, one can find a complex matrix of various mandates, enticements, review processes, and state agency requirements. In broad terms, most of the 10 states require or at least encourage planning at the local and regional levels and authorize some form of review to measure plans for consistency. Here is an overview of common elements found in the different states' growth management plans.

Who Must Plan?

In Florida, Maine, Oregon, and Rhode Island, municipalities must submit plans for state review. For different reasons, the legislatures of those states concluded that planning at the local level was necessary. In Rhode Island, a state with only 39 municipalities, it did not make much sense to build a planning process with a regional emphasis; instead, the Rhode Island law requires towns to coordinate with contiguous municipalities. Florida, struggling to handle explosive growth, decided it needed to move quickly and powerfully to protect its water resources.

The planning mechanisms of these four states have been described as "state dominant" or "top down" approaches because of the statutory requirement for local planning and vesting the authority to review plans at the state level. Each state has the authority to impose sanctions on towns adopting plans that do not meet required standards.

Vermont and Georgia opted to make local planning optional, but both states require regional plans, which necessitates local-regional cooperation. Both states also have statutory incentives for towns to plan.

One incentive for Vermont towns is that approved municipal plans—that is, town plans that have been OK'd by the regional planning commission (RPC)—have precedence over state agency plans. State agencies do not have to recognize town plans that have not received RPC approval.

In both Vermont and Georgia, municipalities maintain control over land use decisions that have only local impacts.

New Jersey law contains no requirement for consistency in local plans. Instead, counties serve as mediators between municipalities and the state planning commission in a complex but surprisingly effective cross-acceptance process.

Washington State took a more measured approach and mandated that counties with populations beyond a certain threshold or that have grown rapidly in recent years must prepare plans. Planning efforts are under way in 28 of the state's 39 counties. Some have voluntarily come under the program, while others that don't come under the full force of the laws are subject to certain state requirements in their local plans and regulations.

The state least like the others is Hawaii. On this island state with a fragile ecology and a limited amount of land in private ownership, land use policy and regulatory power are vested in the Hawaii State Land Use Commission. It is highly unlikely any other state could adopt a similar state-administered program. Furthermore, the system has become increasingly ineffective over time and has been recently under executive review, with major changes proposed but not adopted as of this writing.

How Do States Check for Consistency?

In terms of a state-dominant approach, Oregon, Rhode Island, and Florida serve as consistency models. Each demands state approval of local plans, while Florida also requires approval of regional planning. In Rhode Island, if a town fails to write a consistent plan, the state will prepare the plan on the town's behalf. Maine, the fourth state with a more top-down process, does not mandate formal certification. Rather, municipalities may submit their plans for review and comment, which places more emphasis on local decision making.

In Vermont and Georgia, where local plans are not mandated, if a municipality writes a plan, both states require review at the regional level to verify consistency. The Georgia Department of Community Affairs has final say in whether to accept local plans recommended for approval by a regional development center. In Vermont, discussed in more detail below, regional planning commissions have the authority to approve or reject local plans. Appeals of RPC decisions go to a special board, the Council of Regional Commissions.

New Jersey, as mentioned earlier, mandates mediation at the county level and has established a new mechanism: cross-acceptance. In simplest terms, officials at the county level are empowered to attain compatibility between local, county, and state plans without any threat of a regional or state veto of a local plan.

How Have States Addressed Urban Sprawl?

Oregon's landmark growth management system pioneered statewide planning in the 1970s with the development of urban growth boundaries (UGBs) intended to limit almost all forms of urban development. "The first and still the most powerful comprehensive effort to contain sprawl by establishing some kind of line within which most urban development will occur was put in place in Oregon in the mid 1970s in the form of urban growth boundaries aimed at containing almost all urban development," writes DeGrove in *Planning and Growth Management in the States*. De-Grove continues:

> All urban-scale development not vested or approved under a difficult exception process was to take place within these boundaries. Population growth projections for a twenty-year period were to be accommodated fully within these boundaries. While not without its faults, the UGB system has been put in place and has contained most urban-scale development in Oregon within the boundaries.

Empowering planners to draw specific boundaries to stop urban growth requires a good deal in intermunicipal cooperation and is not politically feasible in many states, probably including in my own. Indeed, it was fear about a possible state land use plan with lines drawn on a map that scuttled Vermont's first attempt at a growth management planning effort in the early 1970s.

As for a more rural state, Maine provides an example of how to limit sprawl with a planning goal that directs municipalities to identify "growth areas" for the next 10 years out.

Who Requires Concurrency?

Florida is blazing the path in the "pay as you grow" approach toward managing growth, a concept more states should consider. As stated in De-Grove's book:

The concurrency of the growth management systems of the 1980s represents, where fully applied and funded, nothing less than a revolution in what is required of planners and the planning process. A concurrency management system demands a constantly updated management information system that has been, except for rare exceptions, non-existent in the local government planning process. Concurrency demands the data necessary to set levels-of-service for specific facilities. It also requires the preparation of capital facilities programs that are not "wish lists" but are supported by documented funding sources. Another essential feature is the linking of land use transportation as well as other key facilities.

Vermont's Act 200 does not contain concurrency language. Fortunately, Act 250, the regulatory side of our land use statutes, allows district environmental commissions and the appellate Environmental Board—all citizen commissions—to impose proactive conditions on land use permits. In one well-publicized case, the Environmental Board granted a permit to a developer to construct a Wal-Mart in a town seven miles east of Burlington only after significant improvement to the adjacent state highway had been completed.

So What Works?

No one formula guarantees success. But the track record of the 10 states during the past decade clearly shows that certain elements, both in statute and in the political climate, are crucial to the success of growth management efforts:

- *Consistency.* Without it, municipalities and counties would operate with their own definitions and planning goals, which would only intensify the type of destructive competition for development that already exists. Whether through mandatory compliance or incentives, and I prefer the latter, states must strive for consistency in planning at each level.

- *Clarity.* In Vermont and in many other states, citizen boards are primarily responsible for carrying out the provisions of planning laws. Growth management statutes with unreasonable and conflicting planning goals and a confusing process will only discourage the volunteers willing to serve on these boards.

- *Natural resources, economic development, and affordable housing.* Any successful growth management legislation needs all three if for no other reason than to bring together the coalition of stakeholders necessary to win passage.

- *Dedicated funding.* Several states, including Vermont, pledged financial support for their planning efforts but then made cuts to the programs during the recession of the early 1990s. This clearly left some planning advocates dispirited.

- *Political leadership.* Without backing from the governor and legislative leadership, growth management planning is difficult to establish and maintain. Sustained leadership is necessary through passage and implementation of the law.

- *Consensus building.* Given the many stakeholders with a vested interest in the results of any growth management plan, consensus building is crucial before the introduction of the first bill in any state's legislature.

. . . .

The Vermont Experience

The story of Vermont's Act 200 is, in many ways, representative of how states lay the foundation for growth management laws, how the laws get enacted, and the reaction that soon surfaces. In other respects, however, Vermont's experience has been notably different.

Pinpointing the genesis of Act 200 is not easy. It dates at least to 1968, when Deane C. Davis, a Republican known then as a conservative businessman, was campaigning for the governorship. While campaigning that year, Davis was shocked at the level of shoddy development taking place in ski towns. Soon after taking office, Governor Davis appointed an 18-member committee to prepare a package of legislation for the 1970 legislature to address many of the environmental problems he had seen. The committee report led to the passage of Act 250, which applies to a project that involves any of the following:

- Construction of a commercial or industrial enterprise on more than 1 acre of land, or on more than 10 acres if in a municipality with permanent zoning and subdivision bylaws;

- Construction of more than 10 housing units within a radius of five miles;

- Subdivision of property into 10 or more lots;

- Construction of a road if the roadway accesses more than 5 lots or is longer than 800 feet;

- Development above 2,500 feet in elevation, including logging activities;

- Substantial changes to existing developments.

Any project subject to Act 250 must meet 10 criteria—some of which have subcriteria—covering, for example, the protection of water resources, air quality, traffic, municipal and school services, wildlife habitat, and aesthetics.

Although a landmark law, Act 250 was not intended by its sponsors to serve as the only piece of the land use puzzle. As described in the *1988 Report of the Governor's Commission on Vermont's Future,* its framers expected Act 250 to serve as a first step:

> The passage of Act 250 and related measures signaled the emergence of environmental protection as a major political issue. But while the regulatory provisions of Act 250 went into effect on June 1 of 1970, development of the full three-stage planning mechanism called for in the act had only just begun. It was only partially complete when it was finally abandoned six stormy years later. The Land Use Plan, the important capstone of the law, was never implemented. It languished in the state Legislature during the energy crisis years of the early 1970s, and by the middle of that decade was clearly defeated.

In the minds of most Vermonters, for the first dozen years following the passage of Act 250, that law alone sufficiently controlled growth. The huge increase in fuel prices, followed by a massive jump in interest rates and the recession of the late 1970s, tempered growth in Vermont. As the state continued to welcome more residents and businesses, economic forces and Act 250 appeared to keep the rate of growth in check.

In the early 1980s, however, Vermont's growth rate again shot up, and many residents noted that, despite its strengths, Act 250 could not adequately address the cumulative impacts of development. In September 1987, Governor Madeleine Kunin appointed the Governor's Commission on Vermont's Future, a 12-member body that listened to more than 2,000 Vermonters in hearings around the state in the following three months. The 1988 legislature took the commission's recommendations, amended them, and narrowly passed Act 200, with these components:

- A set of state planning goals set in statute that are to guide the land use planning of local, regional, and state entities.

- A foundation in municipal planning. Acknowledging Vermont's strong history of local control, planning would be accomplished at the most local level possible. Planning at the local level was not mandatory.

- A coordinated planning program in which local, regional, and state plans all address the state planning goals and in which local plans approved by regional planning commissions have precedence over state agency plans.

- Explicit authority to levy impact fees for towns with approved plans.

- An appeal/dispute resolution process to address disagreements about land use planning issues between state, local, and regional plans.

- Dedicated funding from an increase in Vermont property transfer tax to support local and regional planning through an annual entitlement distributed by formula.

- Creation and temporary funding of a state GIS (geographic information system).

- A new emphasis on planning for affordable housing.

In Act 200, the legislature created an opportunity for truly coordinated planning that would harmonize local, regional, and state plans around a common set of goals and policies. Under certain circumstances, the law requires state agencies to make their plans and programs compatible with provisions of municipal land use plans, giving towns an unprecedented voice in how state agencies carry out their responsibilities. And the law created a new appeals body composed of people from all levels of government, the Council of Regional Commissions, to hear and resolve disagreements about conflicting land use plan provisions.

Passage of the law required a good deal of political maneuvering, foreshadowing the protests to come. Immediately following Governor Kunin's signing Act 200 into law, there was a lull. But opponents of the law began organizing in the following autumn and by Town Meeting Day in 1989 an orchestrated attack was under way.

Assaults on Act 200 continue today, almost always focusing on the provision requiring regional review of town plans. The consensus that appeared to coalesce during the commission's hearings has dissipated. It is

hard to define all of the reasons for the backlash, but the following are
some:

- *Politically unpopular reviews for consistency by the regional planning
  commissions.* Like most New England states, Vermont has almost no
  county government. In a state where local control has long served as
  a rallying cry, the concept of people from the town next door having
  a voice in your community's affairs struck many Vermonters as foreign. Vermonters understand that a major development in neighboring towns can have a huge impact on their community in terms of
  traffic and tax rates, but many aren't willing to part with a long-
  standing political tradition. With the benefit of hindsight, we recognize that we did not do a good enough job of making local officials
  comfortable with this concept.

  Regional review of local plans remains the focal point for opponents of Act 200. Reacting to what I consider a small but vocal minority of Vermonters, the 1995 General Assembly passed legislation
  to remove this section of our growth management law. I vetoed this
  bill, and fortunately the legislature sustained my action.

- *Incentives not strong enough.* If there is one aspect of Act 200 I don't
  believe most Vermonters understand, it is the importance of the
  incentives contained in the law. Towns seemed unenthusiastic about
  the promise of having RPC-approved plans that take precedence
  over state agency plans. This provision, for example, gives a municipality the authority to veto an Agency of Transportation plan to
  widen a state highway that runs through the community's downtown.

  A second incentive, empowering towns to levy impact fees after a
  certain date if they had an RPC-approved plan, was actually viewed by
  many as a step backward. Municipalities in many other states can levy
  such fees without having a plan approved by anyone, and some Vermont towns had already begun levying impact fees prior to the passage
  of Act 200, so the law infringed on an already growing practice.

- *Too many planning goals.* The 1988 legislature passed Act 200 with
  32 planning goals, a number that intimidated many municipal officials, who viewed the goals as complex, unattainable, and unrealistic.
  Two years later the legislature reduced the number of planning goals
  to 12.

- *The recession.* For many Vermonters, the need for a growth management law became irrelevant as the state went into a recession in 1990.

Act 200 should have been touted more as a way to deal with change, not just growth.

- *Funding.* Related to the above, funds for planning shrunk as the state struggled to balance its budgets.

- *Breakdown of coalitions behind the law.* Although some organizations that supported passage of Act 200 remain vocal supporters of the law, many stakeholders who appeared to have been on board when the Governor's Commission on Vermont's Future presented its report have become silent, maybe taken aback by the shrillness of property rights activists (some supporters, myself included, have been hanged in effigy) or maybe just tired of the battle. Awkwardly for Governor Kunin, she and members of her administration were often the only spokespersons for the planning law when the anti-Act 200 forces fired off accusations. How much better it would have been for a coalition of supporters to step in occasionally to take the heat.

Some opponents of Act 200 will never be persuaded to support the law or any form of growth management, and many of them dream of repealing both Acts 200 and 250. Others will come around, but need to be brought into the process and empowered. Governor Kunin attempted to foster this sort of broad-based support in creating the Governor's Commission on Vermont's Future. Members included a town manager, ski area owner, dairy farmer, and other business people. Their support of the commission's findings made passage of the law possible, but their constituencies haven't stuck by Act 200 through its implementation.

With the advantage of 20-20 hindsight, it is easy to see how Georgia provides a better model for developing consensus in terms of bringing more stakeholders to the table and giving them sufficient time. A 35-member commission was given *18 months* to propose a plan. As DeGrove writes:

> The Governor's Growth Strategies Commission in Georgia is the most impressive example of bringing all the stakeholders to the bargaining table in a remarkably open process. The result was support for the growth management system proposed to the 1989 session of the Georgia legislature by every key stakeholder in the system, including homebuilders, environmentalists and local governments.

For states with a fairly clear division between areas absorbing rapid growth and regions where development has languished, Washington

State's approach merits consideration. As mentioned above, counties in Washington must write growth management plans if their size or growth rate is above a certain threshold or they've experienced a population in crease of more than 20 percent in just the past decade. Two-thirds of the state's 39 counties are planning. As for the remainder, primarily in eastern Washington, they still have many duties to carry out under the planning law, such as identifying critical lands, but can forego more demanding functions, such as designating urban growth areas.

.   .   .   .
Beyond Planning

Valuable as it is, planning alone will not lead to sound land use decisions. States must do more.

Regulation

There's the word, highlighted, for the world to see. A state, region, or municipality can write all the rules it wants upfront and still will need someone to determine whether all parties are operating within the bounds of statute and regulation. Every football player at the professional level steps on the field knowing the rules—but imagine the chaos in a game without referees.

As described earlier, Act 250, Vermont's statewide land use regulatory process, has not hindered economic development. It's not perfect, and the biggest complaint from the development community is a lack—sometimes real, sometimes perceived—of predictability. Predictability comes from better planning and a fair and impartial application of the law. Furthermore, as members of my administration and I have dug deeper into these complaints, we find that Act 250 is often blamed for the consequences of other state regulatory processes and sometimes even decisions at the local level.

Other Initiatives

Even the coupling of good planning and regulation is not enough. State leaders must be more proactive if they want to encourage growth in a way that will protect open land and thriving downtowns.

A SOUND SYSTEM OF TAXATION

The greatest disincentive to good land use planning in Vermont is, by far, our reliance on the property tax. Despite many efforts in recent decades to find other sources of revenue, the Vermont legislature has failed to relieve our cities and towns from depending on the property tax to fund municipal and educational services. The disparity between our communities is staggering: Towns with ski areas and valuable lakefront property within their borders typically have low tax rates and, as a result, well-funded schools and town services. Communities with weak tax bases depend on the state for aid to education, which is never enough to meet the tremendous need. For Vermonters, the disparity in effective tax rates ranges from less than $.50 per $100 evaluation for some "property-rich" towns to more than $3 per $100 evaluation.

This has left many select boards and planning commissions believing that the only way to bolster their communities' financial picture is to attract more development. But residential growth is not the answer. More homes bring more students into the school system, and this influx in turn increases taxes, which creates a vicious circle that left unchecked leaves the town fruitlessly trying to build enough homes to pay for the services required by the residents of these homes—like a spaniel that keeps chasing its tail. As the 1992 study by the American Farmland Trust (AFT) stated:

> In this [cost of community services] study of three Massachusetts towns, AFT found the average ratio of dollars generated by residential development to services required was $1 to $1.12— for every dollar raised by residential revenues, the towns spent an extra 12 cents in direct services. These included education and social programs, public health and safety, highway maintenance and public works, and even local government. On the other hand, the average ratio for farm, forest and open land was $1 to 33 cents—for every dollar raised after the town provided services, 67 cents remained.

Certainly some types of growth will reap property tax benefits. The same AFT study found a commercial/industrial ratio of $1 to $.41, and certainly clean, light industrial businesses are every governor's favorite type of growth.

PERMANENT PROTECTION OF
OPEN LAND AND AFFORDABLE HOUSING

Planning cannot guarantee permanent protection of critical habitat. It cannot guarantee a critical mass of working farms in a region to support the associated businesses that farmers need, such as grain stores and machinery dealers. Nor can it guarantee enough housing will be available to meet the needs of a state's low-income residents. To meet all of these needs, a state must act creatively.

A powerful coalition of conservationists and housing advocates in Vermont came together in 1986 and developed a proposal for a trust fund that would preserve farmland and natural areas and build more afford able housing units. Armed with detailed information about how the federal government was failing in the housing arena, hurting our dairy farmers with a deeply flawed milk pricing system, and consistently underfunding the Land and Water Conservation Fund, coalition members intensively lobbied the 1987 legislature. The result was the Vermont Housing and Conservation Trust Fund, an innovative quasi-governmental entity that encourages partnerships with nonprofit organizations as a way of stretching public dollars further. Funded primarily through our annual Capital Bill, the fund has been a tremendous success: The Vermont Housing and Conservation Board (VHCB) in its first seven years invested nearly $40 million in the development, preservation, and rehabilitation of 3,500 units, leveraging $147 million in other public and private investment; VHCB has helped protect about 25,000 acres of natural and recreation lands and has purchased the development rights on more than 41,000 acres on 122 working farms.[2]

REINVIGORATING DOWNTOWNS

Through capital projects, such as redeveloping Newport's waterfront on Lake Memphremagog, and an executive order directing all state agencies to locate their offices in downtowns unless impossible, we in Vermont have made a concerted effort to keep our downtowns vibrant. To assist the towns in doing this themselves, my administration has created the Vermont Downtown Program, modeled in part after a program developed by the National Main Street Center of the National Trust for Historic Preservation. Our program, operated by the Agency of Development and Community Affairs, focuses on four major activities:

- Bringing key local players together, raising funds, and developing and implementing a plan for action;

- Helping businesses reposition themselves to capitalize on market opportunities, supporting business expansion, and recruiting new businesses to the downtown;

- Physically improving the downtown through building rehabilitation, facade improvement, landscaping, and traffic and pedestrian walkway improvement;

- Better marketing and promotion.

Sometimes this emphasis on downtown requires hands-on lobbying. I traveled to Arkansas in 1993 to encourage Wal-Mart officials to consider building slightly smaller stores in our downtowns rather than on pastures five miles outside of town. The company has responded positively in one corner of our state and intends to build a store in downtown St. Johnsbury, a midsized community in Vermont's Northeast Kingdom. I've also lobbied the U.S. Postal Service to keep its facilities in our downtowns; post offices provide an important part of a community's fabric.

All of this requires innovative thinking, whether the topic is on-farm energy-saving initiatives or exploring the feasibility of commuter rail to alleviate highway congestion. We in state government need to approach problems differently, explore the possibility of partnerships with private businesses and nonprofits, and understand that decisions we make everyday may have an indelible impact on the landscape around us.

. . . .
A Sense of Community

Speaking before the Rutland Rotary Club in 1929, writer Sinclair Lewis summed up his appreciation of Vermont as follows:

> I like Vermont because it is quiet, because you have a population that is solid and not driven mad by the American mania—that mania which considers a town of four thousand twice as good as a town of two thousand or a city of one hundred thousand fifty times as good as a town of two thousand. Following that reasoning, one would get the charming paradox that Chicago would be ten times better than the entire state of Vermont, but I have been in Chicago and have not found it so.

No offense to Chicago—it's a wonderful city and I've enjoyed visiting it—but I don't want a Chicago where I live. And I don't believe most folks in Rockland, Maine, want one either. I would bet the same is true for the residents of Bellingham, Washington; Cheyenne County, Nebraska; Salisbury, Maryland; and Astoria, Oregon.

My entire discussion about growth management derives directly from my belief that we must value our sense of community and control our common fate. For many Americans, even for some who deeply cherish the sense of community, the concept and practice of land use planning seem to go against the grain of American history. But we're slowly learning, that with the frontier closed, healthy economic growth and quality of life today are increasingly and inescapably tied to intelligent land use.

We in state government must assume the leadership for fostering smart land use planning—growth management laws that acknowledge the economic importance of good planning as well as the health and quality of life benefits. Our commitment will involve education and consensus building, no easy tasks in an era of sound bites where the pithiest and increasingly the most vitriolic comments attract the attention of our media.

The challenge is present in every one of our states. Now is the time to respond.

NOTES

1. The most current assessment of these states (with the exception of Hawaii) is John M. DeGrove's *Planning and Growth Management in the States: The New Frontier for Land Policy* (Cambridge, Mass: Lincoln Institute of Land Policy, 1992).
2. For a fuller description of the Vermont Housing and Conservation Trust Fund, see Endicott, Eve, *Land Conservation through Public/ Private Partnerships* (Washington, D.C.: Island Press, 1993).

Ecosystem Management: An Organizing Principle for Land Use

. . . .

Douglas P. Wheeler

Douglas P. Wheeler is Secretary of the California Resources Agency.

. . . .

Every day the *San Francisco Chronicle* carries a small map of California that forecasts the state's probable weather conditions for the next day. On the newspaper's map, California is divided into nine climate zones. In effect, the editors have made a policy call: California's weather, they have said, is too complex to be rendered comprehensible in a simple graphic, and understanding the weather depends on the deployment of equivalently complex tools. To be useful to readers, in other words, the map must be broken down into rational components.

At the California Resources Agency, we have followed a similar logic. On our map, California is divided into 10 bioregions. This map was originally created in 1988 as a product of long deliberations among members of the state's Interagency Natural Areas Coordinating Committee (INACC). Interestingly enough, our map closely resembles other maps of the state's natural hydrology and settlement patterns dating to the mid-19th century, long before urban development projects had obscured the direct convergence between human activities and the natural order. Early settlers, heavily dependent on sustainable forests and fisheries and on subsistence agriculture, showed great respect for natural systems and lived and worked within their contours.

Despite development over the years and the imposition of superficial subdivisions, the strength of natural systems remains evident, and the logic of their alignments compelling. Even the climate zones of the morning newspaper, which range from the cool, wet coastal forests of the far northern Klamath province to the arid heat of desert highlands some thousand miles away, reflect the permanence and diversity of our natural order. Thus, no matter what lines may have been superimposed, or alterations to the landscape made, we return inevitably to the enduring reality of California's bioregions as a guide to the management of natural resources, including the land itself.

The same logic may not obtain in other areas of the United States. Some states are homogeneous enough to escape subdivision. Other states are small enough to be considered as components of multistate regions. Still more complicated are those particularly grand theaters of biological clustering—usually large watersheds, mountain ranges, basins, and estuaries—that imprint themselves on multiple states and sprawl across time and climate zones. Common to many logics organized around biology and landforms, however, is a disregard of jurisdictional boundaries. The cunning and inexorable logic of nature seldom complies with the arbitrary and compromising logic of politics.

. . . .
Background

In California, we are still in the experimental stage of working with this new organizing principle of ecosystem management. Not long after I was appointed California's seventh secretary for resources by newly elected Governor Pete Wilson in 1991, with broad resources management responsibilities at the state level, not unlike those of the U.S. secretary of the interior, I was approached by a coalition of state and federal land managers with an appealing organizational concept. Why not, they argued, agree to pursue our disparate responsibilities—whether emanating from Sacramento or Washington—in a more coordinated manner and, at the same time, along bioregional lines.

The leader of this visionary cabal was an unlikely revolutionary. Ed Hastey had long been state director in California for the federal Bureau of Land Management (BLM), and, in developing programs for multiple use of BLM's vast California acreage, did not always enjoy the support of environmental activists. Ed was nonetheless a canny public land manager who had become increasingly frustrated with overlap among state and federal agencies, lack of clear direction, paucity of valid resource data, and the resulting failure by all concerned to achieve effective land use policies.

To his credit, this "Viceroy of California," as Secretary of the Interior Bruce Babbitt describes him, had earlier experimented with Coordinated Resource Management Plans (CRMPs) in areas with large BLM ownership. But time was running out for California, whose population had doubled since the mid-1960s—and for Ed Hastey, who was nearing the end of a long career in public service. Ed proposed, and I—perhaps too readily—agreed, that we should embrace the deceptively simple idea of fostering regional efforts to promote the conservation of biodiversity and to encourage compatible economic development.

Following execution of a memorandum of understanding (MOU), we created the California Executive Council on Biological Diversity (now the California Biodiversity Council), a collaborative body of more than two dozen representatives drawn from the following: state agencies responsible for land, wildlife, water, parks, agriculture, fish, and forests; the University of California; local governments, conservation districts, and associations; and the federal departments that, collectively, manage half of the state's lands. In its first act, the new council adopted the bioregional map as a basis for coordinating activities.

Invariably, such developments have their origins in earlier events and are built on those sturdy foundations. Although the Biodiversity Council has adopted the INACC map, with its 10 bioregions, there are other ways in which to draw defensible boundaries. In her book *An Island Called California*, published more than 25 years ago, Elna Bakker identified 11 bioregional communities in California.

To be sure, not all of the state's relevant departments have been reorganized along bioregional lines, but we have made especially significant progress within the Resources Agency itself. We have given emphasis to conservation of biodiversity in pursuing the individual missions of the agency's Parks and Recreation, Forestry and Fire Protection, and Fish and Game Departments.

Although to the signatories of the MOU seemingly benign, these concepts of "biodiversity" and "bioregional planning" were not at first well understood or widely accepted by the private sector. At the "Sierra Summit," which I had convened in the fall of 1991 to discuss bioregional planning as a possible solution to resource management conflicts in the Sierra Nevada, representatives of timber and mining companies, some resort operators, and local officials all voiced concern that our MOU contemplated an extension of land use regulation, or the imposition of regional government, or both. Pickets appeared at a series of workshops in small mountain communities, with placards warning of a "Wilson-Wheeler Land Grab" and newly minted buttons with the now-familiar diagonal slash superimposed on the word "biodiversity." Nor were the protesters placated by assurances that state and federal officials only sought to coordinate activities and share information. Those who objected to wasteful, duplicative, and overzealous government were in no way relieved to learn that the MOU was intended to make government more effective.

Ultimately, the principles of our MOU were embraced by additional agencies and, most important, by all of the counties in the state. As a result, we are able to address various problems with an equally various array of skills and instruments. The Council on Biodiversity, which meets quarterly, has become the most important statewide forum of its kind, providing a showcase for grassroots activity in every bioregion and assuring the active engagement of federal, state, and county agencies. Although we had originally planned for the establishment of regional councils, local organizations concerned with the conservation of biodiversity, including many grassroots groups focused on watersheds, have argued against the interposition of a regional structure per se, much as landowners had expressed their opposition to regional governance. Thus, in each of our bioregions, we have a variety of initiatives going on. They are all different, for each is designed to respond in a tailored way to the givens of the biology and the land in each specific region. Some initiatives are more advanced than others: those in the South Coast and the Bay-Delta bioregions lead the way.

In Southern California's five-county, 6,000-square-mile region, the Natural Communities Conservation Planning (NCCP) program, designed to protect the state's remaining coastal sage scrub habitat—home of the California gnatcatcher, a threatened species of bird, and numerous other imperiled species—is the flagship of our experiments. Although our early success in the South Coast region points toward a new way of thinking about the land and its uses, we are aware of our debt to others who have gone before. A regional approach to the protection of San Francisco Bay dates back to 1965. In 1975, a private task force that studied land use practices throughout the state published *The California Land: Planning for People,* a seminal report identifying problems that are today even more acute. Creation of the State Coastal Conservancy in 1976 provided a model for dealing unconventionally and simultaneously with environmental, economic, and social issues, especially those that cross jurisdictional boundaries and require imaginative solutions.

Despite the success of these early efforts, there remains an urgent need to protect California's extraordinary natural legacy. In *The Diversity of Life,* famed Harvard biologist E.O. Wilson puts our task in its largest perspective: "It is reckless to suppose that biodiversity can be diminished indefinitely without threatening humanity itself." Californians have long acknowledged that existing mechanisms are inadequate to safeguard this legacy in the face of mounting population and development pressures. Writing about California's biodiversity in *Living on the Edge,* a new resource guide edited by Carl Thelander, Raymond Dasmann observes that "the view of the natural world as a place to live, and therefore to care for, has not held its own against the view of nature as something to exploit. We have reached our present dilemma: Now we must balance the need to protect and maintain what is left of California's once-renowned biodiversity against the need to care for the well-being of its human population."

Population pressure dwarfs and compounds all other problems. California's population, now 32 million, is expected to approach 60 million before the middle of the next century, but the state's explosive growth has already squeezed the range of policy options and pushed many alternatives to the margins. Population has grown so swiftly that even the projections found in *The California Land,* thought to be extreme in 1975, have been outpaced. More recently, both the private sector Bank of America and the public sector Department of Water Resources have studied our population growth and come to the same conclusion: It is simply imperative that we quickly find proper mechanisms for the optimal distribution of our burgeoning population. The sustainability of our economy and our resources hangs in the balance. Our landscapes can no longer support uncoordinated and haphazard settlement patterns.

In its recently released assessment of the cost of sprawl, *Beyond Sprawl: New Patterns of Growth to Fit the New California,* the Bank of America concludes that "we can no longer afford the luxury of sprawl. Our demographics are shifting in dramatic ways. Our economy is restructuring. Our environment is under increasing stress. We cannot shape California's future successfully unless we move beyond sprawl."

To stand on the flat bluffs overlooking the seaward reaches of the San Dieguito River Park, as I did recently, is to be overwhelmed by an undeniable truth—the relentless power behind the human drive to occupy and master a landscape. To the north toward Escondido and to the south toward San Diego, and packed within five miles of the Pacific Ocean, lies an extraordinary array of human enterprises, each jostling the other within severe limits of space, each competing with the other to claim a place. In the hurly-burly of such vigorous human activity, the San Dieguito valley— the only greensward to be seen in this vista—looks painfully vulnerable and lonely, its protected status notwithstanding.

Unfortunately, this vista carries metaphorical overtones, for much of California's natural bounty, its unsurpassed inheritance of biological treasures, is already at risk. Scientists have estimated—or underestimated, to be more precise—that at least 33 species or subspecies of animals and 30 species of plants have already been extinguished as a direct consequence of habitat conversion or degradation. Of the 47 major habitats and 380 distinct natural communities that blanket California's lands, only a few retain their original characteristics, and virtually all have been fragmented into small remnants.

The quality of basic information on biological resources remains spotty. To initiate the NCCP process on a sound factual footing, conservation biologists first had to gather missing data. In both 1992 and 1993, for example, the scientists literally were compelled to count individual birds. Under emergency pressures, they also had to determine the minimal size of viable habitats for selected species. This discovery of the inadequacy of existing data has led to the development of a large, computerized database, the California Environmental Resources Evaluation System (CERES), at the Resources Agency. CERES compiles critical information on our state's resources from a variety of sources and makes this database more readily accessible along the "information superhighway" to those who need it most.

CERES has been built on earlier efforts to compile resource data, including The Nature Conservancy's natural heritage inventory. The Nature Conservancy, meanwhile, has also identified the loss of habitat as a critical problem for California. Most of our forests have gone through multiple logging cycles, with unknown, but certainly significant, impacts on biodiversity. Grasslands have been converted to large-scale agricultural operations, heavily grazed by domesticated livestock, and occupied by exotic species. At least 90 percent of the state's wetlands have been drained. Numerous rivers and streams have been dammed, channeled, and diverted, with their waters—called "liquid gold" in California—serving the immediate demands of agriculture and sprawling metropolitan populations, often at the long-term expense of fish and other biota dependent on steady and abundant supplies of freshwater. And in the coastal scrub habitats of Southern California, location of the five-county NCCP planning area, residential subdivisions, shopping malls, transportation facilities, and other human interventions have brought natural systems to the threshold of disintegration.

. . . .

New Partnerships

The NCCP program, our pioneering effort in the South Coast bioregion, was recently called "the nation's most ambitious and remarkable application of biodiversity conservation." Our motivations are, in fact, quite simple: California wants to save exposed habitats and ecosystems and to slice through the Gordian knot of legal, political, and social paralysis. All of my experience in this arena, whether in the Resources Agency, World Wildlife Fund, Sierra Club, American Farmland Trust, or the U.S. Department of the Interior, suggests that private landowners and environmentalists alike want a measure of certainty above all else as they pursue their various objectives.

In seeking to provide greater certainty, we could not have tackled a more challenging site for our experiment than the South Coast. Never before has a large-scale program combined resource protection and development objectives in such an urbanized context. Nor has any program so extensively attempted to find common ground and rational process between the conflicting requirements of state and local missions for economic development and land management and the environmental mandates of federal legislation, epitomized by the Endangered Species Act.

In early April of 1991, Governor Pete Wilson took advantage of the annual Earth Day celebrations to announce his support of a range of initiatives that are designed to allow state officials to become more anticipatory and less reactive in their responses to pending resource problems. Included in the Governor's announcement of "Resourceful California" was our cherished experiment in new partnerships. What is needed, he said then, is a means by which "to protect endangered species and their habitat through a process of consultation rather than confrontation." His approval of specific statutory authority (AB-2072) for the NCCP enabled the California Department of Fish and Game to begin the evolution of this still embryonic program. Instead of focusing on the protection of a single species at a time, as traditionally occurs, the new NCCP process would try to conserve entire habitats and ecosystems encompassing numerous species. The one-by-one listing of a single species freights each listing with too much baggage. The new approach allows us to step back and gaze across wider horizons and longer timescales.

No one person is more deserving of credit for the early success of NCCP than Michael A. Mantell, undersecretary of the California Resources Agency. Both Michael and I came to the NCCP from World Wildlife Fund in Washington, where we had been exposed to E.O. Wilson's pioneering work and efforts to achieve sustainability in rapidly developing regions outside the United States. When Governor Pete Wilson challenged us to resolve the endangered species conundrum of Southern California, Michael thought to apply at home the concepts of bioregional planning and ecosystem management that had already proved useful in developing countries.

I came to the problem from a different perspective. As a fledgling at the Department of the Interior, I had helped write that portion of President Nixon's environmental program that was adopted in 1973 as the Endangered Species Act. I knew that misapplication of the act had caused the paralysis about which developers and environmentalists alike complained in Southern California and that ecosystem management could be useful in resolving that impasse—and others like it. More important, our approach could bring broader protection to the California gnatcatcher and associated denizens of the coastal sage scrub than was provided by either the federal or state endangered species laws. Both Michael and I knew that NCCP had achieved the desired degree of "name recognition," despite its alliterative weakness, when we were greeted in San Diego with placards that read "New Cover-up for Corporate Polluters (NCCP)."

As of late 1995, this unique convergence of environmental and economic interests had already survived a series of hurdles. Each success, it should be emphasized, grew out of an unprecedented degree of trust among the various stakeholders.

First, we invited hard science to move into the very center of our process. We created an independent review panel of five nationally recognized conservation biologists, headed by Dr. Dennis Murphy at Stanford University, to evaluate data, prescribe standards for the collection of additional information in the field, and recommend guidelines for integrating the biological sciences into future planning efforts.

We had hoped, as part of our campaign to maintain the integrity of the NCCP process and the incentives for collaboration, to avoid listing the gnatcatcher as threatened or endangered. But Secretary Bruce Babbitt of the U.S. Interior Department ignored our plea and decided to list, while granting a special rule, under Section 4(d) of the Endangered Species Act, that recognizes the NCCP, including its 32 participating private landowners, as a legitimate player in the land use drama. Secretary Babbitt had understood our dilemma and offered Section 4(d) as an incentive for developers to stay in the program. Specifically, the new rule allows partners who agree to produce a plan that protects coastal sage scrub to develop up to 5 percent of the habitat and receive authorization for an "incidental take" of the threatened California gnatcatcher during the planning process. The announcement of the special rule represented an important step in making the federal government a full partner in a

cooperative ecosystem management program and provided further incentive for the continued participation of landowners who might have
otherwise walked away when the gnatcatcher was listed.

The California Department of Fish and Game's NCCP Process and
Conservation Guidelines were completed in late 1993 and merged into the
special Section 4(d) rule. The process guidelines constitute "the rules of
the game" and provide guidance for interactions among stakeholders.
The conservation guidelines, based on the findings of the scientists' review
panel, prescribe the outline of each plan, thus rendering subsequent evaluation, approval, and implementation more rational and certain. These
two complementary documents constitute a blueprint for the immediate
development of 10 subregional preserves in Southern California and the
eventual spread of the model throughout the state. Furthermore, in an unusual display of coordination and collaboration, the state Fish and Game
Department and the U.S. Fish and Wildlife Service signed an MOU that
eliminates the redundancy of parallel regulatory requirements.

Meanwhile, the inevitable urge to turn to the courts for relief has
been tempered. There were challenges to both the March 1993 listing of
the California gnatcatcher as a threatened species and to Secretary Babbitt's novel application of the Section 4(d) rule. Private landowners initially succeeded in getting the four-inch bird delisted, but the listing was
temporarily reinstated pending public review of scientific research that
had buttressed the original listing. As of this writing, the final ruling is
still not known. Nor have the courts taken up a lawsuit filed by environmental groups that challenges the U.S. Interior Department's decision to postpone the designation of critical habitat for our tiny bird.
Fortunately, the chilling possibility of continuing the business-as-usual
uncertainty in the courts has actually sharpened interest in NCCP as a
safe harbor. Developers, in particular, have reaffirmed their commitment
to the NCCP program. In short, the common interest of all parties in
multispecies, ecosystemic planning has been underlined, and court actions have, so far, left the process undamaged.

Finally, it should be noted that the U.S. Fish and Wildlife Service eased
local concerns by issuing a set of "assurances" in August 1994. In effect,
these pronouncements tell nonfederal landowners with approved multi-
species plans that they will not be subjected to further land use restrictions
or mitigation requirements if additional species are listed or other regulatory action required. The progress of the NCCP program in Southern California was explicitly cited as the justification for Secretary Babbitt's pro-
nouncement that "a deal is a deal."

. . . .
Approvals and Appropriations

Now comes the hard part; approving applications for preserves and finding funds for land acquisitions whenever acquisition is required to assure the integrity of the subregional preserves.

As of this writing, the parties are close to complex agreements on a variety of subregional plans—the very heart of the NCCP program. Since the Section 4(d) rule took effect, some 30 projects in San Diego County and 8 in Orange County have either received final approval by wildlife agencies or are close to being approved for consistency with preserve guidelines. More than three dozen other projects are also in advanced stages of review in those counties, even as more comprehensive, long-term preserve plans are being designed.

Meanwhile, interested stakeholders recently initiated a long-term planning process in San Bernardino County, and an agreement was recently reached with Riverside County to have its multispecies planning effort meet NCCP requirements. Each county plan will encompass thousands of acres and embrace many cities and partners. Even Los Angeles County, long recognized around the world as a metaphor for problems associated with urban sprawl, will protect several thousand acres of its remaining coastal sage scrub habitat on the Palos Verdes Peninsula.

Nevertheless, it is to San Diego and Orange counties that we turn to taste the true ingredients of success. In these counties, the nuances of the NCCP process are revealed in all their complexity.

In San Diego County, where 4,200 square miles are home to 24 plant and animal species listed or proposed as threatened or endangered and another 300 considered vulnerable, three subregional plans are being developed. The Multi-Species Conservation Program, encompassing almost 580,000 acres in the city of San Diego and southwestern San Diego County, stands out as one of the largest, most ambitions, and most complex of all regional plans in the United States. This program, which affects a great variety of interacting species and habitats and is anchored in the city's Clean Water Program, involves no fewer than 11 cities, adjacent lands in the county, and a system of corridors connecting diverse preserves. The North County Multiple Habitat Conservation Program, organized by SANDAG, the regional consortium of governments, covers 610,000 acres in 10 of the county's northernmost jurisdictions. The third plan, covering over 1,000,000 acres of land in the eastern two-thirds of the region, mostly owned by the U.S. Forest Service and Bureau of Land Management and the county's park and recreation department, is intended to complement the other two by establishing both a wildlife corridor system and a desired degree of "connectivity" among all three.

In Orange County, there are two plans in the works that cover approximately 340,000 acres. The Southern Orange County NCCP is noteworthy because this subregion includes large sections of coastal sage scrub habitat that are still relatively undeveloped, including lands reserved until now for military uses.

In fact, we are willing to engage, as partners, any entity with holdings that include eligible lands, whatever the entity's official status: the military, as noted, and other federal agencies, including such exotic ones as the Resolution Trust Corporation (RTC); private corporations, owners of individual parcels, and, especially, developers; nonprofit groups, trusts, foundations, and conservancies; and, of course, other organs of state and local government. The California Department of Parks and Recreation, for example, has signed an agreement with the Fish and Game Department, the NCCP manager, to help identify, evaluate, and enroll appropriate state parklands in the program. So far, six park sites are enrolled. Similarly, the U.S. Interior Department's Bureau of Land Management has made 176,000 acres within San Diego County available for conservation planning. Land assets once held by failed savings and loan associations and now being redistributed by the RTC are being evaluated for their habitat potential and possible inclusion in the NCCP program. To relieve the burden on private landowners, we have given priority to the inclusion of public lands whenever they meet eligibility criteria.

Similarly, our funding for research, administration, and acquisitions must come from multiple sources. The financial resources of the state and federal governments are simply insufficient for underwriting the multiple requirements of an effective NCCP program.

For example, the National Fish and Wildlife Foundation, a nonprofit organization that supports natural resource partnerships throughout the nation, has supplemented federal funding with matching donations. The federal government has contributed $2 million for planning, and Secretary Babbitt has pledged support for continuing efforts in the five-county NCCP region. The city of San Diego has spent another $3 million. Local governments in San Diego and Orange counties are providing staff time and technical advice.

California's financial plight, however, is not a well-kept secret. The state is just recovering from a deep and traumatic recession. Steeply rising medical and welfare costs leave little margin for discretionary spending. Governor Wilson estimates that unfunded federal mandates alone cost the state about $8 billion annually. More than two-thirds of California's counties are currently insolvent. Opportunities to increase property taxes are severely limited. Bond measures are difficult to justify in the current political climate: California's voters rejected a $2 billion bond issue for parks and wildlife as recently as June 1994. And, in a rare instance of true bipartisanship, the Reagan, Bush, and Clinton administrations have all withheld funds from the federal Land and Water Conservation Fund, formerly a prime source of funding for states wishing to purchase wildlife habitat.

Clearly, it is time to be creative. Secretary Babbitt displayed such creativity in December 1994 when he announced to the quarterly meeting of the California Biodiversity Council in San Diego that he would provide federal funds to assist NCCPs through a previously ignored provision, Section 6, of the Endangered Species Act. And the state has done its share by funding the start-up of NCCP and authorizing the establishment of Habitat Assessment Districts, through which local governments can generate revenue to acquire habitat.

On the state and local levels, it may also be feasible to acquire less than fee interests—including development rights—as an alternative to outright acquisition. The state has promulgated guidelines and has encouraged consideration of tax credits, increased reliance on publicly owned lands, and broadened incentives like California's Williamson Act for owners to participate in voluntary habitat stewardship.

Another possibility involves using funds from such programs as the federal Intermodal Surface Transportation Efficiency Act of 1991 to mitigate for transportation projects that have had adverse impacts on the land and biological resources. A small proportion of the $1.6 billion in federal funds provided under the Conservation Reserve Program, part of the 1985 federal Farm Bill, might also be made available to help property owners with ecologically valuable lands become willing stewards of their holdings, much as the Wetlands Reserve Program has encouraged protection of that ecotype.

· · · · · · · ·
Replicating the Model

The success of the NCCP program in Southern California, admittedly qualified and fragile, has encouraged us to transport the model to other bioregions in the state and adapt its underlying principles and processes to different sets of circumstances. Not without a touch of foolhardiness, we have dared to apply the model to the most intractable problem of all—the sharing of the limited resources that meet in the delta formed by the confluence of the Sacramento and San Joaquin rivers above San Francisco Bay. This has been a war zone for decades, and the battles have been fought over water. What land-based development is to the South Coast bioregion, water diversions are to the Bay-Delta bioregion.

The 1,600-square-mile estuary in the Bay-Delta ecosystem abounds in biodiversity. It is home to some 400 species of fish, mammals, reptiles, amphibians, and birds, including half the shorebirds and waterfowl that migrate on the Pacific Flyway. Two-thirds of California's salmon swim through the estuary each year, including the endangered winter-run chinook. The threatened Delta smelt also swims these waters.

Unfortunately, California has a semiarid climate. Its waters—most of which, if left untamed, would flow freely through the estuary—are also needed to irrigate the nation's largest and most productive agricultural industry and to slake the household thirsts of the populous south. Most of these waters begin as snow in the Sierra Nevada. Before the melted runoff reaches San Francisco Bay, however, it moves through a dauntingly complex network of dams, waterways, pumps, and canals that supply gigantic water systems managed by both the state and the federal governments. Virtually every individual in California, not to mention every economic interest, is affected by the management of these systems.

The latest round of battles began almost a decade ago. In 1986, a state judge ordered a new balancing of the region's resources. In 1987, the U.S. Environmental Protection Agency (EPA), applying the standards of the federal Clean Water Act, declared the state's water quality too poor to sustain the region's biota. Over the next few years, numerous plans were proposed and rejected for one contentious reason or another. Finally, a newly elected Governor Wilson decided to make the ending of the water wars a matter of high priority. In 1992, he directed a new Water Policy Council to find solutions that would ensure adequate water quality, allow efficient and reliable water exports, fulfill the requirements of fish and wildlife, and protect the integrity of the region's maze of channels and levees. I was joined on the council by representatives of various state agencies that deal with water, natural resources, agriculture, and commerce. The governor also directed the State Water Resources Control Board to adopt interim water quality standards, and he created the Bay-Delta Oversight Council, a panel of citizens representing water users and environmental groups that would help design long-term solutions.

Early in 1993, while the state was working on interim standards, the

National Marine Fisheries Service issued regulations, pursuant to the requirements of the Endangered Species Act, to protect the winter-run chinook, and the U.S. Fish and Wildlife Service listed the Delta smelt as threatened. Both actions implied large, additional diversions of water away from other uses. The state was forced to focus immediately on long-term solutions that reflected the needs of an entire ecosystem.

In September 1993, the four responsible federal agencies involved in the issue responded to the state's frustrations by forming the Federal Ecosystem Directorate (now known a bit derisively as "Club FED") to coordinate their management responsibilities across jurisdictional lines. This step opened the door to an unprecedented degree of cooperation between state and federal officials.

In June 1994, only six months before a court-imposed deadline for EPA to issue final water quality standards, a framework agreement was signed by 12 federal and state agencies with responsibilities for managing water quality, fish and wildlife, and the principal conveyance systems. In essence, the new agreement was a declaration of interdependence. In the new spirit of cooperation, both sides moved quickly toward the achievement of mutual goals for regulatory certainty, long-term environmental protection, and predictable water supplies. Club FED and the Water Policy Council, for example, worked together to establish a seasonal supply regime for the two vast storage and delivery systems that traverse California and to stabilize the natural systems of the estuary.

The basic story line here is short and simple: In the beginning, complexity reigned; paralysis and uncertainty were the results; gradually, however, a cooperative spirit began to emerge; enthusiasm mounted as solutions became evident. The story, of course, is still unfolding, with the final chapter only now being written and edited. Nevertheless, the state's water users are already pleased with the plot. They simply want an end to the uncertainty of fragmented, piecemeal management. Like the policy makers in state and federal agencies and the chiefs of the operating water projects, they seek practical resolutions for long-standing conflicts that will avoid the drastic consequences of direct collisions with the Endangered Species Act.

On December 15, 1994, all of this hard work snapped into sharp focus. California and the U.S. government signed an agreement that will, for the first time, allow state officials to manage ecosystems as whole entities rather than regulate one industry, one resource, and one species at a time.

The new arrangement establishes limits on how much freshwater can be diverted from the estuary to agricultural and urban areas, thereby supplying our endangered fish species with enough stream flows to survive annual migrations and to keep salty intrusions at bay. Although farmers and city dwellers will sacrifice part of their current allotments, their compensation will take shape as an absolute guarantee of delivery. In relinquishing about 10 percent, some 400,000 acre-feet, of their current draw in normal years, they are, in effect, trading water for certainty.

Indeed, the guarantee—and, in particular, its application during drought years—was the final domino to fall into place. At virtually the last moment before the court-ordered deadline, Secretary Babbitt agreed to have the federal government underwrite the costs of supplying additional water, should it become needed due to unforeseen circumstances, beyond that which has been contributed by the state's water users.

As we sought to bring government processes more nearly into conformity with natural systems, our experiences in the South Coast and Bay-Delta bioregions also revealed the emergence of a new "institutional ecosystem," the shape of which should influence further efforts to balance economic and environmental objectives. First of all, we have learned to tackle complex environmental issues on a scale suited to their solution. Although the scale of workable solutions to the habitat crisis of Southern California and the conflicts of water use in the Bay-Delta estuary are necessarily broad—in both instances nearly as broad as the bioregions themselves—the tenets of integrated resource management are applicable in smaller settings as well.

The Council on Biodiversity has compiled a long list of watershed subgroups in the Klamath and Sierra Nevada bioregions, each of which is an avid practitioner of ecosystem management. It is critically important to involve all stakeholders, no matter how checkered the history of earlier relationships. Until all parties acknowledge the legitimacy of one another's objectives, and agree to collaborate on the problem-solving exercise, no real progress can be expected. In fact, the role of government then becomes secondary, as the truly interested parties seek an alternative to continuing—and wasteful—controversy.

Just as the gnatcatcher in the South Coast and the Delta smelt in the Bay-Delta have served to galvanize this new "institutional ecosystem" in their bioregions, the northern spotted owl has had a similar effect in far northern California. Although not everyone, including the state of California, approves the federal government's "Option 9" prescription for management of national forests in the Klamath province, we do recognize that it reflects a new commitment to ecosystem management. Equally important, the program has included a Community Economic Revitalization Team, whose members are making funds available to promote sustainable development in the bioregion. The federal and state governments are also cooperating to improve resources planning in yet another of California's bioregions, the Sierra Nevada. Following the Sierra Summit, Congress authorized an ecosystem study of the Sierra Nevada by the U.S. Forest Service. The Sierra Nevada Ecosystem Project is the first of its kind and is intended to offer management strategies that integrate economic and environmental objectives. A report of its findings is due at the end of 1995. It is difficult to overstate the significance of business participation in this effort, and with it the articulation of economic, as well as environmental, costs and benefits.

In each instance, we sought to engage the entire suite of stakeholders, whether public or private. But there also emerged an unanticipated interest on the part of the general business community, which has come increasingly to understand the connection between economic growth and environmental protection.

The landowners of Southern California were, of course, directly affected by the outcome and were, thus, essential participants in development of the plan. The role of business in finding agreement over water quality standards for the Bay-Delta bioregion was not so well defined at first. The usual combatants in California's water wars—agriculture, urban users, and environmentalists—welcomed business to their ranks when a formidable array of corporate leaders reminded President Clinton and Governor Wilson that continued disagreement, and the resulting uncertainty of water supply, would have seriously adverse consequences for the state's economy as a whole. Just prior to the December 15, 1994, agreement between California and the U.S. government, the California Business Roundtable urged compromise in the interest of economic recovery: "Moving beyond gridlock and reaching a compromise on water is critical to sustaining the economic recovery underway in the state. We implore you to do everything in your power to ensure that the goal (of satisfactory water-quality standards) is achieved."

Because its credibility is derived from scientific theory, ecosystem management can succeed only when sustained by sound, or at least defensible, science. As noted above, it was recognized from the beginning that NCCP could not succeed unless well grounded in conservation biology. Even when there are inadequate data, or genuine disagreement among scientists, as in the case of the enormously complex Bay-Delta estuary, agreement can be found within the "range of reasonable science," subject to modification as new information becomes available. The establishment of protocols for extensive monitoring in the Bay-Delta estuary is an essential element of the December 15 agreement. Despite legitimate disagreements among scientists about the likely effects of new water quality standards, it will be readily possible to determine whether the desired result has been achieved and to modify the water quality regime as necessary. As we learn more about the functioning of ecosystems, we will rely less on rigid prescriptions and more on adaptive management of their component parts.

．　．　．　．　．　．　．　．
Managing Complexity

Although I believe that we are well served by these principles, and by the larger shift toward bioregional planning, I am laboring under no illusions that would lead me into declaring that the state of California has suddenly decided to launch a direct attack on the problems of land use and growth management. Indeed, there has been virtually no response to the comprehensive recommendations of the Governor's Council on Growth Management, published in 1993. In *Strategic Growth: Taking Charge of the Future, A Blueprint for California,* we attempted to examine all elements of the state's physical infrastructure, including housing, transportation, energy, and municipal facilities in light of California's rapid growth.

Not surprisingly, the council concluded quite cautiously that regional planning "of some sort" and "in some circumstances" would be required to deal with issues that transcend the fixed boundaries of political subdivisions. As we discussed the relevance of "airsheds" and "commutersheds" and even "milksheds," I wondered aloud to my colleagues whether we had come full circle, to the acceptance of watersheds—or even bioregions—as the organizing principle for growth management in 21st-century California. The popularity of E.O. Wilson notwithstanding, my suggestion was dismissed, and our final report contained only passing reference to ecosystem management.

The indifference to conventional growth management is even more inexplicable. When I challenged a graduate student at Harvard's Kennedy School of Government to explain the absence of public and political support for growth management, John R. Christiansen identified, among other reasons, "the lack of a clearly focused intellectual framework." Until this framework is established, perhaps as the result of renewed interest by the business community in the economic implications of unplanned growth, California like many other places will continue to approach growth management in an incremental manner, using the tools at hand.

Thus, our efforts at bioregional planning would more accurately be described as a policy of loose and indirect containment for the somewhat limited purpose of protecting biological diversity. In effect, we surround our problems with a complex weave of flexible limits and variable inducements. At one and the same time, we work a problem top down, bottom up, and side out. We nudge the problems into a framework with edges that are both fuzzy and real. But within that framework, we leave the interested stakeholders with plenty of room to innovate. We try to still the big sticks—the Endangered Species Act and the water quality standards of the Clean Water Act, for example—while we negotiate solutions that rely instead on incentives, trade-offs, cooperation, scientific reality, and regulatory certainty.

It should be evident by now that we are sailing toward the far shores of a new world of governance. The familiar universe of prescriptive policies no longer obtains. The crisp efficiencies of command-and-control hierarchies are increasingly irrelevant.

We have found in ecosystem management a means corresponding closely to the logic of natural functions by which to protect those systems, and to foster compatible human activity. We have also developed a new kind of "institutional ecosystem" by which our environmental and economic objectives can be achieved. In acknowledging the legitimacy of these linked goals, we have opened the planning dialogue to all stakeholders and transformed the roles of government and the private sector. After 25 years' experience with a model that favored regulation over collaboration, and confrontation over cooperation, the parties to ecosystem management in California now demonstrate a shared commitment to sustainable use and perpetuation of our extraordinary natural legacy.

Transportation: A Key Element in Sustainable Communities

James Lighthizer

James Lighthizer is former Secretary of the Maryland Department of Transportation, former County Executive for Anne Arundel County, Maryland, and former Member of the Maryland State Legislature.

Transportation should be a servant of community development, not its master. To that end, or that said, it is essential we achieve far greater integration of transportation and land use decision making. In fact, if we are to achieve sustainable communities that protect natural areas and retain vital urban open space, we must develop transportation systems that preserve and enhance community development goals.

In the United States, transportation planning is too often viewed as one discipline and land use planning as another. Transportation planning has largely been the domain of professional engineers driven primarily by federal and state transportation policies and procedures. Land use planning has been handled basically by local governments. There has been an inadequate understanding that the two are vitally connected. Even when some awareness exists, moreover, techniques for making the transportation/ land use connection are undeveloped. This is a major failing of our transportation policy process.

From the close of World War II to the present, federal and state governments have done a remarkable job in constructing a surface transportation system. The crowning achievement, of course, is the Interstate Highway System, started during the Eisenhower administration and now essentially completed. An unanticipated and, from a land use perspective, undesirable side effect resulting from the construction of this system is that America began to sprawl.

This was not entirely unanticipated. Thirty years ago Daniel P. Moynihan predicted many of the very problems at issue today. In April

1960, in a brilliant, forward-looking article entitled "New Roads and Urban Chaos"[1] he wrote:

> It is becoming increasingly obvious that American government, both national and local, can no longer ignore what is happening as the suburbs eat endlessly into the countryside. Since the spreading pollution of land follows the roads, those who build the roads must also recognize the responsibility of the consequences.

When Senator Moynihan became Chairman of the Environment and Public Works Subcommittee on Transportation in 1990, he became the chief architect of a revolutionary new law called ISTEA (see below).

Sprawl has emerged for many socioeconomic reasons, but two key factors have contributed to it: (1) land use planning decisions made at the local level and (2) surface transportation policy and decisions made mainly at the federal and state levels, although but not in conjunction with one another. Sprawl is not only eating up more and more land, it is stretching our transportation infrastructure to the financial breaking point. According to the Chesapeake Bay Foundation, total developed land in my state, Maryland, has increased from .18 acres per capita in the 1950s to more than .60 acres per capita in the 1990s. Quite simply put, if we continue to make land use decisions as we have in the past 50 years, we will be unable to pay for the transportation network of highways that connect our communities.

As we stretch farther and farther out into the countryside we find that our cities are in decline; more recently, we find the inner suburbs declining as well. So we are not only creating unsustainable development patterns through suburban and exurban sprawl, we are denigrating existing communities as we expand.

In urbanized states such as Maryland, sprawl threatens to engulf increasingly limited rural and natural resource as well. Office parks are developed at densities that are solely dependent on the automobile. Much of the new development constitutes a false economy requiring greater and greater highway and infrastructure funding while urban infrastructure is underused and urbanized areas experience disinvestment. The amount of land being consumed by sprawl development is astonishing. Between 1985 and 1990 alone, an area three times larger than the city of Baltimore was converted from natural uses to urban uses, and at only a fraction of the density.

Another casualty of poor coordination between transportation and land use planning is the use of alternatives to highways. Transit systems and services have continued to decline because of highway construction and automobile-oriented development beyond existing urban communities. Even when new transit systems are created, there is often insufficient emphasis on land use that will encourage transit ridership. Thus, a vicious circle: highway construction at the urban edge encourages sprawl, and sprawl creates land use patterns that can only be served by highways. Alternatives decline, and transportation users are left with no option but to drive.

How can we make transportation decisions that will encourage reinvestment in existing communities, encourage economic development and competitiveness, protect natural resources and rural areas, improve air quality, and maximize the use of existing transportation facilities, while minimizing transportation expenditures? To do this, we need to broaden participation in transportation decision making and we need to consider land use in transportation and the long-term results of our decisions. If we do a better, more rational job in linking transportation and land use, we can achieve these goals and develop sustainable communities.

The remainder of this paper offers thoughts and suggestions gleaned from more than 15 years of experience with these issues, starting in 1979 after I was elected to the Maryland House of Delegates. While serving on the House Ways and Means Committee, the principal tax writing committee of the Maryland Legislature, I was involved in funding transportation-related projects. I became much more involved in the land use side in the 1980s when I was elected county executive of Anne Arundel County, a large and fast-growing suburban area of some 400,000-plus residents. Anne Arundel County, like all Maryland counties, is the primary land use planner and, in effect, makes all the essential decisions on how land is used, including all zoning and land subdivision decisions. Finally, my transportation experience covers four years as secretary of the Maryland Department of Transportation—a 10,800 employee agency responsible for all state highways, mass transportation, port, toll, and airport facilities throughout Maryland. Thus, over 15 years, I tackled all three sides of the "iron triangle" that drives sprawl: finance, land use planning, and transportation service delivery.

. . . .

Land Use at the Local Level

As Anne Arundel county executive (in essence a county mayor), I focused on local land use issues and relied on recommendations from professional

planners, citizens, business representatives, environmentalists, and others
involved in community development. On the basis of this advice, I recognized the need to undertake a progressive management program that
provided for growth in and adjacent to existing communities, adequate
public facilities, farm preservation, urban renewal, development impact
fees to discourage sprawl, and protection of critical areas adjacent to the
Chesapeake Bay. Land use was basically a local issue and transportation
planning was highway oriented through a cooperative process with the
state and a regional planning body. Development policy was determined
at the local level and often competed with neighboring jurisdictions. We
vied for industrial and commercial development projects to increase our
tax base and to provide jobs without any real consideration for how this
might affect nearby counties or Baltimore City.

During the 1980s, the regional economy was largely geared to building
suburban office/industrial parks and single-family residential subdivisions. Major highways that would serve development, if not built by the
developers themselves, were built by the state. The county, through its
state elected officials, competed for transportation funding. By the mid-
1980s, the counties surrounding Baltimore City contained more office
space than the city itself. Disinvestment continued to occur in Baltimore
City. Given the institutional, economic, and political dynamics within the
region in the 1980s, a local county executive had to emphasize and opti-
mize land use from a local perspective. This remains largely unchanged.
County executives are elected locally, and voters typically do not have a
regional or statewide perspective, especially if this means subordinating
local objectives to regional ones. In this way, local jurisdictions participate
in and encourage a cycle of investment and disinvestment in their regions.

In transportation planning, state agencies typically interact with the
local jurisdictions, developing a rational statewide highway network and
cooperating on local land use. In one case that comes to mind, the State
Highway Administration agreed to build no interchanges through a rural
segment of an interstate highway linking Baltimore with Annapolis,
Maryland's capital. The road was planned cooperatively, and the county
and state agreed that interchanges would be eliminated to reinforce farm
and rural preservation in the area. In this case, we decided that the *community* values realized through elimination of this interchange out-
weighed the *economic* benefits that interchange construction would have
on new business locations. Of course, I still competed to locate this business elsewhere in my jurisdiction.

Although cooperative state-local processes can yield results like this, typically there is insufficient attention given to understanding the linkage between land use and transportation. While as officials we realized that more coordination and careful, interactive planning was needed, our political, social, economic, and institutional circumstances did not facilitate a change in policy development or implementation. Our goal as county executives was to attract more economic development to our counties, so we zoned land and developed the transportation plans "needed" to accomplish that objective. The result was logical, but irresponsible. In the Baltimore-Washington metropolitan area, the amount of land zoned for development outpaced the amount of land needed for such development by a factor of 20. This result reminds me of the wisdom of H.L. Mencken, the famous Baltimore native who observed that "for any problem there is a solution that is logical, simple—and wrong."

. . . .

ISTEA and the Maryland Planning Act

When I became Maryland's transportation secretary in early 1991, it was immediately apparent to me that the state could not afford all of the transportation projects needed to serve land use determined by the towns and counties. Early in my tenure, two major pieces of legislation, one federal and one state, gave me some of the tools I would need to begin to address this imbalance.

In late 1991, U.S. Congress passed the Intermodal Surface Transportation Efficiency Act (ISTEA). Much has been written about the early experience in implementing this remarkable legislation, but I would like to highlight a few of the innovations from ISTEA that I think make transportation accountable to other community goals.

- *Demand Management.* ISTEA builds on a history of federal planning and environmental review requirements that place a strong emphasis on proving a selected alternative is the most efficient and cost-effective means to address a transportation need. Because of ISTEA's links to the air quality planning process and requirements for project review, agencies essentially must prove that there is no alternative to a project catering to cars before anther road can be built. As a result, transportation agencies are scrambling to evaluate options ranging from traffic operations improvements to land use considerations as part of highway planning studies.

- *Flexibility.* ISTEA lets states put federal funds where they are most needed, not where categorical slots dictate. For example, states can decide to transfer funds from highway categories to mass transit categories. In 1989, Maryland's six-year capital program devoted 60 percent of its funds to highways and 24 percent to transit. By 1996, only 56 percent will go to highways. This proportion could be reversed in another state, but the point is that the decision to invest in a particular part of the system is up to local decision makers.

- *Planning.* ISTEA is innovative because it explicitly ties transportation investment to regional and local land use plans. In the best situations, local governments are getting together, comparing land use plans, and developing transportation programs that meet the goals of the region. Even in regions where cooperation remains more a goal than a reality, ISTEA at least promotes a forum to recognize what needs to happen. Given a long history of antagonism between transportation agencies and the people whose neighborhoods are affected by new projects, ISTEA emphasizes long-range planning. The response of many states and regional planning organizations has been "visioning," an inclusive process that lets citizens, bureaucrats, and elected officials talk about the goals of a plan in a cooperative environment. Visioning its best manifestations, visioning makes transportation the servant of community development rather than its master. Visioning is the process of deciding what you want your community to look like, and then building transportation systems that get you there.

- *Innovative Financing.* ISTEA has raised expectations about transportation financing tied more closely to users—for example, toll financing and "congestion pricing." Congestion pricing is the practice of charging users of a particular facility a higher price to use that facility during peak periods of demand; normally, the higher charge would be made when the facility is operating near or over capacity. At this point, there is a lot more smoke than fire, and states and regions have to understand that pricing mechanisms can be a two-edged sword. If congestion pricing pushes commuters and employers out of congested urban centers to the rural periphery, the end result is worse. Without aggressively enforced land use plans, no transportation program will work.

- *Enhancements.* Finally, ISTEA recognizes that it was time for transportation agencies to give something back to communities and requires states to set aside a portion of their federal funds as "enhancements" and use these on community and environmental amenities.

Maryland moved aggressively to take advantage of the program, setting up a competitive process that requires a 50 percent match from the local project sponsor. Now several years into the program, we have built fish ladders and bike trails, acquired Civil War battlefields and greenways, restored historic train stations, and landscaped dozens of facilities. The enhancements program does not make up for poor planning decisions or create high-quality communities in and of itself, but it builds goodwill with citizens and helps transportation agencies be a part of the communities they serve.

The second major piece of legislation that affected transportation and land use in Maryland when I was transportation secretary was the Economic, Growth, Resource Protection, and Planning Act. Enacted by the Maryland General Assembly in 1992, this legislation resulted from a series of studies and commissions commencing in the 1980s that searched for ways to minimize the impact of growth on the state's natural resources, including the Chesapeake Bay.

Generally, Maryland's local jurisdictions have been progressive in adopting modern growth management programs, and Maryland's courts have been supportive. Although Maryland has had a statewide planning function for many years, the state does not play a substantial role in developing local land use plans and controls. The "where and how" of growth is defined at the local level.

Maryland has, however, enacted a number of meaningful laws that structure the planning process and protect selected resources. These laws include planning enabling legislation, statewide erosion sediment control standards, statewide reforestation requirements, and strict protection and preservation of land adjacent to the Chesapeake Bay. In adopting the 1992 planning act, the Maryland General Assembly reached a compromise on the contentious issue of land use.

In 1991, Governor William Donald Schaefer proposed legislation with strict requirements for counties and municipalities, including specific land use densities. This met with strong opposition from the counties, and the legislature declined to enact the legislation. As an alternative to prescribed densities, the act approved in 1992 established seven development policies, imposed certain planning requirements and deadlines, and set in place an oversight commission to provide stewardship for a continuing effort to encourage better use of state resources.

The 1992 act set forth the following seven visions as the state's growth policy:

- Development is concentrated in suitable areas.

- Sensitive areas are protected.

- In rural areas, growth is directed to existing population centers and resource areas are protected.

- Stewardship of the Chesapeake Bay and the land is a universal ethic.

- Conservation of resources, including a reduction in resource consumption, is practiced.

- To assure that achievement of the above, economic growth is encouraged and regulatory mechanisms are streamlined.

- Funding mechanisms are addressed to achieve these provisions.

The planning act is flexible, but it requires that local jurisdictions amend their comprehensive plans and development regulations to be consistent with this growth policy. In addition, state capital projects must be consistent with the growth policy and adopted local plans. The act also establishes a statewide commission of appointed citizens to provide guidance in implementation of the act's provisions and to report to the governor and General Assembly on progress made in managing growth throughout the state.

By mid 1992, these two laws, ISTEA and the Maryland Planning Act, had set in place a vastly improved institutional framework for transportation and land use decision making. ISTEA provides a framework that encourages more rational planning with flexible implementation. The Maryland Planning Act, on the other hand, sets overall state policy that begins to define clearer goals for land use and transportation. The act gives Maryland direction in its use of ISTEA.

. . . .

Transportation Decision Making and Planning in Maryland

I want to discuss several experiences in Maryland that have guided my understanding on ISTEA and helped shape my opinions or prospects for achieving transportation decisions for more sustainable communities. In two of these cases, I affected specific project outcomes that demonstrated how transportation decisions can be changed when larger goals are considered. On a broader front, Maryland has undertaken a multijurisdictional, multimodal planning project that, although still in process, can become a model for rational transportation and land use planning. Finally, I shall describe how Maryland maximized one aspect of ISTEA flexibility in establishing a creative ISTEA enhancement program.

I should underscore that I have enormous respect for the quality of management at the State Highway Administration in Maryland. The following two cases, however, illustrate how improved results can be gained when transportation decisions are influenced in a cooperative way by larger community goals and constituencies. As the appointed secretary of transportation, I brought a different perspective to the department. As a lawyer, politician, and former county executive, I brought a different viewpoint to transportation decision making.

Route 50 is an east-west interstate highway connecting Washington, D.C., with Annapolis. In reviewing the plans for a segment of that road, I thought the engineers were going to eliminate a lot more trees than necessary. I, therefore, directed the State Highway Administration to redesign that section of the road with an emphasis on using more of the median strip and less of the buffer on each side. The results were that the road was aesthetically more pleasing and the environment was protected. I also requested the State Highway Administration to convene an informal citizens committee with representatives taken from various communities along the road, and to consult with the committee as we proceeded through design and construction. Simple actions such as these can vastly improve the aesthetic quality of highway projects without compromising transportation objectives, can reduce community impacts, and can avoid antagonizing the public, who become partners in the project rather than opponents. However, outreach must be constant, community values must be given equal weight with transportation values, and the decisions of the consultative group must be implemented.

Late in 1991, I received a call from a concerned citizen in Westminster. She informed me that the State Highway Administration, in its efforts to repave the town's Main Street, had run up against some specific engineering standard that concerned her. The consequence of compliance was that the road would have to be much wider than she believed necessary and would also destroy many of the ancient trees that add so much charm to the community. The state highway administrator and I visited with the woman several days later, decided that we could make the road conform to the community's standards—not the highway standards—and save the trees. The results were a reconstruction of the road in a way that added to the community ambiance. Here again, common sense and communication

made the Maryland Department of Transportation a partner and not the
problem. As in the Route 50 example, a committee made up of elected and
appointed city officials, business advocates, and citizens was created to
participate in the redesign of the road. The improved design would not
have occurred without input from outside our agency.

The "Route 301 Corridor Study" is an example of how transportation
planning should, and I believe will, be done in the future. This study follows a Maryland/Virginia effort commenced in 1987 that examined
eastern and western bypass alternatives to relieve congestion on the
beltway around Washington, D.C. Preliminary costs in 1989 indicated
that construction of an eastern and western bypass would range up to
$3.3 billion. In 1991, in the face of strong opposition from citizens and
elected officials, the Maryland Department of Transportation (MDOT)
dropped all plans to study or pursue an eastern bypass. The more rural
and outlying suburban jurisdictions tended to oppose the bypass primarily on land use and environmental grounds. The Washington Board
of Trade, some business leaders, and higher density communities near the
beltway continued to support the bypass. As a result, in part, of the
bypass study, there was significant distrust between community groups
and MDOT.

In 1991, MDOT began discussing future transportation needs and concerns with key environmental groups. It became clear that future transportation study of the area would need to be multimodal and include related growth management and environmental issues. MDOT hired a
facilitator to interview key stakeholders in the affected five-county area to
determine opinions and support for a new study. A total of 250 people
were ultimately interviewed. Overwhelmingly, they felt that—although
the bypass was rejected—there should be a cooperative study of transportation needs.

The study area includes five counties east of Washington, D.C., with a
total land area of 1,940 square miles and a population of about 1.4 million people. The largest county contains 729,268 people and the smallest,
51,372. Land use is diverse, ranging from high density mixed use areas
served by the Washington subway system to suburban development and
rural farm communities. Some of the counties provide for dense growth
areas and strong rural preservation; however, much development is low
density, ranging from one unit per three to five acres up to four plus units
per acre, serving commuters. Although the majority of the study area is
undeveloped, the trends point to more auto-oriented, low-density residential development beyond the old suburbs.

The purpose of the new study is to examine transportation needs and related growth management and environmental issues. The goal is to build consensus on multimodal transportation solutions and related growth management options for the 50-mile corridor. There are no predetermined solutions. The study will consider highway and transit options—bus, HOV (high occupancy vehicle), light rail, and commuter rail. The study will also consider recommendations to bring growth management into consistency with state and local development policy.

There are 75 members on the task force, including state and local elected officials; state, local, and federal employees; environmentalists; business advocates; and so forth—a diverse group. They were identified as leaders through an interview process and appointed by the governor of Maryland. The group is chaired by the president of a local community college. There are two vice-chairs—one an environmentalist and one a businessman who supported the bypass alternative. All of the local planners/directors are members. The committee has four subcommittees: Transportation, Growth Management, Environment, and Education and Information.

The study committee has been deliberating approximately two years and expects to deliver a report to the governor in 1996. At this point, it has developed a vision for the corridor and is examining transportation options to serve that vision.

The ultimate solution to the transportation problem in southern Maryland is being driven from the bottom up, not through the traditional top-down process that has led to so many problems in the past. The new process is in accord with the ISTEA legislation in that it provides for substantial citizen involvement, coordinates pertinent governmental actions, and is expected to obtain a result supported by the local community. It is important to stress that this is an honest process. It is not a subterfuge for some preconceived notion of transportation planners, but rather a legitimate process that will determine what type of surface transportation solutions are recommended, consistent with the financial realities at the time.

. . . .

Enhancements and ISTEA

One of the more remarkable parts of ISTEA is the enhancement section. Under this section, 10 percent of each state's share of Surface Transportation Program (STP) funds are set aside for enhancements. The kinds of projects that can be funded include:

- Pedestrian or bicycle facilities;

- Acquisition of scenic easements and historic sites;

- Scenic or historic highway programs;

- Landscaping and scenic beautification;

- Preservation, rehabilitation, and operation of historic transportation buildings, structures, and facilities, including historic railroad facilities and canals;

- Preservation of abandoned railroad corridors, including conversion for bicycle and pedestrian trails;

- Archaeological planning and research;

- Mitigation of water pollution due to highway runoff; and

- Control and removal of outdoor advertising.

Given the broad nature of the enhancement objectives, we at the Maryland Department of Transportation decided to attempt to interpret this program as liberally as the Federal Highway Administration would permit. In doing so, we set up a comprehensive effort with specific criteria and approval requirements. Additionally, we created a panel consisting of members of other government agencies, including the secretary of the Department of Natural Resources, the head of the Maryland Historic Trust, and the state highway and mass transit administrators. The group is chaired by the secretary of transportation. We encouraged nontraditional transportation-related projects. In addition, although ISTEA requires a 20 percent local match for enhancement projects, we decided to require a 50 percent match. This means that half the total cost of a project must be borne by someone other than the MDOT, whether an individual, group, or another governmental agency. We were able to require a higher match because of the huge demand we encountered for project funding. In this way, we leveraged more local funds, expanded the local funds dedicated to enhancement projects, and were able to participate in more projects. Additional criteria used by the panel in considering applications included the proposed project's relationship to other plans and programs, geographic distribution, and the question of whether the project would otherwise be funded.

The results of this program have truly been remarkable. In approximately three years, there have been some 110 projects of varying complexity approved, including the first enhancement project in the United States approved by the Federal Highway Administration (a hiker-biker trail that surrounds the Baltimore-Washington International Airport). The size of the awards have ranged from $10,000 to $3 million. The types of projects have varied from construction of fish ladders—a mechanical device that allows fish to migrate up streams that had been cut off by construction of roads—to hiker-biker trails to the preservation of Civil War battlefields.

Maryland's program is considered by many to be a model for the rest of the United States. It set up a fair, flexible process soon after enactment of the law. This was important to ensure that there would be no arbitrary decisions and to "push the envelope" before the various bureaucracies set up so many rules and regulations that the program would stall.

As a consequence of involving other government agencies, we were able to enter into a memorandum of understanding whereby the Maryland Department of Natural Resources pledged some $5 million of its Program Open Space funds as a 50 percent match for ISTEA funds. This resulted in a $10 million program for purchase in fee and easements of important parcels of land on Civil War battlefields at Antietam, South Mountain, and Monacacy. The 3,400 acres covered represent one of the largest efforts to protect Civil War battlefields in the history of the United States. The rationale behind this expenditure was the protection of views seen from state highways. In the absence of the enhancement program, the battlefields may have been lost forever.

Conclusion

From my experience, it is clear that we can no longer afford business as usual in land use and transportation planning. Transportation itself is of limited value unless it serves broader community goals. Whether we are transportation professionals, land use planners, elected officials, community leaders, or just plain people, we must determine what kind of communities we want first and then carefully integrate transportation decisions to serve our community goals.

Recent legislative changes under ISTEA provide a vastly improved institutional framework for integrating land use and transportation planning.

My experience illustrates that when we bring diverse groups into transportation, we improve decisions in ways that enhance the quality of our natural and built environments. Across the country, we are at a point where protecting our natural resources and revitalizing our urban areas depends on our ability to plan, build, and preserve a transportation system that supports community development goals.

NOTES
1. Daniel P. Moynihan, "New Roads and Urban Chaos," *The Reporter,* April 14, 1960.

Across the Barricades

• • • • • • • • • • • • • • • • • • • •

William K. Reilly

William K. Reilly is former Administrator of the U.S. Environmental Protection Agency and Visiting Professor at Stanford University.

• • • • • • • •

The modern revolution in environmental protection that began in the United States during the 1960s has achieved stunning successes, particularly in reducing pollution. We are restoring the Great Lakes to health; fecal coliform, algae, nutrients, and toxics are all way down. Two-thirds of the country's rivers and streams are fishable and swimmable. Our 1990-model automobiles emit 98 percent fewer tailpipe hydrocarbons than 1970 models did. The air in the nation's cities has been cleansed of more than 60 percent of the particulates and 96 percent of the lead concentrations that characterized urban air a quarter-century ago. Statistics tell the story one way. The Hemlock Society, the organization that offers advice to those who want to depart this world, tells it another. It has warned members against relying on the lethal effects of carbon monoxide emissions from any automobile manufactured after 1993. This advisory marks true progress.

• • • • • • • •

The Land Debate

Our triumphs on pollution controls notwithstanding, we have conspicuously failed to make the same progress on land use. Except for those instances where federal, state, or local governments have simply bought and preserved land, as the federal government has done in the national parks, development around cities has too often resulted in the degradation or obliteration of streams and forests, groundwater and wetlands. Many beautiful landscapes have been carved up and subdivided, without regard for topography, meandering streams, and other defining natural features, into housing and commercial developments. Episodic floods, the result of paving floodplains and channelizing rivers, clear-cutting forests and destroying wetlands, are reminders of our failure to integrate human developments within natural systems.

With the advantage of hindsight, it is obvious that dealing with land use issues is far more complicated than attacking pollutants, however dangerous and pervasive the latter may have become. Land use issues are highly decentralized and inevitably engage the vested and emotional interests of multiple participants. Americans feel strongly about the ownership of land and the right to exploit that ownership without undue interference. Every land use debate must be resolved locally, and solutions in one community are often not applicable in a neighboring one. Thus, the deceptively clear objective of using the land efficiently and productively becomes clouded by a storm of competing claims.

Consensus on what constitutes "good" land use is hard to achieve. There is no pollutant to measure and eliminate. Tastes vary: Some people prefer the old, the traditional, and the quaint; others what is new, stylish, and sleek. Thus, the search for better land use arrives quickly at a recognition that good land use decisions involve consensus-building, inclusive processes, respect for private property, and compromise among many competing interests. Although America's experience with land use has not achieved the same success as the battle against pollution, we have learned enough to begin to rethink land use problems. The nation's most formidable environmental challenges concern land use, and I believe that, to make real progress, the land use issue itself must be reframed. The components for such a reframing of the land use challenge are at hand.

A primary reason for the failure to manage our lands rationally is the continuing lack of consensus about the proper reach of government and public authority in constraining the behavior of private landowners. Instability and unpredictability have characterized this tension from the very beginnings of the European settlement of the North American continent. Much of American history can be seen as a repeating saga of land-hungry immigrants arriving with the paramount goal of finding a piece of secure property. Oscillations in public policy reflect the inherent contradiction of trying, at one and the same time, to honor and to control this defining American drive to possess and develop private property.

The sense of pride in the ownership of a piece of real estate is indeed fierce, and public officials trifle with it at considerable risk. The recent revival of this pride, embodied in a nationally vociferous property rights movement, has found powerful champions in the U.S. Congress. As a result, the Congress elected in November 1994 has moved swiftly to advance an array of proposals that will alter and complicate the land use equation. The goal of this movement is the recognition of the principle that a drop in the value of land as a result of either wetland or endangered species regulations is the equivalent of a "taking" of the land by common law right of eminent domain—that is, of the power of the state to take private property for public purposes requiring payment of just compensation to the owner.

At first glance, it is hard to argue with this principle. Indeed, many ardent conservationists, although concerned about the complexity of its application in practice, accept the principle as a traditional manifestation of American fairness. Others, however, find it flawed in its distorting simplification of the multiple factors and complex interactions that create value and in its implicit rejection of a common good that rises above the sum of private interests.

Many are the determinants of land value. And most are not inherent in the land itself. According to a study produced in 1994 by the National Association of Home Builders, the value of a house varies with its surroundings. Environment, in fact, is the single variable that is most determinant of value. Quality of neighborhood, availability of park, beach, pond, or stream, or even distant views of water or mountains are more important to the value of a dwelling than are square footage, appliances, swimming pools, or number of rooms. Yet the common assumption that an American enjoys a Constitutional right to absolute control over property, even if it diminishes the value of a neighbor's land or a whole community's landscape, is a compelling fact of political life, although courts have consistently found that police power regulations may permissibly reduce land values, provided the purposes furthered are sound and the residual economic value remains substantial.

While the lasting effects of recent and prospective legislative and judicial moves to buttress the rights of property owners are still far from clear, newspapers are already being filled with a rising tide of competing or confusing claims. In April 1995, for example, the *Wall Street Journal* reported that corporate farmers in California's Central Valley will claim reimbursement at market rates for the "taking" of their allotments of subsidized water. At risk is a recent and historic agreement that would divert a part of the agricultural allotment to the restoration of salmon runs. A lawyer for the Natural Resources Defense Council questions, "The public is already subsidizing irrigation that is devastating the environment, and now we have to pay even more to make it stop?"

Meanwhile, a group of Western ranchers is claiming a private property right to graze their cattle on public rangeland. Any restrictions, including those designed to restore the public's lands to ecological health, are viewed as a taking under the Fifth Amendment of the U.S. Constitution. The owner of a 90,000-acre spread in Wyoming insists that hunting restrictions are a taking of his private wildlife for which he must be compensated.

The surreal could become real in some local jurisdictions, as the countless decisions of zoning boards and planning commissions affect everyday life. A property owner, for example, might demand compensation for being denied the right to subdivide a piece of property, in spite of the fact that the decision was taken to spare other property owners the inconvenience of increased traffic congestion and other potential problems. A distressed director of a planning agency in Denver, quoted in a *Wall Street Journal* article, predicts that takings legislation pending in Colorado would mean "a nightmare of dueling appraisers and dueling lawyers."

Land use has become a domain of bewildering complexity, where the facts are often in dispute, the variables are many, the interests entrenched, the politics intense, the equities unbalanced, and the consequences immediate. The tendency to resort to abstract theories and polarizing arguments has led to a paralysis of policy in some cases and to a desecration of landscape in others.

Not all of our land use problems are new. In fact, none of the arguments about "takings" or public rights and benefits is new. The power relationships among their various proponents have changed, in Congress and many state legislatures and in the courts. That is what has given new urgency to a familiar debate. Although the "property rights" advocates are presently gaining influence over the "public interest" proponents, measures that result in lengthy arguments among appraisers and in more frequent recourse to the courts and in accelerated development of wetlands and floodplains should inspire care and caution in all parties. The moment cries out for a new reconciliation. I suggest we look for it in the experiences of problem solvers who are crossing the barricades and reframing issues in a manner that does recognize and balance public and private interests.

. . . .
Engage the Scientists

Where to begin? My preference is to begin with science. Shortly before I took office as administrator of the U.S. Environmental Protection Agency (EPA) in February 1989, I asked EPA's Science Advisory Board (SAB), an independent body of scientists and engineers, to answer two questions: What are the principal threats to health and ecology? To what degree do EPA's programs, priorities, and allocations conform to scientific priority?

The concept used to determine threats and develop priorities is comparative risk assessment. Comparative risk assessment helps establish priorities under conditions of severe budget restraints, especially in light of our new understanding that the tools of the past, the instruments that shaped great environmental achievements—large public expenditures and tight regulations—will be largely unavailable in the future.

In response to the first question, the scientists gave a surprising answer: criteria air pollutants (those six priority pollutants listed in the Clean Air Act—ozone, carbon monoxide, sulfur dioxide, oxides of nitrogen, particulates, and lead); indoor air pollution, on which EPA was spending nothing at all; toxics and pesticides, as they affect the industrial worker or farm applicator, not as residues on food or products; and, in the realm of ecology, upper atmospheric ozone depletion, climate change, destruction and fragmentation of forests, and loss of species. At that time, EPA was spending about 15 percent of its budget on those issues. Conspicuous by their absence from the scientists' list were oil spills and hazardous wastes, to which the bulk of EPA resources were allocated.

Another insight emerged in response to the second question. Of the great problems that remain, many are land related, even the pollution problems. More than half of the water pollution problem in the United States is now the consequence of runoff, derived from city streets, roofs, farmland, forestry, and construction sites. Now that the large plants and factories are under control, air pollution problems are also increasingly a function of many diffuse and decentralized small sources that are spread across the landscape. Moreover, the SAB highlighted the need to place greater priority on basic natural systems—on ecology, in other words.

EPA and other government agencies had deemphasized the significance of estuaries, lakes, rivers, wetlands, groundwater, forests, grasslands, and wildlife. The restoration of degraded lands, such as the overgrazed lands in the Great Plains and the strip-mined areas of West Virginia, Ohio, and Pennsylvania, has received virtually no priority. EPA itself, having been conceived in 1970 to protect the environment, had in fact evolved into a health-protecting agency, a mission it carried out with great success. But the agency allowed its ecological priority to fade in comparative importance, and the SAB called for a restoration of ecology to parity with health. The SAB's rationale was that even as many pollution problems were brought under control, ecological systems across the nation were being degraded.

Such systems do not require the same blanket of plans and permits, inspection and enforcement, as pollution sources, for natural systems possess a remarkable characteristic: self-regulation. Left to their own devices, natural systems tend to organize their own energy and nutrient flows, absorb and recycle their own wastes, and control their own pathogens, including those that affect human well-being. The self-organization of natural systems works to our advantage. It reduces the need for expensive, and often clumsy, regulations and remediations. This posits the possibility of a different, less adversarial approach to ecological protection than to pollution control.

Comparative risk assessment is not without controversy, particularly among environmentalists. The Sierra Club says it will lead to a triage that justifies the abandoning of cherished priorities. Unfortunately, triage is likely to happen anyway. Risk assessment is just a tool for making painful decisions as rationally as possible. To the degree we understand real threats, we will be able to deploy scarce resources better and attend to the broken bones, not just to the abrasions, of everyday life.

Consultations with scientists can provide unique opportunities to reframe a debate or build a consensus. Science is the secular religion of the United States. Its practitioners enjoy broad respect and authority. To the degree that scientists can us help think through problems, we will reduce the level of noise that surrounds debates on the environment and the use of land.

·   ·   ·   ·   ·   ·   ·   ·
Love Thy Resource

The SAB's advice to take ecology more seriously came at a time of reconsideration of EPA's program to rescue our great bodies of water, the Great Lakes and Chesapeake Bay in particular. Part of the challenge, I believed, would involve taking advantage of the reservoirs of goodwill that people have for natural features and resources near their homes. Thus, I began the process of reorienting the agency's resources around these well-loved features of the American landscape. Stop talking about effluent levels and parts per million, I advised EPA staff, and start talking about Lake Michigan. Our "geographic initiatives" focused on the overall health of the great watersheds and landforms that shape entire ecosystems. In each case, we tried to identify and target the primary sources of pollution, and we brought all of our programmatic expertise to bear—air and water— quality programs, waste-site cleanups, permitting, enforcement, research, and so forth. In the year after our reinvigoration of the Great Lakes program, we invested more enforcement activity in the Great Lakes than we had devoted to the entire country the year before.

Our projects brought federal, state, and local governments, farmers and other private landowners, business and industry, civic organizations, and academic institutions together to protect specific, valuable, and productive natural resources. When citizens recognize and understand the impact of their activities on a place they know and love, they are often receptive to the call for stewardship. A complex community can be mobilized on behalf of a treasured resource—Chesapeake Bay, Narragansett Bay, Puget Sound, the Gulf of Mexico, or the Great Lakes, for example— much more readily than by a patchwork of complicated, government-imposed policies and regulations. People begin to see the connection between the condition of the resource and their own activities—the problems caused by, say, dumping used oil down the drain or the consequences of building too close to a shoreline.

Chesapeake Bay's popularity follows its tributaries and extends far into the hinterlands of eastern North America. Thus, seemingly distant people are increasingly aware of the impacts of their behavior on the sustainability of the great estuary and its amenities and economic activities. Farming practices miles upstream along the Susquehanna River in Pennsylvania have a profound impact on the health of Chesapeake Bay. Pioneered in Pennsylvania, the bay's nutrient management program has become politically viable and a national model. Today, the bay states have almost 200,000 acres under nutrient management plans and have cut potential pollutants by millions of pounds.

EPA's 20 national estuaries, which are nominated by governors and selected in a competition based on an appraisal of likely local interest and commitment, are dollar-for-dollar one of the most effective environmental programs in the nation. Through the program, all major interests are convened in a series of efforts beginning with characterization of the problem—of Corpus Christi Bay, for example, or Long Island Sound— and then proceeding to a selection of consensus-priority responses. No other program is as useful in educating and involving diverse interests and in obtaining support for action. All because the people who live around such a resource typically do love it!

. . . .

Guerrilla Negotiating

In confronting this generation of environmental problems the issue is no longer General Motors, it is the general public, the millions of individuals who make countless choices every day about throwing away used oil or keeping their car's pollution control system maintained or leaving their floodplains and wetlands alone. From the challenge of controlling a relatively small number of very large and visible sources of pollution we confronted in the 1970s—refineries, pulp and paper plants, steel mills, chemical factories, which we have brought largely under control—we now have to confront a very large number of sources that is each responsible for an amount of pollution that is individually small but huge in the aggregate. Needless to say, it is difficult for government to influence these decisions with only the heavy stick of punishment in its repertoire.

While strong, predictable, and reliable enforcement is essential to environmental policy, we need to reward socially productive behavior rather than simply penalize the bad actors. We have to fashion programs, as we have begun to do in other areas of public policy, that draw on the desire to solve our country's problems, that recognize the presence of statesmanship in the economic and regulated sectors, and that assume the possibility of both enforcing the law and joining with property holders and business leaders in addressing environmental and land use problems.

My experience at EPA reinforces this view. We discovered, for example, that it was taking up to five years to register a new pesticide. During that period, older chemicals that are invariably inferior to modern chemicals from the point of view of health and environment were typically kept in production. We crafted an initiative that said if a chemical company proposes a pesticide that does not accumulate in the environment, does not cause cancer in test animals, but does have a number of other positive characteristics, then we will put that company at the head of the line and give its proposed pesticide a fast-track registration, cutting as much as two years off registration time, an economically significant benefit.

We asked American industry to reduce emissions of the 17 highest-priority toxic substances by 50 percent beyond what the law requires. Those results were achieved—a year early. Nothing that I could have specifically ordered industry to do would have obtained such significant reductions in lead, cyanide, and mercury in an equivalent period of time. By responding to our request in its own way, American industry was also able to discover a variety of new technologies and approaches. Similarly, we developed voluntary schemes to promote energy conservation that encouraged companies to reduce lighting expenditures by changing to newly available technologies. And more office space than exists in Boston, New York, Chicago, San Francisco, Los Angeles, Detroit, and Dallas is now committed to those energy-saving programs—more than four billion square feet of commercial space.

From the outset of efforts to implement the 1990 Clean Air Act Amendments, we pursued a collaborative and collegial process. Historically, many proposed clean air regulations have languished in the courts. Where possible we elected to negotiate first rather than litigate later.

We drew on a process that EPA had used with some success in the past—negotiated rulemaking, where representatives from industry, states, environmental groups, and other interested parties sit down together. In the right circumstances, these unlikely gatherings enable EPA to hammer out agreements that meet tough environmental goals in economical ways. The agreement provides greater certainty about the fate of regulations. Once agreement is obtained, all parties commit not to litigate a rule.

This experience encouraged action to enhance the beauty of one of America's most spectacular landscapes: our "Navajo Rule," an unprecedented agreement among government, industry, and environmentalists to clear the skies over Grand Canyon National Park. The agreement calls for a 90 percent reduction in emissions from the Navajo Generating Station, which is responsible for the wintertime haze that obscures park vistas. By making clear EPA intended to act alone if necessary, but was willing to bring all parties together and ask them to negotiate a consensus solution, we achieved greater reductions—at less cost—than the preliminary proposal EPA had originally made, preserving for visitors the striking breadth and depth, the vivid palette of reds and golds, of a national treasure.

· · · · · · · · ·

The EDF Model for Controlling Runoff

To see how cooperation and flexibility offer possibilities for the future, consider how the Environmental Defense Fund (EDF) has proposed to control nonpoint source pollution in California's San Joaquin Valley. Substantially more than half of the pollution of most of America's rivers, lakes, and estuaries began as runoff from farms and fields, forest and construction projects, land development, and parking lots. The size of the problem is suggested by the reduction in pollution from farm drainage necessary to achieve a key water quality standard in California's San Joaquin River: an estimated 80 to 89 percent, a tough challenge indeed.

Since enactment of the Water Quality Act of 1972, various efforts have aimed at dealing with the runoff problem, and many local governments have implemented more or less effective controls such as requirements that disturbed soil on steep slopes be covered and planted, that settling ponds be constructed in new subdivisions, that buffer strips be left along streamsides in farm- and forestlands. Nevertheless, runoff remains the largest component of the nation's water pollution problem that is largely unaddressed by an effective national policy.

Runoff pollution does not yield to the combination of policy instruments that cleaned up the Great Lakes and other water bodies, which included federal aid for constructing wastewater treatment plants as well as regulations to reduce pollution effluents. If it does not come from a pipe, the water cannot be run through a plant and purified. If the problem is seen as one of diffuse drainage over extensive land surfaces, issuance of permits to each involved landowner, followed by individualized monitoring and enforcement, is impractical.

There are too many sources each responsible for relatively small amounts of pollution. To this problem, at least when large irrigated farmlands are involved, EDF brings a fresh perspective. It is possible, says Chelsea Congdon of EDF in *Plowing New Ground*, to measure much of the irrigation water entering and leaving agricultural properties. The problem is less diffuse than has been generally believed. Provided that water pollution can be measured, responsibility can be assigned and reductions credited. If reductions can be measured and credited, a new system of controls can be devised, one that is based on incentives and that encourages trading among sources of pollution to foster cost-effective corrections.

This is a decentralized solution to a decentralized problem. The point is to create value in pollution reductions and then watch the market begin to work. Several other decentralized problems that remain unaddressed— influencing landowners not to destroy their wetlands, or drivers to submit their vehicles for regular smog checks, or car owners not to discard used oil in their backyard or the toilet—all require incentives. Protecting endangered species is another example of such a problem.

The AFT Experiment

Elizabeth Scott-Graham of The American Farmland Trust (AFT) has proposed to increase and enhance habitat for endangered species in the Central Valley of California, which contains more than seven million acres of irrigated farmland and more than 200 species of plants and animals that are already listed, or are candidates to be listed, as endangered. Far from being detrimental to the region's landowners, the AFT proposal will enable them to improve the habitat value of agricultural lands while at the same time preserving flexibility in the use of their lands.

Administration of endangered species law has resulted in prohibitions and restrictions on cultivation of farmland if that land was settled by a listed species when it lay fallow. The law has prompted farmers to plow land they have no intention to farm, simply to preclude species from nesting on it. Farmers decried the law and resented the energy, time, and cost entailed in ensuring against the arrival of endangered wildlife. But they considered they had no choice but to ward off wildlife if they wished to retain their options to cultivate.

The AFT proposal calls for the U.S. Fish and Wildlife Service and the California Department of Fish and Game to offer a "safe harbor" from liability and from further restrictions and increased penalties under both the federal and state versions of the Endangered Species Act (ESA). The farmers who enter into agreements with the agencies would undertake model projects to demonstrate the effectiveness of this approach to other farmers who may wish to encourage the spread of wildlife habitat on their lands but fear the serious disincentives to conservation.

There are two options. Under Section 10(a) of the federal ESA, land owners who establish an approved Habitat Conservation Plan would be granted a permit that allows the "incidental take" of an endangered species while engaged in normal agricultural practices. Alternatively, using ESA's Section 7, farmers could obtain protection from liability by enhancing habitat under the Conservation Program of the U.S. Department of Agriculture, which provides cost-share grants to farmers who create or restore habitat. Similar agreements will be offered by the California Department of Fish and Game. These proposals do not necessarily require the removal of land from production. Typically, they would involve ditch banks, canals, tailwater drain areas, and those strips between fields where hedgerows or windbreaks can be planted. Species in such areas would be protected. Species which invaded fallow or cultivated land would not be.

Because few data and guides are currently available on how best to enhance habitat on farmland, AFT suggests the adoption of a phased approach beginning with habitat enhancement for the endangered San Joaquin kit fox. Farmers will benefit because this species is an opportunistic forager and an effective predator of ground squirrels and rabbits, serious pests of field crops like alfalfa. Although the kit fox has become endangered primarily because of habitat lost to irrigated cropland, small numbers live and breed in and next to irrigated farms, using artificial dens and man-made structures for cover. Encouraging kit foxes on farmland would not only increase numbers of this species but would also provide bridges between populations on public lands in the valley and the larger populations on private and public lands around the valley margins.

Other species use farmland that is otherwise unoccupied during certain seasons or, like the kit fox controlling rabbits and squirrels, work congruently with the overall interests of the farmer. Planting cottonwoods on a corner of a farm would provide nesting habitat for Swainson's hawks, which forage in row crop fields. Alfalfa farmers can implement certain post-harvest grazing practices that encourage habitat for the mountain plover. Narrow strips of habitat can be used as corridors for the occupation and dispersal of Kangaroo rats. Wetlands can be created out of tail-water ponds. Revegetating canals and ditches can provide habitat for spadefoot toads, red-legged frogs, snowy plovers, and slough thistle, all of which are listed as endangered or candidate species.

AFT has long believed that most farmers want to see increased wildlife on their lands, but have been kept on the defensive because of the threat of liability, including civil and criminal penalties, and the cost of habitat enhancement. Farmers need to be convinced that protecting endangered species brings benefits that outweigh costs. AFT has already enlisted a number of farmers who have agreed to participate in the habitat enhancement effort provided they can be assured, by written agreement, of protection from liability. This project promises to bring farmers, environmentalists, government managers, scientists, and others together to find local solutions to the problems of managing and sustaining resources for the benefit of all.

In both the EDF and the AFT examples, environmentalists have engaged farmers seriously, grasped the validity of their interests, and then proceeded to craft a consensual solution. Achieving a working consensus is the essential, unavoidable precondition for bridging the barricades.

. . . .
Great Plains, Great Plans

Cooperation and flexibility are also being tried on a much larger scale. The EPA regional office in Kansas City launched its Great Plains Initiative in 1992 in response to a variety of ecological and health concerns, including the very ability of the Great Plains to sustain biodiversity and economic activity into the next century. The Great Plains Partnership (GPP), as it is now called, was designed to address problems on varying scales of diversity and complexity involving multiple participants and landscapes.

The GPP is a voluntary alliance. It includes representatives from EPA, the Western Governors' Association, The Nature Conservancy and other nonprofit organizations, Native American tribes, the International Association of Fish and Wildlife Agencies, the National Association of Soil and Water Districts, the state of Minnesota, the province of Manitoba, the U.S. Fish and Wildlife Service and other agencies in the Department of the Interior, the U.S. Department of Agriculture and various agricultural organizations, and other entities, including groups of landowners in central Canada, northern Mexico, and the middle of the United States. The complexity and sweep of this coordinating structure reflects the on-the-ground diversity of a vast bioregion, one that occupies the heart of an entire continent and that overflows with a volatile mix of challenges and opportunities. Involvement of local landowners is considered pivotal.

The project wisely moved first to shore up its scientific underpinnings. In December 1993, the Great Plains International Data Network was formed in an effort to bring coherence and accessibility to widely scattered sources of important information. Starting with The Nature Conservancy's Natural Heritage Data Center Network and various governmental and academic databases, the Great Plains network already connects more than 120 separate participants. Many of them are strictly local in focus.

Among the concerns underlying creation of the GPP were the long economic decline of the Great Plains, the region's vulnerability to natural disasters, epitomized by the 1993 and 1995 floods in the Midwest, and the uncertainties of global climate change, which could be accompanied by changes in precipitation, shifting biological regimes, and the like. The most impressive responses to date have come at the grassroots level, where local efforts, usually delineated by the boundaries of a specific watershed, have developed into *de facto* demonstration projects for the larger bioregion.

The Iowa River Corridor Project, for example, projects the vision of a three-county, 49,500-acre, and 45-mile-long mosaic of private and public lands characterized by uses that can accommodate floodwaters, such as farm- and pasturelands, parks and other recreation lands. Using private and public partnerships, the objectives of this endeavor are to provide landowners with a broad menu of assistance options based on proved principles of floodplain management; manage public lands for the natural

diversity and functions of the river system; use the natural resources of the
floodplain to improve water quality; provide an educational opportunity
for stakeholders in other watersheds; and evaluate the economics of alternative uses of the floodplain and its lands. Management will be limited to
allowing the re-establishment of bottomland forests, wetlands, and floodplain prairies.

A variety of easements, buyouts, and sustainable land-management
practices are being offered to the Iowa project's landowners. Several
AmeriCorps volunteers based in the area are helping out—for example,
making personal contacts with landowners to explain the complex ease-
ment-planning process. The entire enterprise is largely focused on the
ethic of land stewardship. Wetlands restoration and conservation are
placed in the context of the landscape as a working whole. While wetlands function as the "kidneys," they lose their ecological importance in
the absence of the rest of the body.

The Great Plains Partnership assumes that an integrated approach
based on natural and human communities is the most effective way to
ensure economic and ecological sustainability and the best way to set
meaningful goals, achieve efficiencies in the use of government resources,
and give stakeholders a voice. Ultimately, the result hoped for is a region
capable of accommodating episodic flood surges without loss of life or
property.

. . . .
Wetlands and Habitats, Science and Technology

Cooperative and flexible approaches may be applicable elsewhere as
well—as a way to address, for example, the often contentious land-use
issues of wetlands and habitat protection. The Endangered Species Act is
perhaps surpassed only by wetlands regulations as the most unpopular
weapon in the federal arsenal. It was a serious mistake to fashion a law
that focuses its firepower to protect a single species at the moment of its
maximum danger, at the very moment when a conflict over the use of a
particular piece of land is likely to be at its most protracted and difficult.
The staffs of Governor Pete Wilson in California and U.S. Secretary of
the Interior Bruce Babbitt have together worked on an approach to
ensure species protection well in advance of the emergence of a polarized
controversy.

The system involves determining the species that exist on a property
and that require a particular habitat, examining the development pro-

posed for the area, and reconciling the two before the train wreck occurs. This approach, in my view, must be the way of the future. It takes a larger, systemic view of living resources and of development needs and plans, and enlists science and economics early in the process of reconciling the two, and it does this well in advance of a specific conflict.

In applying the same system to wetlands, it is possible that systematic surveys, classifications, and scientific delineations are likely to be the most productive means of sidestepping protracted fights over property rights and environmental values. Of all of President Bush's environmental positions, his commitment to "no net loss" of wetlands was among the most difficult and least popular. Long battles were fought over delineating what, in fact, constitutes a wetland. The inability of government agencies to promulgate definitive maps in advance of a development proposal, making unmistakably clear what is and is not wetland subject to federal regulation, is a significant contributor to wetlands controversies. Just finding out whether land is in or out of the wetlands category can be a time-consuming and frustrating affair for a landowner. That is unfair and intolerable.

The Bush Administration vigorously administered wetlands laws and was the first to put landowners in jail for repeated and egregious violations. More interesting is the fact that every single case was brought to our attention by a complaint from an adjacent landowner—by neighbors whose basements were being flooded or whose property was being washed out as a consequence of a change in wetlands or floodplains upstream. The National Academy of Sciences has recently reported on the criteria that should govern wetlands delineation. The Academy report provides a basis for laying to rest one of the major issues in contention. A serious commitment to mapping the nation's wetlands according to the Academy's approved criteria should now follow.

I am not at all certain that we have sufficiently exploited some of the modern technologies that science has available to address many land-use problems. In early 1971, while a member of the staff of the President's Council on Environmental Quality, I proposed the use of satellite imaging and aerial photography to determine the precise configuration of wetlands in the United States. With such a determination in hand, I hoped we would be able to identify areas in which tax advantages could be provided, rapid depreciation for construction, for example, denied. The Internal Revenue Service was prepared to accommodate the proposal, but insisted on absolute clarity about the precise lines delineating the lands to be afforded special tax treatment. Having just left the Army, I was aware of high-resolution aerial photography that would have made that proposal viable. The Defense Department was then unwilling to allow civilian access to these monitoring instruments. Now, however, they are available, and we should use them.

I was reminded of this recently when Secretary Babbitt ran into difficulty in trying to obtain access to private property in the West for government scientific researchers to complete biological surveys. Obviously, if property owners object to such surveys, they should have the right to keep researchers out. But much about land and even about species can be inferred from aerial photography. No intrusion need be involved.

Meanwhile, the importance of incentives and mitigation in solving long-standing environmental problems should be given higher priority. Disney World is expanding in Florida without great controversy largely because the company identified large, long-degraded, and important tracts nearby that will be upgraded, restored, and protected. Wherever significant wetlands are scheduled for destruction—in the building of highways and airports, for example—it is important to restore at least their equivalent elsewhere in the vicinity. Funds for this purpose are available now in transportation law.

To those interested in the future of land policy, my message is straightforward: reframe the issue; negotiate at the beginning with principal stakeholders; defer to science as the best compass for turbulent times; focus on rewards and incentives; develop decentralized approaches to decentralized problems; and exploit new technologies. Only with a diversity of approaches will we break the current stalemate and begin to establish a new, consensus-based approach to protecting America's most productive and threatened landscapes.

Metropolitan Development Trends of the Late 1990s: Social and Environmental Implications

. . . .

Christopher B. Leinberger

Christopher B. Leinberger is Managing Partner of Robert Charles Lesser & Company, the largest independent real estate advisory firm in the country.

. . . .

The metropolitan growth trends over the past two generations have propelled the United States toward a future of decentralized, low density development that will consume land many times faster than the underlying population or employment growth. A basic understanding of how this process works has only begun to emerge over the past decade. It should be emphasized that this process is in constant evolution and permutation, always following the volatile changes of the real estate business cycle. The social and environmental implications of this evolution are still not well understood, a failure that carries serious implications for the future cohesiveness of American society.

The fundamental organizing units of our metropolitan areas over the past 30 years have been and will continue to be "metro cores." Metro cores are the location of the vast majority of export[1] and regional-serving[2] jobs in the metropolitan area and include the original downtown, the early alternative locations to the downtown, centers in what are now called the inner suburbs, as well as the more far-flung outer suburbs. The newer cores are also known as edge cities, urban villages, and activity centers.

The growth of metro cores has roughly paralleled the private sector real estate booms of the past 35 years. The private real estate industry—which includes developers, investors, and construction, marketing, and management professionals—is one of the largest industries in the economy, with over $3 trillion in commercial and industrial assets alone, and one of the most cyclical. In terms of economics it has higher highs and lower lows than any other industry, including auto production. These real estate cycles generally last 6 to 10 years from peak to peak, though this varies depending on the particular product type (office, industrial, housing, etc.) and the local metropolitan economy.

As table 1 shows, metro cores in our metropolitan areas established themselves during particular real estate upturns—except for the original downtowns, which has been around since the initial settlements. In the following decade, the next real estate upturn generally resulted in explosive growth of the metro core, followed by maturation and then stability or decline. Determining the course of growth or decline of these metro cores is paramount in assessing metropolitan development trends of the past few decades and projecting these trends into the future.

. . . .

A History of Metro Cores from 1960 to 1994

First Generation Metro Cores

Prior to 1960, the main concentration of export and regional-serving jobs existed in or near downtown, referred to as the first generation metro core in table 1. In addition, the downtown and adjacent areas provided major regional shopping for the metropolitan area and a large concentration of housing for most socioeconomic groups, many times including a large concentration of upper-middle and high-end housing.

Starting before World War II, but accelerating rapidly afterward, most American downtowns lost their upper-middle and high-end housing to the suburbs, regional retailers expanded in suburban regional malls, and the vast majority of industrial and office jobs relocated or were created outside of downtown. Generally speaking, most downtowns today only capture three types of office users—professional services, financial services, and government—all of which are stable or shrinking in their number of employees. Most of the industrial users that remain downtown do so for either historical reasons such as low, below replacement, occupancy costs or for rail service, which has become much less important for industrial users in recent years. While regional-serving retailing may maintain a presence downtown, it is a mere shadow of its former self. With few exceptions, few downtowns have significant upper-middle and upper income housing nearby.

For the most part, downtown employment relative to metropolitan employment growth has been in decline. Downtown Baltimore grew by less than half the rate of the metropolitan area as a whole over the last 25

TABLE 1   Types of Metro Cores

Generation	Character		
(Beginning Decade)	Urban or Urbanizing	Suburban	Semi-Rural
1st (Pre-1960s)	All Downtowns		
2nd (1960s)	Bala Cynwyd/Philadelphia	Northlake/Atlanta	
3rd (1970s)	Buckhead/Atlanta	Tysons Corner/Washington, DC	
4th (1980s)		Schaumburg//Chicago	Fairlakes/Washington, DC
5th (1990s)			Hoffmann Estates/Chicago

Source: Robert Charles Lesser & Co.

years. It held 13 percent of the region's employment in 1970 but only captured 6 percent of the employment growth in the last 25 years. Thus, its share of the region's employment had dropped to 11 percent by 1994.

This relative decline has, naturally, affected the office market. Downtown Los Angeles, the heart of the fastest-growing metropolitan area of our time, contained 60 percent of all occupied office space in Southern California in 1960 but only 22 percent in 1985; and it absorbed only 11 percent of the net new space between 1985 and 1992. The trend was masked by a gleaming new skyline which replaced millions of square feet of obsolete space, but that skyline also hid soaring vacancy rates for most of the last decade. There is very little chance that vacancy rates will decline enough over the next decade to warrant increasing rents to the point of justifying new construction in most downtowns—except for the occasional government sponsored build-to-suit office buildings, which are of dubious economic merit.

Second Generation Metro Cores

The 1960s saw the tentative emergence of the second generation of metro cores, providing new office and industrial space two to six miles from downtown. These metro cores offered for office and industrial users an alternative to downtown for the first time.

Examples of the *office-oriented* second generation metro cores include the Stemmons Freeway metro core in Dallas, the Mid-Wilshire in Los Angeles, the Northeast Expressway metro core in Atlanta, and Bala Cynwyd in the Philadelphia area. Time has shown that most of these second generation office-oriented metro cores have failed, although there are a few exceptions, such as Bala Cynwyd. Today, the second generation metro core office buildings, mostly built in the 1960s and 1970s (though there were a few, unfortunately, built in the 1980s), only compete on price, generally renting under $15 per square foot (gross) for office space, well below replacement costs. These metro cores have generally become seedy in appearance, and crime has become a factor as the neighborhoods around the metro core have deteriorated. Most regional-serving retailing has left and most of the high-density housing, particularly rental, has declined in value.

What caused this demise? These second generation metro cores fell victim to a decline in nearby neighborhoods (Stemmons Freeway in Dallas and Mid-Wilshire), poor transportation access to executive housing (Mid-Wilshire and Uptown in Phoenix), or linear suburban development patterns and poor retailing which created a "no there there" syndrome (Stemmons Freeway, Uptown Phoenix, and Northeast Expressway). For example, there were few services and no adjacent housing to help provide a "heart" to an otherwise 9-5 employment center. The few second generation office-oriented metro cores that are successful continue to have good access to executive housing and superior retailing and have evolved a more urban fabric (Bala Cynwyd and Chevy Chase in the Washington, D.C., area). These lessons are important to keep in mind as time catches up with subsequent generations of metro cores.

The second generation *industrial* metro cores (City of Commerce in Los Angeles, Sunnyvale/Santa Clara in the San Jose area, and the Shipyard in Houston) quietly established the concept of the industrial park during the 1960s and 1970s and generally continue to maintain their value to this day. Because industrial-oriented metro cores only have one type of real estate use, a utilitarian cluster of inexpensive metal and block buildings, they are generally immune to most social ills and demographic shifts in the local area, as long as the transportation infrastructure remains viable and crime can be kept out.

Third Generation Metro Cores

The big story in real estate of the 1970s and 1980s was the establishment and explosive growth of the third generation metro cores, particularly office-oriented metro cores. The growth of Tysons Corner outside Washington, D.C., Perimeter Center outside Atlanta, West Los Angeles and Costa Mesa/Irvine/Newport Beach in the Los Angeles metropolitan area, and the O'Hare area in Chicago attracted more attention than any other real estate trend over the past two decades. In fact, every metropolitan area in the country, regardless of size, saw the appearance of at least one third generation metro core during the 1970s and its subsequent fast growth in the 1980s. Even Tyler, Texas, population 77,000, has a third generation office-oriented metro core on the south side of town, surrounded by its high-end housing district, built around the only regional mall in the area, Broadway Square, which gives its name to the metro core.

Tyler's Broadway Square metro core is typical of all third generation office-oriented metro cores, whatever the size of the metropolitan area: it is located adjacent to the vast concentration of upper-middle or upper-end housing districts in the region. All such metro cores in the country have this characteristic because the bosses live in the high-end housing districts and want to minimize their commutes and the commutes of the firm's senior management. As in Tyler, most of these metro cores are anchored by a regional mall. In addition, all third generation office-oriented metro cores have depended on automobiles as their nearly exclusive means of access and are generally located adjacent to a major limited-access highway, such as Tyson's Corner on the I-495 beltway outside Washington, D.C., or Costa Mesa/Newport Beach/Irvine metro core on I-405 in the Los Angeles metropolitan area.

Although originally working from a small base, the growth rates of employment and occupied office space absorption in these metro cores during the 1970s were at least twice and often three or four times as fast as the average growth in their respective metropolitan areas. During the real estate boom of the 1980s, most third generation metro cores grew one and a half to two times as fast as the metropolitan growth rates; this relatively lower growth rate was a reflection of the larger base achieved at the beginning of the decade. Many third generation, office-oriented metro cores had more occupied office space by the end of the 1980s than did the metropolitan area's first generation downtown, in spite of having barely been in existence for two decades. Following the real estate depression of the late 1980s and early 1990s, these metro cores generally saw healthy growth in employment and office absorption but at rates that were only slightly higher than the metropolitan average. Surprisingly, some third generation cores began to grow relatively less rapidly than the metropolitan area as a whole for the first time.

One reason for the recent slower growth of third generation office-oriented metro cores is continuing dependence on the automobile. Many are reaching a point of traffic saturation, and it is either too costly or not politically feasible to increase the highway capacity serving the metro core. It appears that once a third generation metro core reaches a certain size, measured in the amount of total commercial space, highway congestion deters companies from locating there. A second and related reason is the rise of politically potent neighborhood opposition to additional growth and traffic congestion. Most prevalent on the West Coast and the Northeast, this antigrowth sentiment comes from the most vocal and well financed of neighborhood groups in the metropolitan area: the upper-middle and upper-end households surrounding these cores. A third reason for the slowing of growth has to do with a "character": All of these third generation metro cores initially had a suburban character, which included relatively low densities and surface parking, characteristics that led to up-wards of 70 percent of the land being dedicated to moving or parking cars and very little pedestrian circulation. Some cores continue to maintain that character, while others have begun to evolve toward a denser urban character. This split between *urbanizing* third generation, office-oriented metro cores and those that have retained a *suburban* character seems to have an impact on future growth prospects.

Industrially oriented third generation metro cores, which appeared in the 1970s and grew rapidly in the 1980s, are also located on limited-access highways, generally interstates, and provide convenient truck access to other metropolitan areas. Flanking the third generation office-oriented metro cores, and located farther away from downtown than the second generation industrial metro cores, these third generation industrially oriented cores are generally linear in shape, stretched out along the highway. Like their second generation counterparts, these cores will not usually include regional retailing or high-density housing; they are simply pragmatic concentrations of industrial and warehouse buildings strung together by acres of surface parking lots.

Fourth Generation Metro Cores

The emergence of fourth generation office-oriented metro cores in the 1980s occurred 4 to 12 miles further out from the third generation cores, although moving in the same direction—away from the center city. This generation is characterized by its very low density, semi-rural character. Fair Lakes on I-66 west of Washington, D.C., and Plano on the Dallas Tollway on the north side of the metropolitan area were laid out as very low-density, heavily landscaped campuses. These cores were the most overbuilt in the 1980s as fringe development tends to be, but they appear to be recovering the fastest during the 1990s, because developers were sidelined by the early 1990s downturn in real estate, and there was no more supply added to the inventory.

Like the office-oriented metro cores, the fourth generation industrially oriented cores have also moved four to ten miles beyond the third generation. They have repeated the pattern of locating along interstate highways and on the flanks of the same generation of office-oriented cores. Examples include the Vallwood metro core in northwest Dallas, White Marsh on the northeast side of the Baltimore metropolitan area (combining office and industrial), and the Carlsbad/Palomar Airport metro core in San Diego County.

. . . .

Effects of the Development Pattern

Some of the social and environmental implications from pursuing this development pattern over the past generation are seen in:

- *The geometric increase in the physical size of our metropolitan areas.* For example, the population of Metropolitan Chicago grew by only 4 percent between 1970 and 1990, but the land area of the region grew by approximately 46 percent. The Los Angeles metropolitan area, had a population growth of 45 percent during the same period but nearly tripled in size to approximately 5,000 square miles, equal in size to the state of Connecticut. This geometric increase in size tended to take place in only one direction in most metropolitan areas, except for the five largest which experienced growth in multiple directions. For example, Washington, D.C., extends approximately 12 to 15 miles from downtown to the east and southeast, but 35 to 40 miles to the west and northwest.

- *The monopoly of the automobile.* Because of the lack of building concentration at either the point of origin or the point of destination, the only transportation option in these new metro cores is the automobile. While there are some notably successful transit systems—heavy rail, light rail, bus, and van or car pooling—the capital and operating costs become prohibitively expensive the more decentralized the development. Exclusive reliance on automobile transportation means increased oil consumption, pollution, and traffic congestion—which, in turn, leads to the demand for more highway construction. The percentage of the middle-income household's budget devoted to ownership and maintenance of cars has risen to 20 percent, more than is spent for food (19 percent) and only slightly less than is spent on housing (25 percent). Obviously, lower-income households may have tremendous difficulties in devoting the required amount to own and maintain a car or cars.

- *The growing isolation of center city residents.* Nearly all absolute job growth and the vast majority of corporate relocations have taken place well beyond the easy reach of the original metro core. Minorities

are especially affected because they tend to live on the opposite side of
the metropolitan area from where new jobs are being created. Transit
connections to the new jobs are few, and those that exist generally involve multiple transfers and commutes of well over one hour in each
direction.

- *The development of socially and economically homogenous new
  neighborhoods on the fringe of our metropolitan areas.* The neighborhoods around the new metro cores, generally townhouses and detached homes, are of much lower density and much larger size on average than any before in the nation's history, a trend that promotes
  personal privacy and isolation.

- *Consolidation of retailing into historically large, efficient outlets for
  most needs.* Generally, only high-end apparel and restaurants occupy
  small special places. While the efficiency of historically large outlets
  has driven down prices, vastness and depersonalized character have
  eroded any sense of community.

- *The privatization of public spaces.* The current development process
  generally does not build commonly owned public spaces, particularly
  pedestrian-scale spaces. The main public space in most of the new
  communities developed over the past generation is privately owned
  retail space, spread out in miles of "strip centers" and malls. Inas-
  much as these large retail outlets are national chains, there is a tendency for strip retail to have a sameness to it, a "could be anywhere"
  character, blurring regional character.

Creating a Metropolitan Model

A model of how our metropolitan areas have evolved over the past generation can be developed by using research from metropolitan areas
throughout the country. Upper-middle and upper-end housing tends to
heavily concentrate in most metropolitan areas.[3] By knowing where this
housing is located, and by understanding the limited access highway
system, it is possible to know where most employment growth took place
and where most development will take place. Placing a point in the downtown and drawing a roughly 90 degree arc that encompasses the high-end
housing concentration, defines the "favored quarter." This is where up-
wards of 80 percent of all commercial real estate activity and job growth
took place over the past generation. The vast majority of new housing development (upper-end and entry-level) lies within or immediately adjacent
to the favored quarter.

This model is shown in figure 1. Prototypic locations of the four generations of office and industrially oriented metro cores are shown, as well as the concentration of high-end housing, bracketed by the boundaries of the favored quarter.

. . . .
Learning from Atlanta

Atlanta provides one of the best examples in the country of these metropolitan development trends because it has been growing so quickly and because there are few geographic barriers to distort underlying forces. Atlanta's favored quarter lies north of downtown and includes more than 90 percent of the housing priced over $300,000 (see figure 2). The metropolitan area has a beltway built in the early 1970s that defined the northern boundary at the time. Opened adjacent to the beltway in 1973, the Perimeter Center Mall (#11) was considered to be on the absolute edge of the metropolitan area; hence its name.

Since 1983, the downtown (#1) has seen its occupied office space grow only two-thirds as fast as the growth in occupied office space throughout the region. Downtown had nearly a third of all occupied space in 1983 but only a quarter of all occupied space a decade later. It needed to grow 50 percent faster than it did just to maintain its 1983 market share. The second generation Northeast Expressway metro core (#13) had nearly 12 percent of all occupied space in 1983 but only 7 percent in 1993. It would have had to grow more than five times as fast just to maintain its market share of occupied space.

In contrast, the metro core around Perimeter Center (#11) grew from under five million square feet in 1983 (14 percent of the region's occupied space) to over 14 million square feet in 1993 (almost 20 percent of the regional total). It grew 75 percent faster in net absorption than the region as a whole. In fact, the favored quarter captured over 80 percent of all net employment growth since 1983 and nearly all of the relocations from within the region.

Because of the push to the north, the fourth generation metro cores along Georgia 400 (#9), those surrounding the Marietta Town Center mall (#7) and those around the Gwinnett Place Mall (#14) grew from almost no occupied office space in 1983 to nearly four million square feet of space in 1993, capturing 12 percent of the metropolitan area's growth from a standing start. In addition, these cores were the sites of most of the large owner-occupied buildings put up during the decade, which are not

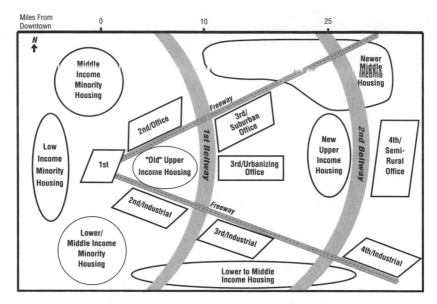

FIGURE 1   Predominant Metropolitan Growth Model in the Favored Quarter—
1995. *Source:* Robert Charles Lesser & Co.

counted in the figures, including the regional headquarters of AT&T, Honda, and Siemons.

The location of new employment in these three fourth generation metro cores has led to two consequences: first, development of new housing projects up to 35 miles north of the downtown, even further north of these metro cores, continuing the geometric expansion of the metropolitan area; second, a heated political debate over whether an outer beltway should be constructed to connect these three metro cores and eventually encircle the metropolitan area. This new beltway would be 12 miles from the "inner" beltway—just 20 years ago the northern physical boundary to the metropolitan area.

•   •   •   •   •   •   •   •   •

Future Trends

What do these trends mean for the future development of our metropolitan areas? The underlying trends of decentralized metro cores and expanding metropolitan areas appear to be continuing and may even be ac-

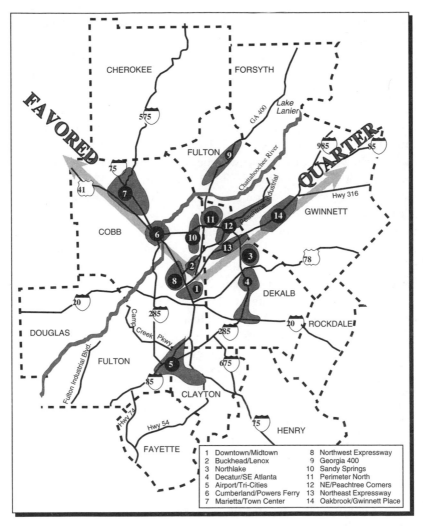

FIGURE 2   Metro Cores Atlanta Metropolitan Region. *Source:* Robert Charles Lesser & Co.

celerating. But this is a case of continuity with variations. Future growth and development will take place in different locations in the 1990s.

Downtowns

There appear to be three options for our downtowns: stability, moderate decline, and severe decline. Downtowns only have three employment sectors that they consistently capture — professional services, finance, and government—stable sectors at best. This means that the relative employment base of downtowns will continue to shrink.

The most optimistic future for downtowns is that they will remain relatively stable, with employment declining a little in relative terms. In the few downtowns that are stable, a significant amount of high-end housing is located in or adjacent to the downtown, particularly detached housing that was generally built 60 to 100 years ago and is still highly valued. Because the bosses want to keep their businesses close to their housing and their housing is close to downtown, they are inclined to locate downtown, even if the business is not in one of the three downtown-oriented employment sectors. A second reason for stable downtowns is vibrant retail, facilities not only for the local population but, very importantly, for tourists. A successful convention center, professional sports facilities and tourist attractions, particularly if they are linked by easy and safe pedestrian connections to the rest of the downtown, adds to this vibrancy. Unfortunately, only a few of the country's downtowns fall into this category—for example, Washington, D.C., Seattle, Portland (Oregon), San Francisco, Midtown New York, and Boston.

The majority of U.S. downtowns will continue to experience moderate decline, with employment and offices growing at only half the rate of the region as a whole. While some upper-end housing exists in many of these downtowns, it is not sizable nor is it growing. For some of these downtowns, the retail may in fact be flourishing. There may be a successful convention center, professional sports facilities and tourist attractions that add to the appeal; yet these assets ultimately do little for underlying employment. Downtowns falling into this category are becoming healthier and may eventually move into the stable category, like Denver, or are solidly in this category and likely to stay there, like Baltimore and San Diego. Other downtowns in this category—Atlanta after the Olympics (unless the "Olympic legacy" does indeed result in a change of recent trends), Philadelphia, Los Angeles, among others—could slip into the severe decline category if remedial action is not taken, because all product categories (office, industrial, housing, and retail) are in relative decline.

Many downtowns are already experiencing, and will continue to experience, severe decline. Employment and office growth will be half or less than the amount in the rest of the region and may even decline absolutely. Downtowns in severe decline have virtually no upper-end housing or any retail base, except for a small amount serving offices, and little prospect that any will be built. If there is any convention business or professional sports facilities, their impact is very limited because visitors attend an event and immediately leave when it ends. There is virtually no entertainment or urban vibrancy. In essence, there is "no there there." The downtown that is probably in the most severe decline is Detroit, but there are many others in this category, including St. Louis, Tampa, Phoenix, Dallas, Houston, and Jacksonville.

Investment and new development will likely focus on the few stable downtowns and some moderately declining ones. Denver is an excellent example of a moderately declining downtown which is being turned around. The revival high-end residential, entertainment, retail, and restaurants in downtown Denver will be followed by the revival of the hotel industry, especially since the opening of the new professional baseball stadium in the summer of 1995. Unfortunately, these positive trends will probably not spill over into office and industrial product types because job growth is relatively weak compared to the region as a whole.

Second Generation Metro Cores

Second generation metro cores that are office-oriented will continue to lose employment relatively and possibly absolutely, like severely declining downtowns. Few today have existing retail or high-end housing bases, nor will any be built in the near future. There will be little in the way of investment-grade opportunities in second generation metro cores. Examples of these metro cores include the Northeast Expressway area in Atlanta and the Stemmons Freeway area in Dallas.

But there are exceptions to the rule. Bala Cynwyd in the Philadelphia metropolitan area will continue to remain a viable metro core with high lease rates and successful retailing and high-end housing, assuming the fear of crime from the city, which is literally across the street, does not overpower it. And there has been a revival of second generation office-oriented metro cores in the Washington, D.C., area due to the success of Metro, the longest subway system in the world and the safest in the country. The inner suburban subway stops, such as Court House, Ballston, Chevy Chase, and Bethesda, have all been relatively successful over the past decade in gaining employment, partially helped by the decisions of federal agencies to locate near Metro stations. These stations, in turn, have helped create vibrant retail and residential developments within walking distance. This recent success will probably continue for the rest of the decade.

The second and third generation industrially oriented metro cores should continue to maintain their underlying value, assuming transportation is adequate and local crime does not become a problem.

Third Generation Office-oriented Metro Cores

As mentioned above, third generation office-oriented metro cores appear to be dividing into two categories. The first are those that are "densifying" by extending mass transit to the metro core, developing high-density residential facilities (mid-rise and high-rise, rentals and even condominiums), upgrading and expanding the retail base, and generally creating a more urban, pedestrian feel. They are developing a "there there." The urban or urbanizing third generation metro cores will experience faster employment and office-space growth than the metropolitan area as a whole, starting from an already sizable base. Examples of urban or urbanizing third generation metro cores include Buckhead (#2) and Perimeter Center (#11) in the Atlanta metropolitan area, Costa Mesa/Newport Beach/Irvine in the Los Angeles area, Cherry Creek in Denver, and Country Club Plaza in Kansas City. A few fourth generation metro cores are also urbanizing, such as Reston in the Washington, D.C., region (partially due to the success of its new pedestrian-oriented Town Center).

The key to this category's success is that it offers one of the few, if not the only, safe urban environments in the metropolitan area. Active management of such a metro core is essential if it is to be successful. To that end, a core might develop a "business improvement district," a property owners organization, or a transportation management association to assess property owners and provide additional security, maintain common areas, promote events in the common areas, develop programs to manage traffic congestion, lobby for infrastructure improvements, and so forth. The Buckhead Coalition in Atlanta has been successfully planning and lobbying for significant transportation improvements to the metro core, including a new tollway and a mass transit stop. It has also been successful in increasing security and cleanliness and plans to create a more pedestrian-oriented environment.

In essence, these metro cores are the "new downtowns" of the metropolitan area, especially if the region has a severely declining first generation downtown. In the office sector, this category of third generation metro core has seen some of the most dramatic declines in vacancy in the metropolitan area. The effective rents are generally the highest of any metro core. As a result, investors and developers will be attracted to these metro cores.

The third generation office-oriented metro cores which are not urbanizing but maintaining a suburban character and are stretched out along a highway may have a different future. Like most second generation metro cores, they have "no there there." As a rule, if outside social conditions do not change, there is no reason to expect that this category of third generation metro cores will decline in the short term (three to five years). But there are some examples of third generation office-oriented metro cores that are showing signs of decline.

Research has shown that the white population has an aversion to shopping or living in a community where there is more than a 20 percent to 25 percent minority population. Whenever a community or shopping center goes over this line, it becomes virtually 100 percent minority very rapidly. This kind of change generally first affects a metro core in the demographics of the shopping centers and malls and then the rental apartment housing stock. Both can change very quickly. In an overbuilt local rental apartment market, for example, owners can offer minority occupants low rents in a better neighborhood than they live in. Where this has occurred, the new minority residents have tended to have children who attend the local elementary schools initially. White flight from the school district occurs, generally in a rolling fashion as the minority children get older and enter junior and senior high school.

The impact on the surrounding single-family housing, which almost exclusively will have a majority white population, and the office market is delayed. There has not been enough experience around third generation metro cores to document this impact or how fast it occurs. Conventional wisdom, however, suggests that there will be a decline in values, white flight from the neighborhoods and a movement of office users to alternative metro cores when their leases, which generally average five years in length, expire.

This kind of decline occurred in the Greenspoint metro core in northwest Houston. After the complete turnover of 6,000 rental apartments immediately northeast of the Greenspoint Mall to low-income families, a perception grew that crime was sharply on the rise. A murder outside the mall resulted in headline news in a metropolitan area numbed by one of the highest homicide rates in the country, even though the crime had no connection with the metro core. As of the summer of 1995, office tenants were not leaving in a panic but certainly the fourth generation metro cores in the region, such as The Woodlands to the north of Greenspoint, are benefiting. This same phenomenon may be starting in such metro cores as

Southfield in the Detroit metropolitan area and Cumberland/Powers Ferry (#6) in Atlanta, though the outcome is not a foregone conclusion.

Even if demographic changes do not occur, it is likely that employment and office growth in this suburban nondensifying category of third generation metro cores will be equal to or less than the growth of the metropolitan area as a whole. Office vacancies will not decline as fast as in the suburban-style third generation metro cores and, more significant, effective rates will stay below replacement levels, which means little new space can be developed even if vacancy rates drop below 10 percent. Retail and rental apartment properties might not recover in value in these metro cores compared to the increase being achieved throughout the country. Examples of suburban third generation, office-oriented metro cores that should not experience dramatic demographic changes include Tyson's Corner in the Washington, D.C., metropolitan area, King of Prussia in the Philadelphia area, and Encino/Ventura Boulevard in Los Angeles.

Fourth Generation Metro Cores

During the late 1990s, the bulk of employment growth will occur in the fourth generation, office-oriented and industrial metro cores. During the early 1990s, when very little speculative space was developed in the United States, the vast majority of owner-occupied relocations and expansions took place in fourth generation metro cores: J.C. Penney moved its headquarters to Plano at the fringe of the Dallas metropolitan area; Sears moved its headquarters to Hoffman Estates, 45 miles northwest of the former downtown Chicago Sears Tower; pharmaceutical R&D facilities located on limited access Route 422, eight miles northwest of the third generation King of Prussia metro core; and the corporate headquarters of U.S. Borax relocated to Valencia on I-5, 30 miles from its former home in downtown Los Angeles. All of these examples testify to the employment base shift to fourth generation metro cores.

These cores have primarily seen owner-occupied construction since 1990. The first speculative office development of the mid to late 1990s will probably also occur in fourth generation metro cores. Some of the best investment opportunities, next to those in urbanizing third generation metro cores, have been and will continue to be purchasing the existing fourth generation office buildings. Development opportunities will span every product type as middle-level and upper-level housing is built nearby, leading to regional and neighborhood-serving retail. Hotels will be developed to satisfy the need generated by the employment growth, and entertainment will be needed because existing facilities are too distant. In essence, fourth generation office-oriented metro cores will be nearly self-contained, extremely low density "new towns," developed by market forces with little or no government interference.

The future health of fourth generation metro cores is predicated on their still being in close proximity to high-end housing. For example, the executive living near the Buckhead or Perimeter Center metro cores of Atlanta would not be terribly inconvenienced if the office was moved to the Georgia 400 metro core (#9). Although the highway is congested going south during the morning rush hours, the executive would be driving north, against traffic. The 12- to 15-mile drive would only take 12 to 15 minutes.

Another reason for growth in the fourth generation metro cores is their abundance of land, which allows the development of very low density, semi-rural projects. In addition, the tax burden in the fourth generation communities is much lower than the metropolitan area average because the infrastructure is so new that it is less costly to maintain and there are virtually no social problems—for example, no welfare to provide yet. The political climate is generally pro-growth. Elected officials actively court new jobs and the resulting increase in tax revenues.

The underlying reason for the growth of the fourth generation metro cores is undoubtedly fear. In spite of the fact that violent crime in this country has remained stable over the past 20 years according to a Department of Justice survey (supposedly FBI statistics, which show an increase are mainly a result of better record keeping and more reporting), the perception persists that crime has become significantly worse. Much of this perception is based on rapidly growing gang activity, which is wrongly assumed to be a predominate factor in every minority community regardless of its socioeconomic base. The majority white population moving to the residential districts serving fourth generation metro cores sees the move as a way to ensure safety.

The Potential Emergence of the Fifth Generation Metro Cores

The emergence of fifth generation metro cores during the 1990s will probably not take place to the extent that the fourth generation metro cores developed in the 1980s. Significant capacity remains for development in the latter. Still, industrially oriented fifth generation metro cores have emerged led by owner-occupied warehouse development. This type of development can take place well beyond the existing fringe of the metropolitan area because interstate-accessible land can be obtained more cheaply and, given the comparatively few employees in a warehouse, there is less need to locate near large clusters of worker housing. Examples of fifth generation warehouse metro cores can be found northwest of Atlanta on

I-75, between Atlanta and the Tennessee border; and in Harford and Cecil counties, northeast of Baltimore County on I-95, toward the Delaware border.

. . . .

Social and Environmental Implications for the Future

Metropolitan area development trends in the United States have many social and policy implications for our nation, including the following:

- The future will witness a continued and growing isolation of the poor and working poor in the central city (and increasingly the inner suburbs) away from new employment opportunities.

- At the same time the inner suburbs will probably decline rapidly, especially because there will be virtually no new or relocating jobs and few cultural and civic institutions to claim general regional support, in contrast to downtowns that have received considerable regionwide financial support for these institutions and have slowed decline over the past 30 years. A decline in property values and educational standards in public schools and a rise in crime will undoubtedly follow.

- The declining tax base of the central city and inner suburbs will exacerbate existing social problems, and their costs will increase. This could lead to the takeover of more central cities and inner suburbs by their respective state governments. This may also lead to more regional tax sharing, as is being proposed in the Minneapolis/St. Paul metropolitan area, building on a limited commercial tax sharing that is presently in place. The Twin Cities pioneered regional tax sharing 20 years ago, and they are considering a far more aggressive tax sharing plan focusing on building more affordable housing in the favored quarter.

- Geometric increases in urbanized land use will continue at a rate of at least 8 to 12 times faster than the underlying employment and population growth.

- Given the pattern of growth toward fourth generation metro cores, air and water pollution will worsen and traffic congestion will increase because of nearly exclusive reliance on the automobile for transportation. Because of the general lack of interest in building more limited access highways on the fringe of our metropolitan areas, traffic congestion on former "farm-to-market" country roads will not improve.

This is both the best and worst of times for our metropolitan areas. The majority of our population is living in the largest and highest quality stock of housing in the world, while the post-industrial economy is producing the highest average living standard and is the most efficient of any nation. On the other hand, sterile and visually abusive commercial strip retail development and little sense of community or regional distinctiveness detract from our quality of life. The environmental costs are huge and, if the economics of oil-based automobile transportation ever radically change, we will have painted ourselves into a corner with few good options.

The opportunities for the underclass, which tends to be minority, will only get worse as job opportunities move ever further away from where they live. There is virtually no affordable housing on the exploding metropolitan fringe. The underclass will concentrate in ever-increasing numbers in the very political jurisdictions that do not benefit from these trends.

As a nation, we continue to ignore the negative consequences of how we are building where 75 percent of all Americans live. During the 1990s, the move of new and relocating employment to fourth generation metro cores will, literally and figuratively, place in concrete how we live, work, and shop for the next 30 years. In so doing, it will set the stage for many environmental, economic, and social challenges.

NOTES

1. Some industries "export" goods and services outside the metropolitan area, bringing new cash into the economy. Export industries include software, transportation/ distribution, and so forth. Providing approximately one-third of the area's employment, these are also some of the highest paying jobs in a metropolitan area and tend to concentrate in metro cores.

2. Regional-serving industries service the household and business sectors of the metropolitan area. They are concentrated in metro cores, as are export industries. They include most lawyers and other professional services, the media, real-estate developers and contractors, regional food distribution, and so forth.

3. This is true for nearly all metropolitan areas except the largest five—
   New York City, Los Angeles, Chicago, San Francisco, and Philadelphia—and those that have special geographic features, such as access
   to water in Tampa/St. Petersburg. The multiple number of high-end
   housing concentrations in the five largest metropolitan areas modifies
   the applicability of this model to them.

Our Critical Forest Resources

· ·

John A. Georges

John A. Georges is Chairman and Chief Executive Officer of International Paper Company.

· · · · · · · ·

As chief executive officer of a corporation that owns and manages over 6 million acres of land in the United States, I deal with land use decisions and policy making every day. Land is vital because it supports, on a sustainable basis, the natural resources on which our enterprise depends. Naturally, we view these resources in business terms. However, they are also fundamental components in current discussions about the ecosystem, economic enterprise and development sustainability, and certainly about land use sustainability.

International Paper has owned land in the United States since the corporation was founded in 1897, but total acreage has varied over the decades. For example, in the mid-1940s my company owned about 3.1 million acres. This total rose to a high of 7.6 million in 1976 and has been just over 6 million for the last five years. Currently, almost all of this acreage is in a publicly held limited partnership, International Paper Timberlands, Ltd. International Paper holds a majority interest in the partnership.

Unlike most of our competitors, whose forests are run as cost centers to provide fiber for their mills, our company's forestry operations are a largely independent profit center. Although the company's mill system is a preferred customer, it is not the only customer. All potential buyers are able to bid on timber sales, and those buying fiber for company mills must compete effectively. Thus, the forestry business' goal is to generate a favorable return for the partnership unit holders rather than solely to provide fiber to company mills.

This independence offers significant advantages, not the least of which is a market-driven focus. Because it operates as a profit center, the forestry business is more likely than its competitors to use the most cost-effective forest management practices. For their part, the mills are more likely to incur the market cost of fiber rather than an artificially subsidized one. Mills with fiber shortages must pay a premium for premature harvest of timber on partnership lands. Cost is calculated as if the timber were allowed to mature into sawlogs, and the premium paid can be substantial.

Being a profit center also brings challenges to our forestry operations. Short-term market pressures can make long-term investments more difficult to justify. This is especially problematic given the nature of the forestry business and the need for long-term investments in reforestation and research. The forestry business must compete for corporate capital with all other businesses. The long-term focus of forestry and the inherent uncertainty of the enterprise are major challenges that must be addressed in the competition for capital.

While cost is incurred by owning and managing forests, my company's landownership gives some flexibility not available otherwise. As mentioned, it can serve as something of an insurance policy for mills during times of fiber shortage. The ability to sell more timber than budgeted, as well as selling nonstrategic lands, provides the opportunity to take advantage of favorable market conditions.

The fact that we own land and know its capability is an advantage in other situations as well, such as logging in wet weather. Probably the most significant advantage when logging during wet seasons is to know the precise location of sites that are accessible and loggable. Because we have a comprehensive soil survey covering all of our lands, we are able to target operations based on soil and site conditions. Our harvest strategies generally hold all-weather logging sites in reserve for use in wet weather while scheduling sites without year-round accessibility for harvest during drier seasons. We are also more likely to supplement supplies with fiber purchased from other landowners to enable us to hold our all-weather logging sites as insurance against fiber shortages during wet weather.

So it should come as no surprise that forest product industry executives and personnel think seriously about natural resource sustainability. For instance, my company holds an annual world fiber supply conference to review the dynamics of forest fiber production on lands around the world. Our experts see a very challenging long-term picture as a result of a diminishing forestland base.

These challenges are immense. Barring some cataclysm, it is now highly probable that the global population will reach something on the order of 10 billion by the year 2050. The U.S. population will reach something close to 300 million in less than 60 years. The real test of sustainability, in its most elemental definition, is whether the individuals and families that comprise this population can have a meaningful and challenging quality of life. For the population to thrive, the life-support system—the biosphere—must remain undegraded in both its structure and function as well as supply the amenities—the natural beauty—that contribute so much to our well-being.

Because food, fiber, and space to support us come by and large from the land, land is central to considering the quality of the human future. Now that we are effectively combating pollution, the central environmental question of our time revolves around how land will be used. This is the question Pat Noonan, Henry Diamond, and others explore in this volume.

Nothing about land is static. In highly protected landscapes or landscapes subject to intensive human use, there is constant change, making it difficult even to take a snapshot of the character of the American landscape and have a sense that we know accurately its state at any given moment. Still, we have to know the condition of our lands before we can judge the sustainability of the renewable resources (the food or fiber) we take from them. With any luck, we can look at past patterns of change in the landscape to paint a clearer picture of these current conditions. Although projecting historic trends is a common practice, it has been as often as not proved to be wrong as much as it has right, so we must view such projections with caution.

I have attempted to put together an inventory of land use in the United States. To help give a clearer picture, I have arrayed the inventory as a spectrum from the most protected lands to the most developed categories of human uses bounded by the urban core. To develop figure 1, I have drawn on various federal and state sources, especially the recently published *Summary Report—1992 National Resources Inventory* of the U.S. Department of Agriculture. Drawing on these many sources unfortunately leads us to a set of numbers that do not add up to the exact total acreage of the United States, but the data fairly accurately reflect the general conditions in broad categories at the present time.

If we aggregate all state and federal parks, state and federal wildlife refuges, and federal wilderness areas, we have a reasonable measure of the protected natural areas of the United States, 217.6 million acres. We attempted to obtain data on as many land use divisions as possible for both private and public lands, as well as the data to provide an estimate of the

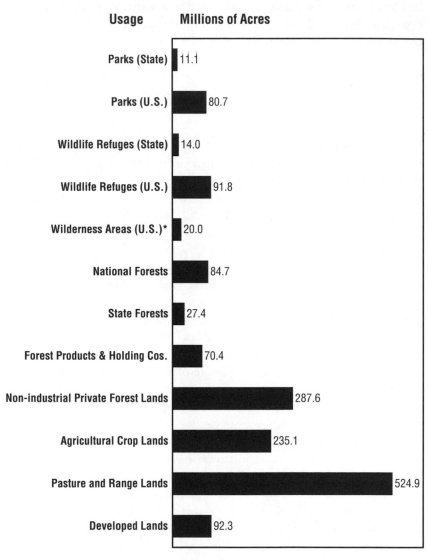

Usage	Millions of Acres
Parks (State)	11.1
Parks (U.S.)	80.7
Wildlife Refuges (State)	14.0
Wildlife Refuges (U.S.)	91.8
Wilderness Areas (U.S.)*	20.0
National Forests	84.7
State Forests	27.4
Forest Products & Holding Cos.	70.4
Non-industrial Private Forest Lands	287.6
Agricultural Crop Lands	235.1
Pasture and Range Lands	524.9
Developed Lands	92.3

*Also included in other totals.

FIGURE I   U.S. Land Use, 1992 (Excluding Alaska). *Source:* National Association of State Park Directors; National Park Statistical Abstract; U.S. Fish and Wildlife Service, *Annual Inventory Report,* 1992; Powell, et al., 1992, Forest Resources of the U.S., U.S. Department of Agriculture Forest Service, General Tech Report RM234; Summary Report 1992, National Resources Inventory (U.S. Soil and Conservation Service).

land in some degree of protected status. The wilderness acreage is isolated in a separate category, and the other public land categories do not include any wilderness areas. At the other end of the spectrum, the category of developed lands, a fair approximation of the amount of the landscape we consider so manipulated as to be effectively precluded from use for either food or fiber production or natural resource protection constitutes 92.3 million acres. Between these two categories exist the national and state forest multiple-use lands, lands held by forest product and holding companies, nonindustrially owned private forestlands, agricultural lands, pasture- and rangelands. These lands comprise about 1,230 million acres. It is this universe on which the future sustainability of our American landscape will turn.

The policies, programs, and market dynamics affecting these lands will determine whether or not we will continue to be sustainable in food production and in fiber production for building materials, furniture, paper, and other cellulose products. It is these lands that also will determine whether we maintain water quality, open space, recreation, biodiversity, and the amenities associated therewith.

Just as land does not support ecosystems that are static, the human uses of land are not static or fixed. If the uses of private land are not economic, the land quickly converts to uses that are. The lands that are in agriculture and forest management are subject to intense economic pressures, and, if those pressures become too great, farmers will sell for development, private forestland will be subdivided, whether we want that to happen or not. Not only are the sustainable enterprises of food and fiber production essential to human welfare lost, so too are the environmental, recreational, and amenity values that go with those uses. If we cannot maintain our land base in these uses, it is rapidly converted, in various development sequences—ranging from ranchettes to second home pieces of pastoral landscape for urban dwellers to shopping malls and classic suburban sprawl. Seen in this light, the advocates of not producing fiber from well-managed forests are in fact advocating the conversion of forestland to uses that will not only not produce fiber but will not provide any of the water quality, open space, recreation, and species protection values that are associated with such forestland.

Developing sound polices and programs for these lands should be an opportunity to bring together the interests of all groups concerned about these issues. Working together in a positive and mutually reinforcing way will require public policy dialogue among public interest groups, industry representatives, and government very different from the altercations that have been characteristic of the past, especially the recent past.

Let us start with industrially owned forestland, which means land owned by the natural resource companies that since the turn of the century have been affording increasingly wise stewardship to a very substantial land base. The industry has been very concerned about its landscapes and the management of renewable natural resources. This is economically rational—our land is the source of our raw material, and sustainable management of the resources insures future raw material supplies. More than any other group, government, or individual, the forest product industry has managed its lands with a long-term perspective.

Clearly, the forest industry operates today in a highly regulated environment. Most people have little trouble envisioning manufacturing facilities as regulated entities. However, these same individuals often appreciate less the regulatory framework within which forest management must be conducted. Federal regulations affect forest management across all of our 6.2 million acres. State (and increasingly local) regulations add another layer of complexity, and vary widely depending on the region and state. Generally, regulations are more comprehensive on our lands in the Pacific Northwest and the Northeast. Fewer state and local regulations exist in the Southeast, but their frequency has increased consistently in the last decade.

Although the total regulatory burden is important to my company, we are just as concerned about consistent interpretation and implementation of federal regulations that truly reflect Congress's original intent in enacting the legislation. We increasingly encounter substantially different interpretations of the same federal regulation from one area to another of our ownership. Additionally, interpretations often differ through time. Such variability makes it unnecessarily difficult for us to develop the long-term plans necessary for forestry. Add to this the increasing involvement of the courts in either preventing or imposing specific management practices on private landowners as a result of citizen and environmental organization suits. Cumulatively, these factors greatly multiply the cost of practicing forestry as well as the uncertainty we face in an already inherently uncertain long-term activity. Two federal statutes affect forest management the most—the Clean Water Act (CWA) and the Endangered Species Act (ESA).

Forest management in wetlands is statutorily exempted from the permitting requirements that the CWA imposes on many other land uses. This "silvicultural exemption" is evidence that Congress believed forestry is an activity compatible with maintaining wetlands functions and values. Over the past decade, regulators have been increasingly restrictive in interpreting the silvicultural exemption. They have done this by challenging specific forestry activities (such as mechanical site preparation) conducted in wetlands; refusing to apply the exemption in certain stand types (such as mixed pine-hardwood stands); and expanding wetlands designation to sites that do not exhibit wetlands hydrology. The interpretations vary widely among regulators in different sections of the country and over time.

The ESA is the other federal regulation that has the greatest impact on forest management. Private landowners are responsible for not taking (that is, killing, harming, harassing) federally listed species, while the federal government has both take and recovery responsibilities. The ESA is an act in serious need of repair. Although my company supports the original intent of the ESA, we do not agree with the manner in which the act is being administered. For example, attempting to work within the act to complete a habitat conservation plan (HCP), as we have done with the Red Hills salamander, is a herculean task. The HCP process is theoretically open to all private landowners. However, in reality, it is only available to large, corporate interests with the money, personnel, and time to navigate the byzantine administrative maze.

Another issue that must be confronted is the social and economic impact of listings under the ESA. Given the necessity of allocating scarce fiscal resources to today's social problems, we would be irresponsible if we failed to evaluate critically the resources required to administer the current endangered species program. Just how much of the nation's resources should be allocated to this effort? Which species should be saved? Should entire regions' economic health and social welfare be decimated to save endangered species? Obviously, these are not simple questions, and answers will not come easily. Citizens must be willing to debate these issues openly so that legislators can make informed decisions in the current reauthorization debate and beyond.

Both the CWA and ESA apply to all private landowners—large and small, industrial and nonindustrial. However, nonindustrial private landowners have much less flexibility than industrial owners. For example, the silvicultural exemption is only applicable to "ongoing" forestry activities. Companies like mine have an easier time passing that test, because we are daily performing a variety of forestry activities.

Nonindustrial owners with small acreage are likely to go several years without active management of their forests. This makes them very susceptible to challenges from regulators over the absence of ongoing forestry operations.

Similar differences exist in dealing with the ESA. In most cases, corporate landowners have the ability to work around listed species because of the large acreage under management. We also have the resources to work through the administrative red tape associated with the ESA. We even have the option of setting aside small acreage to protect prime habitat for listed species in exchange for more management flexibility in less desirable habitat. On the contrary, nonindustrial owners generally own small amounts of land, often less than 50 acres. One red-cockaded woodpecker colony in the center of their forest can eliminate any opportunity for management. As noted, nonindustrial owners have little or no effective access to the habitat conservation planning provisions of the ESA. The lack of financial resources can keep these landowners from working within the act and from challenging agency rulings under the act.

In spite of having to contend with the regulatory uncertainty, our industry has not been static. We keep improving. In September 1994, the forest products industry adopted a very challenging set of sustainable forest management principles and policies. While this certainly reflects concern over the quality of the environment, industry members recognize that sustainable management is critical to maintaining over the long haul the fiber base on which our industry depends. And it is this type of sustainable economic enterprise on which a very significant part of the future quality of life depends.

We seek to work with the scientific community to further develop measures of sustainability to monitor ecosystem health and guarantee reliable production of fiber, while maintaining other resource values as well, without degrading the underlying ecosystem. Our new principles address sustainable fiber production, but they do so within the broader context of protecting related resources. For instance, the principles provide for stream and water body buffer zones, the establishment of wildlife corridors, and the protection of unique habitats. In effect, the forest products industry is agreeing to achieve public purposes that traditionally have only been achieved through public acquisition. We know there will always be insufficient public funds available to protect enough resources by outright acquisition.

Taxes are obviously a cost of doing business for a large company such as ours. Given the long-term nature of the forestry enterprise, the amount paid in taxes can have a substantial impact on profitability. The greatest challenge exists when taxes are assessed based on the highest valued use, which is almost always development. The population movement from urban to suburban areas and the increased desire for second homes in rural settings have contributed substantially to this issue.

Our company has been successful in negotiating reassessments in many areas. Even when land is assessed for forestry, the tax rate is often tied to productivity. Local officials generally do not have accurate data on productivity. The fact that we have a comprehensive soil survey of all our lands means that we have good measures of current and potential productivity. In a number of cases, we have used this information to convince local officials to reassess property values, yielding a lower tax bill. The opportunity to seek reassessment is available to all landowners, but in actuality most nonindustrial private owners have no better data on land productivity than local officials, giving them limited ability to argue convincingly.

In our experience, the concept of tying taxes to sustainable management practices is not widespread, but it is being explored in some locales. The chief challenge here will be ongoing monitoring to document implementation of sustainable practices. Decreased assessments on lands under some type of long-term conservation agreement are now found in more and more places. This as well as other forms of tax relief can serve as an incentive to keep land in forest cover. Clearly, there is a need for more innovative approaches of this sort. On the other hand, one cannot ignore the need to provide tax revenues from some other source to offset the decreased income that results from more favorable tax treatment of forested land.

In the future, it is likely that only limited acres of unique significance will be candidates for the allocation of public resources and acquisition. The future of sustainability therefore will be, as it should be, a function of the success or failure of the management of private lands. All owners of land should be cognizant of these responsibilities, which are reflected in the forest principles our industry has adopted. While we are committed to continuous improvement, I believe that the lands owned by the forest products industry are, from any vantage point, in good hands.

Many public lands, other than unique treasures such as parks and wilderness areas, should be privatized with the public holding development rights and private parties responsible for managing them sustainably—that is, contributing to the economy and the environment. With properly conceived and executed programs, these lands could be better

managed in the public environmental and economic-social interest by
such privatization.

It is clear we must be innovative if we are to leave future generations a
sustainable landscape that provides essential economic and environmental benefits. Traditional notions of zoning, regulation, and acquisition
that have served us to the present are inadequate. As already mentioned,
there are not, nor will there be, sufficient public resources simply to "buy"
land. In fact, it's apparent that the federal government has not adequately
maintained its current inventory of forestlands. Nor are the costs of
zoning and regulation for public benefit equitably distributed.

We will need new devices. One option, for instance, might be trading
or exchanging lands or, more likely, interests in land. Conceptually, a
forest landowner could transfer to a government conservation agency or
a land conservation trust the development rights to a parcel. A state or
federal agency or land trust could transfer land of equal market value to
the forest management landowner while retaining development rights.
The public gains additional acres of protected open space and sustainable
economic activity. The forest management owner gains access to additional acres of forest fiber. Neither party has to put up cash for the benefits gained. It is a win-win, and future generations benefit by a real contribution to sustainability.

The real challenge to sustainability is represented by the future of the
forested lands held by countless individuals and organizations facing the
kinds of problems I have discussed. Although much of this land produces
forest fiber, substantial portions are owned often for purposes other than
sustainable timber production. As a frame of reference, it is important to
note that approximately 70 percent of the fiber used for sawtimber and
paper products comes from private nonindustrial land. Simply put, we
must understand what factors influence the maintenance of this land as
working forestland. Unless we address those factors, we can have little assurance that this resource and conservation base will remain accessible.

The Northern Forest Lands Council provides an excellent example of a
regional dialogue that grappled with the multiple facets of sustainable
forestry. The council was created in 1990 by the governors of the four
northeastern tier states of Maine, New Hampshire, New York, and Vermont with a charge to examine policies and programs that would support
the maintenance of the traditional patterns of land ownership and use
throughout the northern forest. Those traditional patterns consist of a

mix of public and private lands supporting a dynamic recreational and forest resources–based economy.

In part, the council was established because of concerns over the future of forestland and its role in the economic and community life of the region. The council was composed of representatives of government, the forest products industry, environmental organizations, and community leaders. Its work was supplemented by legislation enacted in Congress directing the council to conduct a northern forestland study. Among other things, the council recognized the importance of the policies, especially real estate and inheritance tax policies, that have influenced the character of landscape and the private owners' interest and capability in maintaining the land in the traditional patterns of ownership and use that were so strongly desired by the governors.

The Northern Forest Lands Council recently issued a report addressing and making recommendations on many concerns, including how to assist maintaining the private, industrially and nonindustrially owned forestlands in forest production to provide a continued economic role for the northeastern forest as well as improved water quality, open space, recreation, and species protection. There is growing recognition that a working forest landscape, after full "wilderness" protection, imposes the least impact of any human use of the land. Of course, setting aside "wilderness" itself could be viewed objectively and scientifically as human management, underscoring Rene Dubos' point that, inescapably, mankind now like it or not manages the Earth. The test is to what end. Forest management of land has the least impact on soils, the least impact on water quality, the least impact on species. It is the human use most consistent with maintaining a healthy ecosystem. It needs to be nurtured.

Yet forest management is a threatened use. The threats come from a number of directions. One threat is the continued escalation of real property tax burdens. Real property assessments are typically based on fair market value for the economically "highest" use—that is, on the development value rather than on the forest use value. As development presses farther and farther outward from urban centers, it has the inexorable effect of raising these assessments, pressuring forest landowners to break up and subdivide the land for development, regardless of preference or intention. Although the Northern Forest Lands Council study recognizes these pressures, they are also evident, if less recognized, in the Southeast and Northwest timber areas of the United States.

There are many possible programs and approaches to help alleviate pressure on the forests, ranging from real estate tax abatement programs to easement acquisition programs. But no one is making a concerted effort

nationally or regionally to adopt such programs or to address collateral
issues such as the associated revenue effects on local governments. Nevertheless, a great opportunity exists for national and state policy to emerge
together to achieve the sustainability essential to our future that forest
management lands can provide.

There are also many management issues associated with nonindustrial
private forestlands. Because these lands are often held by owners who recognize them and their timber as their only asset (especially viewed from
the normal perspective of a human lifetime), they want to make the most
profitable use of them to pay for family emergencies or other matters like
the desire to provide homes for children or to send children to college.
These occasions test the commitment to the land represented by sustainable management.

As part of the adoption of its sustainable forest principles, the forest
products industry has an important role to broaden the application of
those principles to other lands producing forest fiber. This role is a very
significant challenge and one that constituencies such as environmental,
fish and wildlife, and other groups could be tremendously effective in supporting. Financial pressures cut across traditional interests. Recently, a
Sierra Club official in the state of Washington cut the timber on his land
to supply needed financial resources, much to the chagrin of many of the
club's members.

The outcome of the ongoing debate about private property rights is of
major consequence to the forest industry. Although much is often made
about the large land base owned and managed by industry, it pales in
comparison to the land base owned by nonindustrial private owners. On
average, industrywide, companies rely on nonindustrial land for two-
thirds of their raw material. The remaining third is provided from a
variety of sources, including corporate lands, national forests, state
forests, and off-shore imports. Thus, the forest industry has a vested interest in the protection of private property rights, especially in protecting
the landowner's choice to manage for forest products.

My company believes that private property rights do not stand apart
and separate from stewardship responsibility, however. One of our goals
is to pass to the next generation of corporate land managers a resource
base that is healthier and more productive than the one we received from
our predecessors. To accomplish this goal, we must understand the inherent productivity and manageability of our lands and implement sus-

tainable practices. We believe this is tangible evidence of responsible stewardship, and we encourage other landowners to use sustainable practices on their own lands as well.

The current private property debate is evidence of our society's apparent transition to a higher level of accountability for private land stewardship. I say "apparent" because I believe it is as yet unclear whether society as a whole is fully supportive of this change. Nonetheless, it seems the view that the public should control public resources is now being extrapolated to private resources. Although this is heresy to some, one can argue it is not totally unexpected. After all, major environmental organizations have made no secret of their desires to hold private landowners to the same standards applied to public lands. But there is another even more obvious reason that this trend is to be expected. When one advocates the sustainable management of our nation's forest resources as a whole, one must acknowledge this goal cannot be achieved without contributions from the two-thirds of the land base that is privately owned. This is especially true in regions of the country such as the Southeast, where private lands account for the vast portion of the landscape.

As our knowledge of ecological processes and sustainability has increased, we have become increasingly aware of the need to manage across landscapes rather than on a tract-by-tract basis. The fact that a given landscape may encompass a multitude of private owners, as in the Southeast and Northeast, presents substantial challenges for landscape management. Additionally, logical land management units from an ecological perspective rarely if ever coincide with political boundaries. An excellent example of this is the checkerboard pattern of private and public ownership in the Pacific Northwest. Attempts to superimpose northern spotted owl circles on this checkerboard ownership (purportedly without a negative impact on private property) clearly cannot be supported ecologically.

My company has advocated for some time using land exchanges in the Northwest to block up ecologically viable habitat to meet adequately society's desire to protect owls and other listed species. At the same time, this will create larger blocks of land for multiple-use management and increase the opportunity for the forest industry to contribute to the economic health of the region. The complexity of federal regulations concerning land exchanges, for all practical purposes, makes this approach unfeasible currently. In spite of verbal commitment to remedying the problem, the federal bureaucracy has made little or no attempt to institute the necessary changes.

Agricultural land has always been cherished in our society. The environmental community has historically worked to protect agricultural use of land. Compare this attitude to that of environmental groups toward forestland, in spite of the fact that agricultural use has a much more serious negative effect on the environment than forest use. Similarly, while the forest industry has supported the application of best management practices (BMPs) to its operations, BMPs have not yet penetrated to the same extent in the agricultural community. That is not to undermine the fact that protection of agriculture and sustainable food production is a very worthwhile goal. Achieving it confronts some of the same issues that face the forest industry, such as real estate taxation based on development value. If the environmental community supports agricultural use of lands, however, it should be positively enthusiastic and energetic in its efforts to maintain working forests.

Another source of pressure on private landowners, and one currently very controversial, is the imposition of policies and restrictions on agricultural lands and forestlands designed to produce public benefit, with the landowner alone bearing the costs of producing that benefit. The public must share in the costs of providing public benefits and values. We must define equitable cost sharing for species, wetlands, and open space protection. Easement acquisitions, reduced assessments, pools of public resources available to assist in implementing best management practices can all serve to provide the values that are sought and at the same time keep public and private costs associated with those values at a minimum.

For these kinds of approaches to succeed, we must create a new partnership among government, private landowners, and other constituencies. Adversarial relationships will not produce the desired outcome. There are important issues of equity and fairness associated with the mix of policies, programs, and principles that can achieve sustainable land use practices. All of us must work together, not to achieve grand designs, but practical, achievable results. This is the true test of sustainability. I am confident that with increasing goodwill on all sides, it can be accomplished.

Land Use Planning: A Farmer's Perspective

Ken Buelt

Kenneth Buelt is a farmer in Oregon and
past President of the Washington County Farm Bureau.

Rational land use is a concept that has been around for many years—a concept that, more often than not, has been accepted in theory and only if it applies to someone else. Whether you advocate land use planning and zoning from an urban or rural perspective, the end result is the same: a calming effect on the process of developing our economic assets in the long term. Those who oppose land use planning and zoning have created a public and governmental frenzy to derail any long-term, focused process in developing our economic assets. In many cases, the debate and turmoil erase the intent of rational land use, which is to provide a cost-effective, stable, long-term picture of our communities and industries and how we will live amidst an ever-growing population. Land use planning is an attempt to monitor the assets of a city, county, state, and nation so as not to squander those assets, an attempt to ensure that everyone will benefit from the stability of using our assets wisely.

Agriculture: An Important Industry That Needs Land Use Policy

Agriculture is the largest and probably oldest industry in this nation, if not the world. Land use on agricultural lands and forestland is of great importance in this country because not only do these lands hold the key to food and fiber production, they also serve as a repository for all other uses. It would be foolhardy for us, as a nation, to assume we can rely on other nations for our food and fiber needs. It therefore behooves us to safeguard our agricultural lands and forestland.

Agricultural land is too often taken for granted. Decreasing acreage cannot meet demand simply through adjusting production. Agriculture is an ebb and flow industry, subject to nature and the elements and requiring a strong and broad land base.

The idea that agricultural lands are a repository for all other uses certainly has some validity. But it is important to remember that an asset once squandered is rarely recovered. If attitudes toward agricultural land were different, we might deal differently with already developed lands and might not be willing to use up land so rapidly. Urban planners and developers would realize just how important housing densities are and not expect farmers to continue to squeeze even more out of each acre of remaining agricultural land.

My views on land use come from at least two different angles. Being a farmer next to a fast-growing metropolitan area in Oregon gives me a perspective on the challenges that face commercial agriculture in a diminishing land supply situation, where farmers are expanding their businesses to meet demand with less land. As a citizen in that same metropolitan growth area, I have an interest in how the region grows and where it grows. I want my tax dollars spent in an efficient manner and livability maintained or enhanced.

. . . .

Oregon's Farmland Protection Policy

The Oregon legislature has attempted to support agriculture by minimizing instability for commercial farms. It has done so in many ways, but the most important step was requiring all cities to adopt urban growth boundaries (UGBs) and prohibiting counties from approving urban-scale development outside them. The idea is not to slow growth or stop it but to make clear decisions about where development will and won't go. The UGB is to contain enough land to meet 20-year growth projections, but no more than that. This prevents taxpayers from being needlessly compelled to finance urban-scale infrastructure on, say, 20,000 acres if only 5,000 acres or fewer are needed.

Outside the UGB, counties are to zone all lands with Soil Conservation Service (SCS) soil capability classifications I-IV as Exclusive Farm Use (EFU). The soil classes are objective measures of limitations on cultivability, are mapped in most areas, and, most important, are understood and accepted by farmers and county officials as indicators of long-term productivity. In Oregon, all 241 cities now have UGBs, and 16 million acres (New Jersey has about 4.5 million acres total) of land outside UGBs has been zoned EFU, with another 9 million zoned for forest management uses based on similar site productivity criteria. In an EFU zone, there are tight restrictions on partitioning (40- to 320-acre minimum lot sizes) and on the placement of farm and nonfarm dwellings.

The Oregon Farm Bureau Federation is a strong supporter of Oregon's land use system as a whole and of restrictions on farmland in particular. In Washington County, the fifth largest agriculture-producing county in the state, the county farm bureau chapter is a particularly strong supporter of the program. I am the immediate past president of the Washington County Farm Bureau.

Under Oregon's system, areas not needed for urban growth are protected from sprawl. The result is that the price of land—agriculture's biggest capital input—reflects agricultural values. Farmers can thus afford to reduce their unit costs by expanding their operations at prices that reflect farm values. Because the program clearly accommodates urban-type development inside the UGB, farmers are not forced to pay residential values for agricultural land, and clearly defined residential areas in cities mean homebuilders do not have to pay industrial or commercial prices for land needed for housing.

In a state that has had statewide planning for over 20 years, most people are aware of the benefits of land use planning. Living between Seattle and Los Angeles in the I-5 corridor, we do not have to look very far in either direction to see the effects of very little planning. Long-term land use planning is a positive force for all parties involved.

Governments benefit from planning city and county alike. When people leave the inner cities to be part of the suburban population, many of the amenities that the city offers—established schools, parks, centrally located business districts, affordable housing—may be unavailable or available only at great cost in the new location. The expense of building away from the fringe of the city core is enormous. Sewers, utilities, roads, road repairs, pollution, traffic control—all are a never-ending financial whirlpool for local governments, which must continue to raise taxes just to cover basic services.

The sprawl approach has been a way of life for many years. Change will not be easy. But if we look back at the basic design of cities earlier in this century, we can begin to see part of the solution: simple grid formations, with smaller lot sizes that will probably lead to more affordable housing and an effort to redevelop older neighborhoods instead of abandoning them and just moving on.

. . . .
The Need for Stability

Farmers benefit from land use planning for one simple reason: stability. Stability in land use creates a long-term atmosphere for effective food and fiber production. Impacts in any agricultural operation are not short term. Many functions are aimed at the production year, but overall the basics— machinery, lime, tile, irrigation projects, field preparations, fencing, and buildings—are ongoing. Without these long-term basics, the output from the operations would be minimal.

There are several different types of agricultural operations inside and outside the Urban Growth Boundary. Intense agriculture such as nurseries and truck gardening can be found inside the UGBs. These operations are generally second- and third-generation enterprises that have adapted to doing business among industrial, commercial, and residential uses. Generally, much of their business comes from the other surrounding uses. Most have retail outlets or are connected to local produce markets. These businesses are long term and would like to stay where they are presently located.

Another type of farming takes place on larger parcels inside the UGB. Usually these parcels are investor owned and leased to farmers, often grain farmers, on one- to five-year leases with a buyout clause if the property is developed before the crop is harvested. These parcels are farmed short term; rarely is lime applied, tiles almost never, and certainly not irrigation systems.

A third type of farming occurs on the urban fringe and usually forms a narrow band around a city. These areas receive most of the long-term inputs for farming, possibly excepting irrigation systems and buildings. The uncertain future is enough for farmers to hold back just a little in case the boundary moves.

The fourth type of operation is located far enough from city boundaries so that all inputs can be used to make a farm or nursery as efficient as the operator wants. Land that is owned by the operator will have buildings, storage facilities, and so on, depending on the type of operation—dryland, irrigated row crop, nursery. Leased ground is usually long term, and it is not uncommon to see leases passed from generation to generation.

This pattern inside and outside the UGB shows how important stability is to farmers. Without stability, the right level of productivity will remain doubtful, and the land will not yield as much as it could. Nonetheless, the challenges for successful land use are enormous.

. . . .

Property Rights

Property rights have clouded land use issues for many years, and the controversy is becoming even more heated. In Oregon, a major effort is under way to weaken our present land use system. What are the rights of private landowners? Can they do with their land what they choose? Should every tax lot outside a UGB be eligible for a homesite regardless of surrounding uses?

Inside UGBs, zoning is pretty well accepted. People have some level of comfort knowing what will happen in their neighborhood and enjoy the stability brought by planning and zoning. Property rights rarely surface as an issue inside a UGB. Local officials who implement long-term plans rarely stray from the course. If land was zoned industrial, commercial, or residential in the initial planning stages, that is where it usually ends up.

But rural lands—lands outside UGBs—are a different matter. Individuals, developers, and local governments feel a need to develop these lands, to convert lands that are presently agricultural to other uses. These lands are where the change to a rural lifestyle—for those who mainly work in the city but want to be hobby farmers—is supposed to happen. And this is the area where the property rights cry is the loudest. Outside of UGBs, many feel it is their right to purchase land and do whatever they want with it without regard to the surrounding predominant uses: agriculture and forestry.

Sound land use planning and zoning can prevent this kind of speculation if local governments have the courage and insight to plan ahead, but normally they do not have the will to do so. Interpretation of statewide land use goals by local governments is the main reason for the uproar over property rights. If policy is sound and stable and backed by a local planning staff, decisions are clear. But when local governments leave a crack in the door that says "Maybe," then all bets are off, and a creative applicant will succeed with a project, regardless of state land use standards.

When an applicant does not succeed, the property rights issue comes into play. And it plays well. State legislators rally around highly emotional issues because, on the surface, this attracts the voters. Underneath all the hype, there is a fundamental question: Should rural property owners' rights differ from those of owners inside a UGB? In Oregon, property rights lie within a zone, and you have the right to do with your land what the zone allows. Inside UGBs, that is accepted as a given. If we can continue to apply that theory to the rest of our lands, as we have done up to now in Oregon, long-range land use planning has a chance. If not, we have government-induced sprawl and the high costs of no land use planning.

People are comfortable with sprawl. It is quick and easy, and they will fight tooth and nail to maintain the status quo. But given some direction and commitment to it, as we have in Oregon, new thinking by the building community comes into play. That building industry, itself driven by stability, will accept and improve on planning in ways that are financially profitable as well as beneficial overall.

. . . .

Farmers and Growth Pressures

Where do farmers fit in this picture? In the years when this nation was first settled, the rivers were vitally important. They provided freshwater, and conditions along them were well suited to settlements. Our major cities and population centers are built along rivers or river valleys, and those valleys have the soil best suited for growing crops. The first settlers knew what they were doing in choosing those fertile soils. As the need for food has increased, farmlands around metropolitan areas have become more important. Today, a majority of America's food production occurs near metropolitan areas.

Farmers deal with this as a blessing and a curse. For many farmers, local population centers are not only the source of customers, but the source of problems that make them want to sell out. Traffic congestion, nuisance suits over farm practices such as odor, dust, equipment movement, and round-the-clock operations, the threat of higher taxes, high land prices—these problems and plenty of others bring instability to farm operations. Most governments' officials look to farmers to provide food and fiber until another use is found for their land—the "highest and best use." Few farmers are willing to tackle the major task of changing that frame of mind. Why should farmers have to lobby on a daily basis to ensure themselves a place in the total economic picture of their county, state, or nation? Is the term rational land use an oxymoron?

Over the 20-some years of land use planning in Oregon, the debates have been long and loud over the desirability of locating new vacation resorts and golf courses in farm zones. Generally supported by the public, the Oregon planning system has remained intact, despite daily challenges. How do we convince the sprawl development side of our communities that there is something for them in the big picture, the long-term picture? Probably in the same way the national transportation system has provided benefits: with incentives to make decisions with considerations of cost to the public, the environment, and businesses. When farmers first confronted the erosion mandates of the 1985 Farm Bill, some flinched—unworkable, too many restrictions on their operations. In the end, those practices saved money for farmers, allowed them to farm more land with less machinery, gave them more free time, fewer hours in the field, and succeeded in reducing erosion.

If land use policy has those same features, planners and developers will learn to adjust and prosper. The debate whether rational land use planning is good or bad needs to change—and soon. If planners and developers could save money in the planning process, be more creative in planning with less cost to the public, be successful in developing this nation's assets as part of the big picture, then we will all benefit in a stronger, more stable economy.

Patience, Problem Solving, and Private Initiative: Local Groups Chart a New Course for Land Conservation

· · · · · · · · · · · · · · · · · ·

Jean W. Hocker

Jean W. Hocker is President/Executive Director of the Land Trust Alliance.

· · · · · · · · ·

> Wherever, at the head of some new undertaking, you see the govern-
> ment in France, or a man of rank in England, in the United States you
> will be sure to find an association.
>
> — Alexis De Tocqueville, *Democracy in America*

In Jackson Hole, Wyoming, a 760-acre inholding in the Bridger-Teton National Forest was on the block for $4.5 million, eyed for a 97-home sub-
division. At stake were two miles of approach road to Grand Teton National Park, pastoral scenic ranchlands, and habitat for bald eagles,
trumpeter swans, grizzly bears, and migrating elk. After 18 months of extremely complex negotiations and a closing involving 15 people and
21 documents, the entire property was protected. Eighty acres had been
transferred to the U.S. Forest Service; the remainder, subject to a permanent conservation easement restricting harmful land uses, was owned by
a private buyer. The whole deal had been planned and carried out by a
local organization called the Jackson Hole Land Trust.

In Illinois, the Chicago-based nonprofit Open Lands Project and its real
estate affiliate CorLands worked for 10 years to acquire 21 miles of abandoned railroad right-of-way from the Penn Central Railroad for use as a
hiking and biking trail and protected habitat for plants and animals. Along
the way, they dealt with the state, two county forest preserve districts, and
four municipalities, worked to placate hostile neighboring landowners, organized supportive conservation organizations and individuals, negotiated
the final purchase price (after starting with wildly disparate appraisals),
and steered a course through numerous other complexities. Finally,
CorLands bought the railroad property for $3.4 million, placed deed
restrictions on the title, and sold various sections to local governments. The
trail was at last in place.

In 1989, the brand new Woodstock (N.Y.) Land Conservancy, composed solely of volunteers, signed a purchase agreement on a 22-acre
cornfield, one of the town's few remaining open fields and highly prized
because of the beautiful view of Overlook Mountain its agricultural use
made possible. The organization's $1,000 down payment was exactly half
of its entire assets; it had five weeks to raise $159,000 more. Volunteers
devoted their summer to raising the money. They developed radio, television, and newspaper ads. A local architect created a rendering showing
what the field would look like with houses on it. Conservancy members
asked neighbors to pledge donations over a three-year period, and 556
people did, including many solicited at the local supermarket. Their efforts attracted a foundation grant and matching funds from two corporations. The Conservancy closed on schedule and leased the land to a local
organic farmer. No government entity was involved in this transaction.

In each of these cases, land was protected because a local organization
put all of the pieces together. These organizations played the roles of coordinator, planner, strategizer, negotiator, community organizer, fund-
raiser, buyer, seller, deal maker. Above all, they solved problems to bring
about land uses in the public benefit.

Each of these groups is a land trust—a private, nonprofit organization
that works with property owners to protect open land through direct, voluntary land transactions. Land trusts protect greenways, watersheds, historic and cultural landscapes, trails, natural areas, endangered habitat,
farm and ranch land—whatever open land is important in their communities and regions.

Local and regional land trusts are by no means the only voluntary organizations helping to shape sustainable land use today, although they are
one of the fastest-growing segments of the environmental movement.
Large national land trusts, such as The Conservation Fund, The Nature
Conservancy, the American Farmland Trust, and the Trust for Public
Land, are key players, too, often providing examples and assistance for
local land trusts. As these national groups seek to protect entire ecosystems, watersheds, and habitat areas, they are increasingly working in
partnership with local land trusts, each drawing on the strengths of the
other.

Other voluntary efforts focus on a specific kind of resource. The national Rails-to-Trails Conservancy, for example, promotes the reuse of
abandoned railroad rights-of-way as trails and greenways, creating recreational opportunities that breathe new life into cities and suburbs. In addi-

tion to their enhancement of human well-being, trails and greenways also serve as "greenways," linear passages that ease the migrations of wildlife and the movements of genetic stock in shifting responses to changes in the environment. More recently, the Rails-to-Trails Conservancy has become a land trust, taking direct action to purchase land for conversion to trails.

Also key are regional advocacy groups like the Greater Yellowstone Coalition, the Piedmont Environmental Council, the Chesapeake Bay Foundation, and scores of others, all of which labor to educate the general public and bring about public policies that foster sustainable use of public and private lands within whole ecosystems. And there are countless groups of citizens in communities and neighborhoods—some formed spontaneously in response to a specific and ephemeral issue, some established for the long haul—that do not protect land directly but work tirelessly as advocates of parks, rivers, or greenways or of responsible land use planning.

There is virtually no way to tally the number of voluntary groups— large and small, staffed and unstaffed, temporary and permanent—that are affecting the use of land in communities across America. From my perspective, however, it is obvious that, as land use issues become ever more complex and urgent, these groups are expanding relentlessly in numbers and influence and will undoubtedly play an even greater role in the future.

The lines between land trusts and other kinds of voluntary conservation organizations are not always crystal clear. Indeed, many traditional land trusts are also assuming advocacy and educational roles, realizing that direct land transactions alone cannot accomplish all that needs to be done. Similarly, advocacy groups, recognizing that hard-won policies may prove to be transient, are turning to the more permanent land protection methods of land trusts. The edges are sometimes blurry, and probably becoming more so. Whatever their points of departure, voluntary nonprofit organizations are converging from many directions to shape the use of land across the country.

Land trusts, however, constitute a particularly compelling and instructive case study—partly because they have grown so quickly, partly because there is a wealth of historical, statistical, and anecdotal information about them, and partly because they provide useful lessons about the role of nonprofit organizations within American public life, especially at the grassroots level and especially in promoting the sustainable use of land.

. . . .

The Land Trust Movement in America

Since 1987, I have been the President and CEO of the Land Trust Alliance, the national federation of the country's land trusts. It has been a fascinating vantage point from which to witness and to help shape the unprecedented growth of a national movement that is changing the way land is protected in this country. In 1994, the Land Trust Alliance identified 1,100 local and regional land trusts, double the number of a decade earlier. With the support of about 900,000 collective members, these non-profit organizations had helped protect over four million acres of land. Together, they form a national grassroots conservation movement that is sweeping the country and beginning to change the way land is used in community after community.

Land trusts are not new in America. Indeed, the first land trust in the world was organized in Massachusetts over a century ago. It was landscape architect Charles Eliot who proposed the establishment of "an incorporated association [that] would be empowered by the State to hold small and well-distributed parcels of land free of taxes, just as the Public Library holds books and the Art Museum pictures—for the use and enjoyment of the public." In 1891, the Massachusetts legislature passed legislation to establish such a corporation, the Trustees of Reservations, and stated that land held by the new group and open to the public would be exempt from taxation.

It was a powerful idea that became the model for Britain's venerable National Trust, founded four years later. In the United States, the Society for the Protection of New Hampshire Forests was established in 1901; on the west coast, the Sempervirens Fund was organized in 1900 to save the region's redwoods, and the Save-the-Redwoods League was founded in 1920. By the mid-1960s, our best records show that there were about 130 land trusts in the United States. In 1981, the number was 431; in 1990, 889; and by 1994, the number had burgeoned to 1,095.

. . . .

Driving the Engine

What has fueled this growth? The answer lies in the growing environmental awareness of the 1960s and 1970s, coupled with the real estate boom of the 1980s, and compounded by government downsizing of the 1990s.

People have begun to recognize as never before the value of undeveloped land. Open spaces have always been deemed nice to look at, of course, providing relief from the visual cacophony of increasingly crowded places. But in the last two or three decades, nearly everyone has seen changes that have affected not just aesthetics but the lives of entire communities and regions. Loss of open space is tied all too clearly to diminishing quality of air, drinking water, plant and animal diversity, and recreational opportunities. Rapid growth—all too often, unplanned sprawl—has brought new roads, disappearing farmland, traffic jams, overcrowded schools, and changed expectations about how people treat one another and the land they live on.

In many parts of the country, the hectic speculation of the 1980s altered forever the character of whole neighborhoods and communities. Meanwhile, the seeds of "small government" were beginning to sprout. Although several state governments actually enacted new programs in the late 1980s to fund open space acquisition, the recession of the early 1990s forced governments at all levels to cut back on land acquisition. At the federal level, the Land and Water Conservation, once a substantial source of support for state and local land acquisition, was hardly being appropriated at all to the states anymore. Simultaneously, strident voices are trying, with sometimes ominous success, to convince lawmakers that more regulation of land use and public ownership of land will result in political disaster, despite the fact that many polls show otherwise.

This is the climate, then, that has driven the dramatic growth of land trusts in the last two decades: growing environmental awareness, painful demonstrations of the consequences of losing open land, and growing political reluctance to regulate private land or even to add to land in public ownership—coupled, I must add, with the innate entrepreneurial spirit that de Tocqueville described aptly so long ago.

These changes in American society have convinced people as never before to take action they can carry out themselves, to rely on their own initiative and the dedication and support of neighbors, and to seek new, creative methods to stem the tide of inappropriate land use and destructive growth they see all around them. Americans have, in ever-increasing numbers, followed in the footsteps of Charles Eliot. They have organized local and regional land trusts.

· · · · · · · · ·
How Land Trusts Work—and Why

Land trusts help protect open land through whatever means will work. They acquire land outright and manage preserves open to the public. They hold conservation easements that permanently restrict harmful uses while leaving the land in private ownership. They design limited development projects to save the most sensitive parts of a property while appropriate building goes forward on the remainder. They devise strategies that encourage responsible farming or timbering while protecting natural and recreational resources. They conduct negotiations and acquisitions at the request of government conservation programs. They use their properties to educate children and adults alike about natural systems. And they tirelessly seek donations—of money, land, volunteer time, advice—to advance the protection and sound use of sensitive lands.

Landowners are usually comfortable working with land trusts, precisely because land trust leaders are typically their neighbors or at least residents of the same region. The land trust, having no governmental powers, is not particularly threatening. And land trust representatives will work tirelessly with landowners to craft conservation plans tailored to the owners' needs and desires, as well to the resources of the land. The land trust can provide information about various ways to protect land and about federal and state tax laws that may benefit the owner who donates land or a conservation easement.

The land trust may also have the capability to help the landowner develop a plan for future use of the property, such as siting a limited development or instituting timbering methods that increase habitat protection without reducing profitability. The most important characteristics of successful land trusts, then, are flexibility and creativity. No matter what resources they protect or what techniques they use, their fundamental approach is that of solving problems.

Unlike many government programs, land trusts do not apply one solution to all situations. The successful land trusts experiment: they take risks, they work closely with landowners, they bring together whatever partners are needed to achieve their desired ends. They look at each land protection project as a new problem to be solved, a new opportunity to try something innovative.

As nongovernmental organizations, land trusts are not, of course, bound by the rules, regulations, and procedures that so often constrain public programs. And one must recognize that those constraining government rules and procedures are often required to ensure protection of the public dollar and avoid abuses. We cannot perhaps expect government to operate with the same degree of flexibility that private organizations can.

Nevertheless, the very lack of bureaucratic constraint makes land trusts exceedingly good at complementing, supplementing, and implementing public open-space agendas. Land trusts can, for example, negotiate donations and below-market acquisitions of land. They can move quickly when government cannot. They have credibility with, and access to, the very landowners who may hesitate to deal directly with government. And land trusts can use a mix of protection tools and funding sources to conserve land.

· · · · · · · · ·

Land Trusts as Partners with Government

Because of these strengths, public agencies at all levels are increasingly turning to land trusts for help in setting aside land for open space. The three stories at the beginning of this piece are examples of projects that could not have been accomplished by government alone.

Another example is found on Long Island, where a few years ago the town of East Hampton passed a bond issue to preserve open space and farmland. However, the town contracted with the local Peconic Land Trust to negotiate the actual acquisitions, because the land trust had more time, staff, and expertise to spend on working out individual purchases. When one property owner, who wanted more money than the town could pay, filed for a subdivision approval, the land trust was able to work out a compromise involving a partial development that protected important farmland while allowing a few suitably located lots, thus satisfying both the town and the landowner.

Successes like these have prompted some governments to go beyond project-specific partnerships. They have created formal roles for land trusts in implementing statewide or regional conservation programs. Such programs exist in at least ten states.

In 1992, the Land Trust Alliance published *Lessons from the States: Strengthening Land Conservation Programs through Grants to Nonprofit Land Trusts*. This report, by Phyllis Myers, documented the growing number of state programs that recognize the value of nonprofit partnerships by channeling funding directly to these groups. The author concluded that such programs "are demonstrating their value in closing the gap between land conservation needs and available funding by drawing on the energy, initiative, and expertise of private groups." She also noted that the resulting partnerships are "helping to strengthen agricultural, tourist, and other resource-based regional and local economies."

Since the report was written, the state of Wisconsin has expanded its bond-funded Stewardship Program to provide modest operating funds for establishment of a new statewide nonprofit land trust. The organization,

Gathering Waters, will not only be a land trust in its own right it is also directed to provide low-cost technical assistance to Wisconsin's growing number of community-based land trusts to strengthen the land trust movement throughout the state. There could hardly be a stronger endorsement of the value of land trusts and their methods in helping to advance public open space objectives.

·   ·   ·   ·   ·   ·   ·   ·

Limitations

Notwithstanding their critical importance, land trusts cannot be depended on to save all the threatened open space in our nation's communities. There are limitations to what community conservation groups can accomplish. Some of those limitations arise from the nature of land trusts; others, from the nature of the job to be done.

First, land trusts as organizations are typically small—over half are operated solely by volunteers. And their resources are limited, with annual budgets often less than $10,000. To be sure, the dedication and creativity of small land trusts produce impressive accomplishments—as with the Woodstock Land Conservancy and the threatened cornfield, for example. But they cannot undertake projects like that every week or every month. Consciously or not, they must exercise a great deal of triage. While one parcel is being saved, inappropriate development may be intractably claiming another.

Second, land trusts are not strong everywhere. Many communities have no such group. There are whole regions where there is still just a scattering of land trusts—and these, perhaps, not very active. Small size and budgets often limit the methods a land trust can use and the expertise it can call on to help carry out complicated projects.

Third, the best efforts of a land trust may not succeed. A landowner may not much care about protecting his property. He may want only to sell to the highest bidder, with willing bidders happy to make offers. Sometimes a land trust can play a critical role in assembling funds to compete in such a market, but often not.

Fourth, parcel-by-parcel protection will never be enough. Whole systems need to be protected—watersheds, viewsheds, habitat, ecosystems, trail systems. It's an enormous job, requiring all hands on deck. Land trusts can be organizers, catalysts, and implementers, but many partners are required.

Fifth, there is a basic level of public responsibility that requires the leadership of public officials and the continuity of sustained public regulation and funding. Land trusts can never substitute for that public responsibility, nor should they. Sound zoning and land use regulation are essential to protect the common good, to ensure that the actions of one individual do not harm the health, safety, and well-being of other individuals and the rest of nature. Local land use planning sets standards and expectations for the community. It protects property values by providing reasonable assurance that compatible uses will be grouped together.

Communities also have an obligation to provide open space for the enjoyment of the public—parks, walkways, natural areas, bike paths, community gathering space, and the like are all part of livable communities. Moreover, clean water, clean air, and safe drinking water all depend on limiting land uses in ways that cannot be delegated to private decision making.

. . . .
Beyond Transactions:
Land Trusts and Land Use Planning

For exactly these reasons, many local conservation groups are expanding their activities beyond land-saving transactions. Using the constructive, problem-solving approaches that bring success in protecting land parcels, they are seeking to bring about better land use planning in their communities by providing leadership, vision, advice, and implementation to the process. In many communities, land trusts are providing the leadership for development or revisions of local comprehensive plans and land use laws.

In Maine, for example, the Brunswick-Topsham Land Trust helped organize an intensive planning meeting, attended by over 700 people, to begin the process of developing a Comprehensive Plan for the town of Brunswick. The land trust continued a leadership role in the three-year process that followed, leading to the adoption by the Town Council of a new conservation-oriented plan.

Though less commonly, land trusts can also be effective advocates for environmentally sound decisions on specific development proposals. The Hillside Trust in Cincinnati is one such local group. Its mission is to "promote preservation and thoughtful use of . . . the fragile and irreplaceable hillsides" of the Greater Cincinnati area. The tools it uses to protect these landslide-prone hillsides include acquisition of land and conservation easements. But the trust also provides informed analyses and recommendations on proposed hillside development.

Theirs is no knee-jerk reaction to development. The trust's approach to advocacy is summed up in its Fall 1994 newsletter: "Our role is that of an advocate of the hillsides and not as a representative of one particular party's interests. The Hillside Trust does not automatically oppose all development on hillsides, despite frequent pressure to do so. . . . [t]he Trust is most often successful in achieving positive results with consultation and . . . education. We work cooperatively with local governments and developers."

The trust's advocacy work is also based on sound research. A few years ago, the trust got some funding and technical assistance from the U.S. Forest Service and undertook research that produced computer-based models for mapping and classifying the hillsides. Its work also resulted in 162 guidelines for development in sensitive hillside areas. In the course of its research, the trust involved ecologists, biologists, soil scientists, geologists, geotechnical engineers, landscape architects, urban designers, planning officials, developers, and attorneys.

The research won the 1993 President's Award from the Kentucky Chapter of the American Planning Association for outstanding achievement in the field of planning. Data from the study have been incorporated into several area GIS (geographic information systems) programs, and many of the guidelines have become part of the Northern Kentucky Area Planning Commission's updated model zoning ordinance.

Not all land trusts are ready to assume such a strong role in local planning. But more and more are concluding that their land saving missions can best be achieved only in a climate of sound planning. One way or another, land trusts are bringing new information, new ideas, and new supporters to the development of balanced, conservation-oriented, sustainable land use plans.

. . . .
Changing How People Think about Land

In the end, we must build a strong political commitment to the wise use of natural resources. People must understand—at a very basic level—the critical role natural systems and open lands play in the well-being of their communities and their lives. Although poll after poll shows that the majority of people do care about the condition of the environment, right thinking and lip service are not enough. People must so fundamentally understand the consequences of land use choices that they will simply not allow short-term gain to win out over the long-term common good. And they must convey that belief over and over to decision makers at every level of government.

Blue-sky thinking? Perhaps. The key lies in education, of as broad a cross section as possible of our citizenry, particularly of our youth.

Here, too, local conservation groups are taking action. The natural areas that land trusts own often become outdoor laboratories for school-children. At least a quarter of all land trusts have some kind of educational programs with their local public schools. Adults, too, benefit from being able to walk the trails and observe the natural relationships that occur on the preserved land.

Education of another kind takes place almost every time a land trust completes a project. Each one becomes a demonstration of alternative land use. A partial development showcases how land can be developed without destroying conservation resources. Land trusts not only tell people about sound land use; they show people, on the ground, what it looks like. That is a powerful message.

As educators, land trusts are a resource that has only begun to be tapped. They need to become much more aggressive about telling what they do and, especially, why they do it. Given the number of communities in which land trusts are now active, and the numbers of people who are members of land trusts (900,000), the potential is enormous.

One of the great challenges before the land trust community today is reaching out across cultural and socioeconomic lines to build new constituencies for land conservation. The love of nature, the desire for outdoor recreation, the need for relief from concrete and crowds—these are universal longings, not the purview of one part of society. Yet too many decision makers and too many communities still view these needs as frills or, at best, amenities that are added to our lives only after more important needs are taken care of.

Land trusts are learning that protecting open space cannot be segregated from the other social and economic aspirations of their communities. They are beginning to join forces with other voluntary groups and with for-profit businesses to cross traditional barricades.

A powerful example is the coalition built in Vermont in the mid-1980s, joining the land conservation, farming, housing, and low-income communities. These groups joined forces to persuade the Vermont legislature to establish, in 1987, the Vermont Housing and Conservation Trust Fund with the goals of "creating affordable housing for Vermonters and conserving and protecting Vermont's agricultural land, historic properties, important natural areas and recreational lands." The Vermont Land Trust convened the initial group, which grew to include organizations such as the Vermont Farm Bureau, Vermont Low Income Advocacy Council, Preservation Trust of Vermont, Affordable Housing Coalition, and The Nature Conservancy.

In its 1995 report to the General Assembly, the fund's administering body, the Vermont Housing and Conservation Board, reported that "the Board is able to respond quickly in assisting municipalities and nonprofits in coping with the adverse impact of development on Vermont's affordable housing stock, its agricultural land, and its environmental quality." By the end of 1994, the Fund had committed over $75 million to provide 3,549 affordable housing units and protect 76,879 acres of land through grants and loans to nonprofit organizations (including many land trusts), housing co-ops, municipalities, and qualifying state agencies.

As they continue to broaden their missions and methods and outreach, land trusts, working with other nonprofit groups, can be the core of a move to change the way people think about the role of land in the social, cultural, and economic life of communities. Only after a fundamental shift in awareness will we be able to mobilize the political will to institute policies and incentives that promote the sustainable use of land and its natural resources.

.   .   .   .

Lessons from Land Trusts: Recommendations

As indicated land trusts alone cannot ensure sustainable use of land. But their growing success should prompt everyone concerned with land use, including policy makers at all levels, to examine the methods of these grassroots conservation groups and the reasons for their success. The lessons from land trusts give rise to a host of recommendations:

1. *We must build strong capabilities at the local level for land conservation.* More public and private money should be directed toward providing technical assistance and support for local governments and nonprofits to increase and institutionalize skills and expertise in land conservation.

2. *Land conservation programs should reward creativity and encourage flexibility.* Government programs at all levels should examine the flexible problem-solving methods land trusts use to protect land. Public agencies should learn about and adopt these methods wherever appropriate and seek opportunities to build partnerships with land trusts.

Government funding programs, such as the Land and Water Conservation Fund, should include innovative grants on a competitive basis for projects that may fall outside established guidelines. There should be a willingness to take some risks, even to see some failures. Successes should be widely publicized, as well as lessons drawn from attempts that don't succeed.

3. *Land conservation programs should stress problem solving and cooperation to the greatest extent possible.* Although there are certainly times when firm tactics are necessary to protect a critical resource, choices should be generally available, creative, and positive.

4. *Federal and state money should be used to stimulate and leverage local investment in land conservation, in both the public and private sectors.* Challenge grants, low- and no-interest loans, and planning and research grants are all ways of using limited public funds to encourage local public and private investment in land conservation.

5. *Governments should try wherever possible to minimize red tape and complex procedures in land conservation programs, consistent with safeguards to protect the public interest to the greatest extent possible.*

6. *Legislators should increase incentives to landowners who want to protect their land.* The "stick" of regulation should be complemented by the "carrot" of incentives. Deductions, credits, and exemptions from federal and state income and estate taxes, as well as local real property taxes, provide powerful encouragement for landowners who are inclined toward land conservation. There is a cost, of course, but it is far lower than outright acquisition and often far lower than the costs of servicing development.

The following examples of changes in federal tax laws would encourage landowners to take voluntary steps to protect their land. They are offered as illustrations; further analysis is needed to determine which would produce the greatest conservation benefits. Many could be adapted for use at the state level as well.

(a) Permit the value of qualified gifts of conservation land and easements to be deducted from federal income tax in an amount that does not exceed 50 percent of adjusted gross income rather than 30 percent, which is the current maximum in most cases for appreciated property gifts. Allow any amount of the gift value that the donor cannot deduct in the year of the gift to be deducted in subsequent tax years until the gift value is used up; current law gives the donor only five years after the gift year to use the full deduction, causing many landowners of modest income to forfeit much of the its value.

(b) Permit the income tax deduction currently allowed for a charitable gift of conservation land or an easement to be an income tax credit, based on some percentage of the gift value, thereby providing an incentive to landowners who do not have a large taxable income.

(c) If an owner of significant conservation property has not permanently protected the land during his or her lifetime, permit heirs of the property to elect to donate the land or an easement on the land for permanent conservation purposes and to use the value of the donation as a charitable deduction from the taxable estate.

(d) Exempt from estate taxes the value of certain kinds of property on which there is a qualified conservation easement, taxing only the value of any retained development rights permitted by the easement.

(e) Provide special financial assistance, in the form of tax credits, tax deductions, or direct payments, to assist landowners who donate conservation easements in managing and improving land for conservation.

7. *Partnerships between public conservation agencies and private nonprofit conservation organizations should become a normal way of protecting land.* Personnel of public conservation agencies and qualified nonprofit organizations should be encouraged to work together. In some cases, public money could be channeled directly to nonprofits for such activities as research, planning, and project execution.

8. *Conservationists need to become informed advocates.* Land conservation practitioners are in a strong, credible position to promote the best use of natural resource lands. They should use that strength to bring informed discussion to the support of sustainable land use.

9. *Conservation advocates need to become educators.* They should reach out not only to inform a broad audience about land-protection methods but to establish a fundamental understanding of the relationship of protected natural resources and open space to sustainable communities and lives.

. . . .
Conclusion

The land trust movement—no longer a few isolated success stories, but a maturing national conservation force—vividly illustrates the influence that citizen action can play in guiding the use of land in sensible, sustainable directions. The same conviction and focused hard work that are found in successful land trust organizations are driving many national, regional, and local conservation groups all across the country.

The leaders and supporters of these nonprofit, voluntary associations do not seek confrontation. But neither are they content to let business as usual determine the future of their communities. By taking direct constructive action to protect open land, to educate and work responsibly with decision makers, and to build a broad, informed constituency for responsible conservation, land trusts and their sister organizations are becoming more and more indispensable to achieving enlightened use of land.

The growth in numbers and capability of these nonprofit groups should be regarded as a most promising development. Everyone who seeks rational and sustainable use of land should encourage and support their expansion.

They can take the privately initiated system of land conservation they have fostered and expand its influence beyond their own numbers. They can use their nonconfrontational, problem-solving methods to teach people that open land is essential for lives that are productive and communities that are sustainable.

Sustainability and Social Justice: The Changing Face of Land Use and Environmentalism

. . . .

Charles Jordan

Charles Jordan is Director of the
Bureau of Parks and Recreation in Portland, Oregon.

. . . .

As suburban sprawl flowed into the countryside during the past 30 years, increasingly irrational patterns of metropolitan growth contributed to a host of social ills for inner city residents, including declining wealth, disappearing jobs, and impoverished educations. In response to this rolling crisis, a new voice—the voice of America's minorities—is finally making itself heard on a broad range of land use and environmental issues.

Environmentalists have rarely concerned themselves with the problems of America's poorest citizens, and the vocal arrival of a new stakeholder initially came as something of a surprise. However, the objectives of the newcomers soon proved to be generally compatible with the traditional goals of conservationists and environmentalists. The advocates of environmental justice want to make sure that land use, transportation, and conservation policies take into account the needs of the less affluent and politically powerless members of society and galvanize black and minority communities into becoming activists for their own environment— the inner city.

In many parts of the country today, inner city groups find themselves collaborating with environmentalists to form all-encompassing social justice organizations in an effort to address issues that affect all Americans, regardless of race or socioeconomic position. This social justice movement is having a profound impact on the way we look at land use issues. For example, white flight and urban sprawl were once seen as suburban concerns. Today, we are beginning to see that in the larger context of urban decay. Today, when we address the downward spiraling dynamics of the inner city, we are beginning to do so in relation to the economic, environmental, and psychological forces currently shaping the suburban landscape.

How we look at things is determined, in large part, by our experiences. As a professional in the field of parks and recreation, I am in the unique position of tending to the needs of both the environment and the people. As a member of the black community, I represent a segment of the population that has seldom been invited to sit at the land use planning table. From this perspective, I shall address some of the issues of the social justice movement as it relates to the sustainable use of land.

.   .   .   .

The Roots of Urban Decay

If we step back and look at earlier trends, we remember that, not long ago, the city was the place to be—not the place from which people were longing to flee. In the 1960s, Charles Abrams wrote the following in *The City Is the Frontier:*

> In our own era, the world's cities are witnessing their greatest surge in man's history. . . . From 1800 to 1950, the proportion of people living in cities with more than 20,000 people leaped from 2.4 percent to 21 percent. Our civilization is becoming urban, and the advance into cities is one of the most spectacular social phenomena of our time. The city has become the frontier.

How relevant are Abrams's words today? In the second half of the 20th century, we Americans have witnessed a great surge of humanity moving away from the city, a vast migration that has transformed the rural landscape no less dramatically than it shaped the earlier cityscape. This phenomenon does not compute as a sociological response to a single condition. It reflects a multitude of desires: personal safety, open space, less congestion, a return to a simpler way of life, and so on. Interestingly, recent studies show that the flight to the suburbs is becoming increasingly diverse. From 1980 to 1990, according to a demographer at the University of Michigan, the black population in the suburbs grew by over 30 percent, the Hispanic by nearly 70 percent, and the Asian by more than 125 percent. In contrast, the white population in the suburbs increased by only 9.2 percent. Whatever the reasons for this exodus, the end result is creating challenges that, at times, seem to defy current strategies.

When we look at the urban landscape today, we see a place far removed from Abrams's happy frontier. Kenneth Jackson, a historian of the American suburb, describes in *Crabgrass Frontier* the new image of the inner city that dominates, and often paralyzes, all thinking about positive change: "The negative results of the urban cycle are the stripped automobiles, burned-out buildings, boarded-up houses, rotting sewers, and glass-littered streets that are common in so many of America's inner cities. In parts of Brooklyn, the Bronx, Detroit, Chicago, St. Louis, Los Angeles, Atlanta, and Cleveland, whole blocks of stores and houses lie vacant. As one federal official noted: "There are some parts of these cities so empty they look as though someone had dropped nerve gas."

What are the challenges we face? Again, in Abrams words, "The history of civilization, from Memphis, Egypt, to Memphis, Tennessee, is recorded in the rise or demise of cities." Perhaps our greatest challenge is overcoming the current "demise."

. . . .

The Evolution of the Social Justice Movement

In my experience, everything tends to get worse before it gets better. From this perspective, I am able to find a silver lining in the plight of urban America. The bitter ashes left behind in the inner city, otherwise so pointless and wasteful, have at least engendered the growth of the social justice movement. Claiming that traditional land use and transportation planners have ignored the needs of poor neighborhoods, the leaders of this movement point out not only that we have allowed our cities and their social services to disintegrate but also that we have compounded the problems by encouraging zoning for potentially hazardous sitings near or in the poorest neighborhoods.

In 1990, I chaired a meeting arranged by Pat Noonan, founder of The Conservation Fund, that was composed primarily of people of color and explored the reasons for their involvement and noninvolvement in the environmental movement. Among those present was Robert Bullard, who had conducted extensive research on the subject of environmental equity. Bullard's findings indicated that because of discriminatory zoning, blacks, low-income, and working-class people have a considerably higher chance of suffering from pollution and other environmental hazards. According to Bullard, "Geographic concentration of blacks in central cities and areas near old industrial plants limited housing and residential choices, and disparate enforcement of environmental and land regulations all increase health risks from pollution."

One of the case studies Bullard presented to the group dealt with

Houston, Texas. During the 1970s, Houston was one of the primary destinations of the great migration to the Sun Belt states. By 1982, Houston had 1.7 million inhabitants, making it the nation's fourth largest city. Again, according to Bullard:

> Houston is the only major American city that does not have zoning, a policy that has contributed to haphazard and irrational land use planning and infrastructure chaos. Discriminatory facility siting decisions allowed the city's black neighborhoods to become the dumping grounds for Houston's municipal garbage.
>
> From the late 1920s to the late 1970s, more than three-fourths of the city's solid-waste sites (incinerators and landfills) were located in black neighborhoods, although blacks made up a little over one-fourth of Houston's population. In 1979, residents of the city's Northwood Manor neighborhood (blacks made up more than 84 percent of the residents) chose to challenge Browning-Ferris Industries (one of the world's largest waste disposal firms) for selecting their area for a garbage dump. Residents mobilized soon after they discovered the construction was not an expansion of their subdivision, but a municipal landfill.

Even more startling than Bullard's overall findings was the black community's organizing against a perceived pollution threat. Historically, black people have rarely taken a stand one way or another on pollution or the condition of their environment. Or, to be more precise, this is the story that we have been led to believe.

. . . .

The Relationship Between Blacks and the Land

Why have blacks and other, less affluent members of society not been participants in land use planning? Part of the answer may be found in the widespread perception that blacks simply do not care about the environment. In point of fact, there are many studies indicating that blacks are not unconcerned. Instead, it is their inherently disempowered socioeconomic status that has precluded their ability to participate.

At the same gathering at which Bullard presented his findings, Dorceta Taylor, then a doctoral student at Yale University, who was pursuing joint degrees in forestry and environmental studies and in sociology, provided a telling critique. As part of her educational focus, Dorceta was examining the historical relationship between blacks and the environment. The following is excerpted from her paper:

> In an effort to explain the black environmental concern from a social psychological perspective, Barry Commoner claims that the disaffiliation of blacks from the environment is due in part to the fact that blacks regard environmental protection as an irrelevant diversion of funds from the plight of blacks. Most blacks have limited economic means and cannot afford environmental concerns because they have to place a higher priority on other basic social needs.
>
> Other researchers have all used the marginality theory that posits that blacks occupy a marginal position in the society because they are alienated from social and economic opportunities. This has had an effect on the number and types of voluntary associations they are affiliated with or the issues they concern themselves with.
>
> Another explanation, the hierarchy of needs theory, assumes that environmental issues are luxury items that can be attended to only after the more basic needs are met. It argues that the middle and upper class have met their basic material needs and are, therefore, freer to focus on aesthetic (environmental) needs. The position is supported by research that shows that the conservation-preservation-environmental movement is composed primarily of people from the upper and middle class.

Other theories considered by Taylor included the possibility that blacks learned, by living through slavery, that the land was a source of misery and humiliation. This concept was supported by Eldridge Cleaver, the former Black Panther leader, who wrote in 1969 that the land was a place of punishment and imprisonment for slaves. However, Cleaver acknowledged that blacks long for land of their own: the land they were promised once slavery was abolished, then subsequently denied. In his essay, Cleaver stated that there

> is a deep land hunger in the heart of Afro-America. It has always been there, just as much so as in other people . . . . even the U.S. Government once recognized that black people must have land, because after the Civil War, black people were promised forty acres and a mule. . . . Booker T. Washington . . . promised to lead black people, like Moses leading his people, to the possession of

some land. . . . Marcus Garvey tapped black land hunger by claiming the continent of Africa for black people.

. . . .

The Need for Inclusion

From my perspective, it is impossible to harbor doubts about the love of black people for the land. In many places, this love may need to be rekindled, but it is certainly there. Why is it important to include the less affluent and politically powerless members of society in the making of land use decisions? What are the costs of not including the inner city in land use planning?

Henry Richmond, former president of 1,000 Friends of Oregon, recently addressed this very question at a meeting of the Greenspace Alliance in Philadelphia. In his speech, Richmond described what will happen as wealthier residents flee the city and the growing number of poor minorities puts a disproportionate financial strain on the services available to the inner city. One of the first services to suffer will be the public school system. The decline in education will have an adverse effect on the work force for generations to come. Cities without an adequate and educated employment base will be unable to attract potential employers.

Ultimately, the systematic weakening of public education and the subsequent disarming of the American work force will affect the lives and bank accounts of even those white homeowners who live in distant suburbs and normally consider themselves insulated from such problems. Their assets are, of course, sunk in the real estate value of their principal residences; they assume those assets are steadily appreciating in value. When retirement arrives, many of these homeowners will want to convert those appreciating assets into other holdings and instruments. Many will find it increasingly difficult to do so. Why? According to Richmond, the reason is plain: "Half the future market will consist of minorities whose earnings are hampered by the curse of ghetto educations and employment unreadiness. If fewer and fewer ill-educated minority Americans can afford to own a home because of low income, the market for home resale will be crippled."

In dealing with land use, American policy makers have habitually overlooked the crucial role of the city. Conservationists, preservationists, and environmentalists, in particular, have neglected to include the less affluent, politically powerless members of society in the discussion—and policy making has suffered as a result. Only by including an excluded constituency can we hope to fulfill our dreams of restoring a balance between urban and rural landscapes. How do we do it?

. . . .
Crafting an All-inclusive Environmental Movement

If we want to engage traditionally disenfranchised populations in environmental causes, we must be prepared to depart from business as usual. What does that entail? First, we need to review carefully the diversity within the ranks of decision makers, especially those decision makers who decide where people will live, work, and play. This means examining those institutions—planning commissions, economic development commissions, and land use bodies—that make decisions for communities and considering the representation of persons of color. This is a difficult task, for the distribution of minorities in such institutions is severely restricted. There are occasional exceptions to the rule, but, generally speaking, one person of color is the limit. And he or she will, more than likely, work for a major corporation with a boss who interacts with other movers and shakers in the community. In effect, this relationship ensures that the token representative does not stray too far afield in pursuit of equity. Is this phenomenon accidental or by design? Is racism the culprit? Or is it just the workings of power? Whatever the answer, the end result is the same.

There is another obstacle that we, especially those of us in the field of environmentalism, employ to discourage the participation of people of color and the less affluent. Our language. Even for those with some field of reference or expertise, environmental terminology can prove daunting. But what of the uninitiated—those whom we inadvertently exclude from the movement by our jargon? It would be interesting to find out how many potential supporters can relate to biodiversity, ecosystem management, biological surveys, nonpoint source pollution, ozone, and a host of other terms clearly explained.

Unfortunately, the language of the environment is obscure and dull. It falls flat. It sounds too elitist. Street gangs have their own culture; musicians and athletes have theirs. But these groups have something that makes many of the rest of us want to understand them—if only to be tuned in to what's happening. The movie and advertising industries are quick to market products using the vernacular of popular culture. We environmentalists need to market our "culture" as well. Indeed, many potential supporters within white communities, too, have been alienated by the increasingly abstract, scientific, and legalistic language of environmentalism in recent years.

Once we learn to communicate, we can earn the trust of those who have never had much reason to trust. Determined to color coordinate the environmental movement, I have traveled over the last seven years to day care centers, penal institutions, churches, neighborhood associations, and street corners in an effort to tell ordinary people why the environment should be important to them. My personal crusade to change attitudes has been difficult but I am more hopeful now than before. I have finally reached the point where I am heard without total incomprehension. Because I talk the talk, I am able to get beyond initial distrust. The process is slow, but essential, if we are going to expand our constituency.

These kinds of issues need to be addressed to make social equity a priority in the environmental movement. Yet it is really no longer simply a matter of the elites being committed or not. For the outsiders are already knocking loudly on the door. The environmental justice movement is no longer willing to consign large segments of the population to sites poisoned by toxic waste. We are dealing with a growing number of highly informed activists. We can either engage in a dialogue that leads to constructive behavior or fight on every issue. That is our choice.

. . . .

How Some Communities Are Doing It

Some cities are already engaging in the dialogue. Although I am not privy to all of the many programs around the country, I do have personal knowledge of some groups that seem to be headed in the right direction.

I am most familiar, of course, with my own backyard. Portland, Oregon, has fared far better than other parts of the country, due in large part to the extraordinary vision that city and state leaders displayed in the 1970s in creating our statewide laws on land use planning. As a result, the city of Portland has a strong tradition of community-based planning that integrates land use, transportation, and other conventional planning area with neighborhood revitalization and economic development. Our region

benefits from a set of state-adopted growth management policies that reinforce Portland's position as the very heart of the entire metropolitan
area. These policies include:

- An Urban Growth Boundary (UGB) that saves a surrounding greenbelt of farmland while simultaneously redirecting the creative forces
of the community inward toward the center. The revitalization of
some of our commercial streets, even those that lie in close proximity
to the "Hood," owes much to the fact that the UGB has only expanded by 2 percent in 17 years. When we restrict the outward extension onto farmland of public investment in sewers and roads, we
create the likelihood that more of the limited funds for public investment will find their way to the urban neighborhoods that are in most
need of help.

- A statewide goal promulgated by the Land Conservation and Development Commission (LCDC) that requires every city and suburb to
plan and zone for its fair share of affordable housing. In the Portland
metropolitan area, this means we have no "single family only" towns
where all vacant land is zoned for half-acre lots as a means of keeping
out the poor. Not all of our communities are affordable to everyone.
Taking the region as a whole, however, this policy has made an enormous difference. It has also made it possible for the UGB to work.

- A Transportation Planning Rule that requires communities to find
ways to encourage transportation by public conveyance, bicycle, and
walking rather than primarily by car. This rule is the least popular of
the LCDC's policies. Nevertheless, it is essential to our vision of the
future. It foresees an urban area with many more vital centers like
downtown Portland, places where walking and transit are as easy and
convenient as using a car. It contemplates more mixed-use neighborhoods where single-family houses and multiple-residence dwellings
are a short walk from a main street that features transit and community retail and other services. These are the kinds of communities
where the poor and the affluent can share the same streets and shops,
the same schools, the same neighborhoods.

- A regional government that offers a framework for solving multijurisdictional problems. No one should overlook the incredible importance of having an elected regional government that can speak for
everyone. As it pursues a vision for the future, it should mature into a
government that will make social justice a cornerstone of its policies.

Managing growth is a priority in the Portland metropolitan region. In May 1995, area voters passed a $136 million bond issue for the purchase of 6,000 acres to be placed under permanent public protection. In November 1994, voters supported $435 million in property taxes for light-rail bonds. Yet some believe Portland is merely a decade or so behind other major metropolitan areas in terms of urban sprawl, congested transportation systems, and deteriorating environments. Many of the signs are already apparent. In the 1980s, Portland's suburbs added nearly 60,000 new jobs, while the city's urban center lost 10,000. The possible expansion of our UGB will be assessed again soon. With more than a half million anticipated new residents moving into the region over the next 20 years, the pressure to push out the UGB will be intense.

For these reasons, I am enthusiastic about a new coalition that recently formed in Portland, one that transcends traditional bounds in terms of collaborative efforts. Called the Coalition for a Livable Future, this organization pulls together environmentalists, church leaders, transportation and land use reformers, and social justice advocates to work on growth management in the Portland area. The mission: "to protect, restore and maintain healthy, equitable and sustainable communities, both human and natural." According to coalition members, it gradually became apparent that there was a natural relationship, an ecology of interests, among the various groups that make up the coalition. They found a direct correlation between environmental degradation in the inner city and white flight to the suburbs. The coalition's primary purpose is to encourage a vibrant urban core and prevent inner city decay and suburban flight and sprawl.

I am also encouraged by the work of Myron Orfield, a Minneapolis representative in the Minnesota legislature. Orfield, who has conducted a comprehensive study of public investment and tax rates in the Minneapolis–St. Paul metropolitan area, says that communities with the lowest average household incomes have the highest per capita tax payments. Needless to say, the highest government expenditures per capita— for new sewers, highways, parks, and schools—are in the wealthy suburbs, which also have the lowest tax rates.

This paradox is hardly unique to the Twin Cities. The same statistics could be generated for any metropolitan area in the United States. In fact, Robert Liberty at 1,000 Friends of Oregon, a local watchdog group that monitors land use policy, has retained Orfield to do a similar analysis of Portland. We "enjoy" a similar stratification. Portland itself has the overwhelming majority of low-income households in its region. Portland and the eastern working class suburbs of Gresham and North Clackamas county are straining under a $10 limit on increases in local property taxes. Yet in Washington County, the wealthiest in the state, the property tax rates are lower. Metro, Portland's regional government, is currently allocating $27 million in transportation resources aimed at implementing the 2040 growth concept, a general policy direction for managing growth in the metropolitan region for the next 50 years. Unfortunately, the money is being spent in a way that reinforces existing trends: $20 million for suburban road projects, only $7 million to city transit, bicycle, sidewalk, and street improvements.

One of Orfield's solutions to this situation is tax-base sharing. This, in effect, distributes the tax burdens and benefits in a more equitable manner throughout a region. For example, a new computer chip company might locate in one county, thereby substantially increasing the country's tax base. A worker at the company might earn only $8 an hour—not enough to afford to live in the area where the job is. In essence, the worker, while contributing to the prosperity of the business and the county, is unable to reap any of the community benefits. In Minnesota, the tax-share formula mandates that 60 percent of a community's tax base goes into a regional pool to address regional transportation and planning issues. Combined with effective land use laws, a shared regional tax base could help reverse urban flight and suburban sprawl.

Meanwhile, in Connecticut, the Yale–New Haven Initiative demonstrates the power of partnerships—in this case, between a large, urban institution, Yale University, and a depressed city, New Haven, in which the institution is a major stakeholder. Included in the initiative are a concerted effort to incorporate urban issues into the university curriculum, a program that offers $20,000 over 10 years to Yale employees who buy homes in New Haven, and a cooperative venture to help children traumatized by crime. The decades old First-Year Building Project at Yale's architecture school is now devoted to the design and construction of houses for low-income New Haven neighborhoods. A "Buy a New Haven" program is expected to increase Yale's purchases from local vendors by 10 percent.

In New York City, a nine-year commitment of some $4 billion has transformed vast areas of blighted neighborhoods by rehabilitating or building more than 50,000 apartments and houses. Parts of the South Bronx, a national symbol of urban devastation, are now showcases exhibiting the benefits of strategically combining grassroots initiatives and participation with public seed money and a great variety of innovative partnerships.

. . . .

Hope for the Future

Although tough battles remain to be fought and destructive assumptions
and prejudices still need to be overcome, there is certainly hope for the fu
ture. I see it in the coalitions that are already beginning to be formed, in
Portland, Minneapolis, Philadelphia, and all the other cities where groups
are starting to understand that we are dealing with a single problem that
undermines both human welfare and the environment.

The issues on our agenda are highly resistant to solutions cooked up in
the nation's capital. Instead, they demand local, multi-interest alliances
that can transcend cultural, economic, and jurisdictional boundaries.
Only then will groups that have traditionally remained small, weak, and
isolated gain the political strength necessary to get the job done right.

In discussing urban justice and the environment, I am reminded of nonpoint source pollution—and of how appropriate it is as a metaphor for
our current situation. Nonpoint source pollution may begin 30 miles upstream, but its ultimate impacts on a watershed may be distributed in such
a way that those downstream will pay the price. In other words, everybody is part of the problem. And everybody needs to be a part of the
solution.

Science and the Sustainable Use of Land

Norman L. Christensen, Jr.

Norman L. Christensen, Jr., is Dean of the
School of the Environment at Duke University.

Land use and resource management were arguably the first human professions. By their skill in managing lands and ecosystems, our ancestors—those nomadic hunter-gatherers of ancient societies—effected a host of environmental changes. They brought about significant impacts, for example, on the diversity and composition of large mammal populations. They transformed vast landscapes by the purposeful use of fire. The Sahel of Africa, the Llanos of Venezuela, and the forest complexes of the southeastern United States make no sense without the profound influence of millennia of human alterations.

The eventual domestication of plants and animals provided the impetus for even more ubiquitous and indelible alteration of landscapes—and for the ecological processes moving across them. Estimates of the worldwide number of human beings during the biblical era (some 3,000 years ago) vary between 300 and 500 million, a population that remained relatively constant until recently. During the last three centuries, however, the patterns and intensity of human land use changed dramatically with the advent of technologies that allowed colonization of hitherto uninhabitable territory. The records also show that land use during this period was driven by local and global fluctuations in climate (for example, the long cycles of drought and plenty preceding the Exodus) that allowed development in marginal areas during favorable periods and caused the collapse of that use during less favorable times.

We are inclined to view land use unilaterally, with landscapes and ecosystems simply responding to human action. Nothing could be further from the truth. Various land uses set in motion cascades of ecological responses, many of which will condition and constrain future uses of the land. Understanding the complex interplay of such cycles of use and change is critical to wise and prudent land use.

The arrival of the Industrial Revolution in the late 18th century brought technologies that greatly increased the human ability to alter the land and increase the supply of food to support expanding numbers of people. Accompanying medical advances increased the likelihood of survival to reproductive age and signaled an increase in our number well beyond the population levels of previous millennia.

In my lifetime alone (something less than five decades), enormous environmental changes have taken place. The carbon dioxide content of our atmosphere has increased by nearly 25 percent, while the forest cover of the earth has diminished by nearly the same percentage. The number of human beings has increased, during this blink of time, by nearly 250 percent.

On any given environmental issue—the increase in carbon dioxide in the atmosphere, the quality of water in streams, or the threat to urban and suburban communities from catastrophic disturbances like fire and flood—one finds land use playing a central and significant role. Thus, it is critical that we consider the connections between land use and ecological change, understand how current land use trends affect the environment, and determine the kinds of change that will be required to ameliorate those effects.

Here, I describe the conceptual changes in ecological science related to land use in the two decades since the publication of *The Use Of Land* (Reilly 1972). I then consider the methods and tools now available to land planners. Finally, I discuss the challenges to bringing the best science to bear in creating the best patterns of land use and land stewardship.

· · · · · · · ·
Scientific Concepts

The past two decades have seen enormous change in the way ecological science views landscapes and land use. The following concepts are now widely available in the public domain, but they also have specifically scientific connotations: populations, communities, ecosystems, and landscapes

Ecological systems and the sciences that study them are roughly organized along a hierarchy of increasing complexity and spatial scale. Individual organisms can be grouped into populations, populations of different species into communities, communities and their nonliving environment into ecosystems, and combinations of ecosystems into landscapes. Critical concepts emerge at each level in this hierarchy. Mechanisms underlying the behavior of components of one level of the hierarchy require an understanding of the behavior of components at lower levels, but the context for behavior at a particular level is set by the higher levels.

Population ecology deals with the behavior of organisms that share a common gene pool—that is, they interbreed with one another and they are reproductively isolated from other groups. At the population level, concepts like rates of growth and mortality, carrying capacity, and genetic diversity are especially relevant.

Outside the laboratory, populations of species interact with one another in the context of complex communities. Populations may influence one another through competition for scarce resources—as, for example, might occur among the varieties of bird species in a single forest that feed on a common pool of insects or seeds. Populations also influence one another through the complex interdependencies of predation and parasitism that define food chains and webs.

The ecosystem level in this hierarchy is critical in the context of discussing the use of land. An ecosystem is defined as "a spatially explicit unit of the planet that includes all of the organisms, along with all components of the abiotic environment, within its boundaries" (Likens 1992). A key element in the ecosystem concept is the acknowledgment of the "chicken and egg" relationship between organisms and their physical environments. The behavior and complexity of the community of organisms not only depends heavily on the surrounding environment but, in ways profound and subtle, shapes that environment.

The landscape concept goes beyond simply seeing the land as a "grab bag" of ecosystems. Rather, it recognizes the importance of spatial scale and connectedness through time and space. Landscape ecologists see the world as a mosaic of "patches," each with a history and a likely trajectory of change that are not only influenced by the interior characteristics of the patch but also by the nature and dynamics of surrounding patches. These patches might be defined in terms of ownerships on some landscapes, or they might be viewed in terms of patterns of human or natural disturbance on others. It may be useful to define the domain of planning as a watershed, but we must also appreciate that the behavior of a particular watershed is conditioned by what goes on around it.

Ecosystem Structures, Functions, Goods, and Services and the Operational Definition of Ecosystems

The goods (commodities and natural resources) and services (amenities, such as clean water and aesthetic beauty) that humans want and need

TABLE 1.   Ecosystem Structures, Functions, Goods, and Services

Healthy ecosystems perform a diverse array of functions that provide both goods and services to humanity.

Ecosystem "structures" include:

- Species composition
- Distribution of resources among species
- Trophic (food chain) structure
- Spatial distribution of organisms
- Spatial distribution and complexity of nonliving components such as woody debris and logs
- Soil characteristics

Ecosystem "functions" include:

- Hydrologic flux and storage
- Biological productivity
- Biogeochemical cycling and storage
- Decomposition

Ecosystem "goods" include:

- Food
- Construction materials
- Medicinal plants
- Wild genes for domestic plants and animals
- Tourism and recreation

Ecosystem "services" include:

- Maintaining hydrological cycles
- Regulating climate
- Cleansing water and air
- Maintaining the gaseous composition of the atmosphere
- Pollinating crops and other important plants
- Generating and maintaining soils
- Storing and cycling essential nutrients
- Absorbing and detoxifying pollutants
- Providing beauty, inspiration, and research

(Christensen et al. 1995)

derive directly from ecosystem structures and functions. These terms are defined in table 1. The usefulness of the ecosystem concept to management is often criticized because of the absence of a rigid operational definition, but this is precisely its great virtue. The concept recognizes that the goods and services depend on processes and that the jurisdictional or ownership boundaries we inscribe on the land often have little relationship to such processes. At the very least, this concept helps identify the patterns of land use that are likely to lead to conflicts and the stakeholders who must be involved in the resolution of those conflicts. In an ideal world, the ecosystem concept could also provide a framework for defining domains of land use planning and management.

How does one actually define an ecosystem "on the ground"? Ecosystem function depends on inputs, outputs, and the cycling of materials and energy, in addition to the interactions among organisms. Ecosystem scientists draw ecosystem boundaries for analytical purposes—that is, in order to measure or monitor particular processes. Depending on the focus of the analysis, even an animal carcass or a rotting log might be defined as an ecosystem. An ecosystem does not have to be a watershed or a lake.

In other words, there is no "natural" system of ecosystem classification. Nor are there rigid guidelines for boundary demarcation. Ecological systems vary continuously along complex gradients in space and are constantly changing through time. Furthermore, no ecosystem, not even the entire biosphere, is closed with respect to exchanges of organisms, matter, and energy.

Boundaries defined for the study or management of one issue, process, or element are often inappropriate for the study or management of others. Watersheds form a useful unit for studying water and nutrient fluxes driven by hydrology but not for tracking trophic dynamics in areas where animals move over great distances. Similarly, the watershed is useful for managing water quality but far less so for managing large vertebrates or air quality. (See table 1.)

. . . .
Ecological Complexity and Diversity

The general tendency in the human management of ecosystems is simplification, focusing on the productivity in those structures or processes that directly benefits the human species. Agricultural ecosystems with one or a few species (such as a wheat field) are not nearly as productive as their more diverse and complex natural counterparts (such as a prairie). But they are certainly more productive of the things humans covet. Humans have always converted ecosystems from complex to simple to secure a productivity that is directly applicable to their needs. Surely the expansion of human populations that was associated with the domestication of plants and animals and with the more recent "green revolution" are a tribute to the success of that strategy. Nevertheless, it is critical to recognize that the long-term sustainability of ecosystems and landscapes across the hierarchies of ecological systems depends on complexity and diversity.

Ecological complexity includes not only biological diversity (the numbers and relative abundance of species and their genetic diversity) but also the complexity of structure derived from woody debris, natural disturbance patches, and landscape heterogeneity. A square meter of prairie might include 20 species of flowering plants, a hundred different insects and spiders, and perhaps more than a thousand species of soil microbes. These species are distributed vertically from the tops of the grasses to the soil surface and at various depths down the soil profile. The complex processes that occur within such a meter of ground depend not only on the variety of organisms but also on their physical arrangement. Casual observations of the structures of a shrubland, an old-growth forest, or a coral reef reveal that complexity is manifest in all terrestrial and aquatic ecosystems.

One might argue that managing for complexity carries significant opportunity costs compared to organizing simpler systems to produce the things that human beings need. Such arguments are certainly at the core of disputes over the importance of old-growth forests or the value of biological diversity. However, one might just as easily argue that simplifying ecosystems also carries costs. In fact, complexity conveys a variety of unique values:

EXISTENCE VALUE

Each of the 10–100 million species inhabiting the earth was produced, depending on theology, by four billion years of evolution or by a few remarkable days of creation. Regardless of the process that produced such complexity, its mere existence provides value to large numbers of human beings who insist on the "rights" of organisms and the complexity associated with them and on our responsibility for their preservation—and who express their commitment in monetary terms by their willingness to support a variety of organizations that attend to the conservation of biological complexity (Smith 1994). In addition, there is already a vast literature that describes the potential commodities and amenities waiting to be discovered in unexplored biota.

PRODUCTIVITY

Diverse and complex systems are more productive than their highly managed counterparts. Sections of ordinary prairie might serve as examples. The various plants in a native prairie produce a variety of rooting patterns. Some plants have shallow, fibrous roots; others, deep taproots. The overall effect is complete exploitation of the soil volume and efficient use of water, solar energy, and soil minerals. This proficiency stands in stark contrast to that of a single-species cropping system. Humans now exploit more than 60 percent of the earth's primary production (photosynthesis), and it has been argued that overall global productivity has thereby been significantly diminished, with sobering consequences for the global cycling of mineral elements and carbon (Vitousek et al. 1986).

FUNCTIONALITY

Much of the diversity in ecological systems relates to the specific functions of organisms, and there is no doubt that the alteration of those functions has created significant land use problems. For example, one important group, now absent from highly developed landscapes, is top carnivores, such as pumas and wolves. In the eastern deciduous forest of North America, populations of white-tailed deer were once regulated by such predators. Today, exploding populations of the deer constitute a serious management problem in those landscapes. Functional importance, however, is not necessarily related to size or abundance. Many chemical transformations in soils depend on specific groups or species of microorganisms whose livelihoods are, in turn, contingent upon webs of other organisms and ecosystem conditions.

RESISTANCE TO DISTURBANCE

Diverse, complex systems are generally more resistant to disturbances than are simplified systems. The stability provided by those multiple rooting strategies in prairies contrasts sharply with the erosion-prone characteristics of tilled, monoculture agriculture. It has recently been demonstrated that diverse systems are far less likely to experience major fluctuations in productivity during periods of stress, such as prolonged drought. Moreover, populations within diverse ecosystems are less susceptible to epidemics of pathogens or predators than populations grown singly or in simple mixtures. Insect predators, such as pine-bark beetle, are much more apt to reach epidemic infestations in plantations than in mixed forests.

RESILIENCE FROM DISTURBANCE

Complexity provides a reservoir of capacities for recovering from disturbance. For example, structural complexity, such as that found in dead snags and downed logs in an old-growth forest, provides critical habitat for the reestablishment of species after the systems are disturbed. Log removal and slash burning, typical of the management strategies prevailing in old-growth forests, diminish diversity and may, in the long term, reduce the rate of ecosystem recovery. Within complex systems, some species are well adapted to early reestablishment and soil stabilization following a wildfire or hurricane, whereas others are, by virtue of their longer lifespans, able to sustain forest ecosystems over longer periods.

LONG-TERM STABILITY

Diversity, whether at the genetic or species levels, is a hedge against catastrophic change. There is ample evidence to show that, as climates change, the relative importance of particular genetic types in populations also changes. In this context, considerable concern has been raised about new breeding techniques and molecular-biological strategies for increasing yields in crop plants and trees. Whether aimed at increasing production or providing resistance to a particular pathogen, these new techniques and strategies may have the unintended consequence of diminishing overall genetic diversity and the ability of species to respond to other insults or changes in their environments. Providing for redundancy is a conservative blueprint for survival.

COMPLEXITY AND DIVERSITY AS INDICATORS OF ECOSYSTEM HEALTH

The connections between ecological diversity and ecosystem health are complex and not always easily predicted. Impacts on one part of the system may, through the web of interactions involving food chains and biogeochemical cycles, be manifest in seemingly unrelated ecosystem components. Nevertheless, the biological diversity of an ecosystem or landscape is a very sensitive indicator of environmental change, and the monitoring of diversity should give land managers early indications of adverse environmental impacts.

Diversity and Complexity as Dynamic Virtues

One of the most daunting characteristics of diversity and complexity is their dynamic character. In a particular patch—in, say, a few hundred acres of forest, shrubland, or prairie that is part of a larger landscape mosaic—plant and animal species may disappear from the patch at one time while new species are immigrating from adjacent patches. Thus, on a year-to-year basis, diversity might vary widely, while over time it remains relatively constant. A fire in the hypothetical patch may result in the extinctions of local species, but invasions from neighboring patches will quickly replenish the losses. The diversity and complexity of a patch can be viewed as a dynamic equilibrium maintained by processes that cause the extinction of local species and the migration of neighboring species. Land use activities that increase local extinction rates or diminish the ability of organisms to migrate on the landscape might severely interfere with this equilibrium.

The paradoxical change in species diversity associated with the creation of natural areas and wilderness preserves is a forceful demonstration of this principle. Wherever diversity has been specifically monitored, the creation of wilderness parks or natural areas intended to preserve a diversity of species has resulted in the opposite—a decrease in species richness. The establishment of a sanctuary also creates opportunity—even encouragement—for development, alteration, and fragmentation of the surrounding landscape. Yellowstone was once part of a contiguous landscape of hundreds of millions of acres; today, it is a two-million-acre island in a sea of human land uses. Activities within the park have accelerated extinctions in some cases (for example, traditional policies toward top carnivores), and land fragmentation and intensive use outside limit the immigration of other species. There are fewer species in Yellowstone today than there were in 1872, the year it became the nation's first national park.

· · · · · · · · ·
The World Has Never Been the Same Twice

It is a general human tendency to believe that the world we know now is the world that has always been, that the climatic conditions we know today are, in some fundamental sense, "normal." We have known for nearly two centuries that the earth's climate has been punctuated over the past two million years by periodic ice ages; as recently as two decades ago, we were still teaching that such events, perhaps four in number, had been

relatively brief anomalies, some 20–30,000 years in length and separated
from one another by hundreds of millennia of "normal" climate. Today,
we know there have been no fewer than 19 such events and that the climatic conditions we enjoy today are representative of only about 10 percent of that time period.

The last ice age ended a mere 12–14,000 years ago, roughly coinciding
with the colonization of North America by humans. During the past 10
millennia, climate across the globe has been undergoing constant change,
and ecosystems have been constantly adjusting. European colonists arriving in North America did not find a continent in climatic equilibrium
but one in flux. Many species are still in the process of migrating in response to those climatic changes.

Our climatic change, while less dramatic than others, has been continuous on the scale of decades and centuries. The present millennium began
with climatic conditions much warmer than today across much of the
Northern Hemisphere, warm enough to permit land clearing and farming
well into Scandinavia—period known as the Medieval Optimum that
lasted up to the beginning of the Renaissance. The beginning of the 14th
century marked a distinct cooling period. Agricultural land in northern
latitudes was abandoned as temperatures diminished and growing seasons became shorter. This cooling trend reached a low point during the
last century, and temperatures "appear" to have been warming since. I
emphasize "appear" because temperatures and moisture conditions have
also varied on the time-scale of decades. It is this shorter variation that
makes long-term predictions about the potential impacts of anthro-
pogenic greenhouse gases, such as methane and carbon dioxide, quite difficult. Nevertheless, although we may not be able to predict the direction
or amount of global climate change with precision, we can be sure of one
outcome: It will change!

Meanwhile, most land use and land management policy presumes
"normalcy" and stasis. Agricultural development in the Central Valley of
California presents a classic example of the consequences of such pre-
sumptions. During the decades following World War II, while irrigation
water was transported from the Sierra Nevada and groundwater "mined"
from confined aquifers, agriculture in this wonderfully fertile valley expanded from the comparatively moist eastern half to the arid western half,
from an area that had formerly been mesic prairie to an area dominated
by desert shrubs and drought-hardy grasses. During the past decade,
drought conditions have severely limited water availability and caused the
abandonment of marginal lands. Natural cycles have their way with the

works of humankind. During favorable climatic periods, human activities often expand into marginal areas, and it is in these marginal areas that humans suffer when conditions become less favorable.

. . . .

Landscapes Are Constantly Changing

We tend to treat the "natural world," those areas that have been less redesigned for human use, as existing in some sort of long-term stasis. We assume that, when not upset by human impacts, those areas will tend to return to some predetermined "stable state," much as a pendulum returns to its nadir position. During the first half of this century, the notion of ecosystem succession following disturbance and leading in a predictable and deterministic fashion to a climatically determined stable configuration of ecosystem structure and function—the famous "climax community"—was one of the unifying principles of ecology. Land use management and natural resource policy presumed that ecosystems would, following disturbances such as wildfire, logging, land abandonment, or mine-tailing reclamation, undergo a process of change leading inexorably to a stable, self-perpetuating community; it was further reasoned that, prior to intensive land use by humans, much of the world existed in such "climax communities."

Now we know that natural disturbances like hurricanes and fires are not only likely to occur but are sometimes the inevitable result of ecosystem change. Furthermore, such disturbances may be critical elements in the sustained functioning of ecosystems.

The role of fire in the shrublands of the Mediterranean or Southern California is illustrative of this point. Fires, whether set by lightning or by human beings, are exceedingly common during the extended summer droughts characteristic of those regions and greatly increase risk to human life and property in areas subject to rapidly accelerating transitions from rural to suburban patterns of life. The reproduction and growth of most native species in these shrublands are stimulated by—and, in some cases, are dependent on—periodic fires. The rapid plant growth that immediately follows such disturbances limits soil erosion and sets in motion a succession of processes that quickly restores the prefire shrub cover. This regrowth also restores, in only a few decades, the availability of flammable fuels and increases the likelihood of another fire taking place in the same area.

Tree-ring data and sedimentary records tell us this cycle of fire and regrowth has been occurring in many ecosystems for hundreds of thousands of years. The systematic suppression of fire in such situations has the effect of increasing the accumulation of flammable debris and the intensity of a fire when it eventually does burn into the area. It is now widely recognized that the fire suppression policies of the first half of this century have created highly flammable landscapes in many regions around the world.

Ecosystem change is inevitable. Ecologists now view landscapes as complex mosaics, patches undergoing continuous change in the wake of unique histories of natural and human disturbances. The trajectory and rate are related to the nature of the particular disturbance that initiates the changes, along with background changes in climate. This pattern conditions and constrains future uses of the land.

The inexorable link between human land use and ecosystem change is wonderfully demonstrated by landscape in the Piedmont region of the southeastern United States over the past three centuries. Broad-leaved deciduous forests, the composition and function of which had been heavily altered through several millennia by Native Americans, were cleared for agriculture in the 17th century. Subsistence farming that relied on relatively long fallow cycles gave way to intensive and sustained cultivation of large tracts of land with little or no fallow or rotation of crops. Loss of top soil and nutrient capital diminished agricultural productivity. This slow decline, coupled with the post-Civil War economic collapse, resulted in the widespread abandonment of land and initiated a process that transformed a landscape of fields and hedgerows into one of extensive pine forests. Pines, not especially abundant in presettlement forests, are well adapted to the soil and microclimates of abandoned fields. Thus, devalued agricultural land was gradually transformed into land newly valued for its timber resources.

The *longue duree* of human use and ecological change continues. When pines are harvested, they are not replaced by young pines, unless conditions similar to the old fields are recreated. In the absence of investments in site preparation and reforestation, cutover pinelands succeed to complex, coppiced deciduous woods, the economic value of which is currently far less than the pine woods. Thus, current land use over much of this region results in conversion of pinelands to deciduous forests, which are quite different from those that greeted early explorers in the region.

This pattern of human use and ecological change is ubiquitous, and it occurs against a backdrop of continuous climatic change. If nature is a shifting, constantly changing mosaic, then perhaps we should conclude that human activities are mere surrogates for natural patterns of disturbance.

Wrong. At no time has the Earth's environment been subjected to the wide extent and rapid rate of change it is experiencing today. Furthermore, many changes, such as extremes of land fragmentation and certain kinds of pollution, have no precedent in evolutionary time. Any notion of sustainability must not only acknowledge the inevitability and necessity of change but also the limits to the sorts of change that ecosystems can tolerate and the thresholds of change beyond which ecosystem function may be permanently impaired.

· · · · · · · · ·
These Patterns and Trajectories Are Inherently Uncertain

There is still a great deal that we do not know about the character of ecosystems and landscapes and the impacts of land use on that character. Even more daunting is the reality that there is a great deal we can never know.

Much uncertainty derives from the need for more information. For example, we understand in general terms that loss of diversity and complexity diminishes the stability of ecosystems; however, we rarely know enough to predict how the loss of a particular set of species will affect the capacity of a particular system to resist or recover from disturbance. This sort of uncertainty would yield to more monitoring and research.

We are beginning to understand that certain classes of events in ecosystems may lie beyond the range of prediction and that "surprises" may be inevitable. While we may know, for example, that large fires or extensive floods will occur on certain landscapes with some probability, we are unlikely to be able to predict the exact time for such events. It cannot be, and should not be, the goal of land managers and planners to eliminate such surprises. Rather, management policies must acknowledge that, given sufficient time and space, uncertain events are certain to happen. Undesirable surprises demand that managers and scientists respond rapidly. Their possible strategies might include holding some resources in reserve to cope with the unexpected and installing programs designed to detect surprises as early as possible.

. . . .

Tools and Methodologies

Over the past two decades, technological and conceptual advances have provided land managers and planners with a wonderful repertoire of tools. Three specific tools have revolutionized our ability to look at land use and landscape change across ranges of time and have provided opportunities to incorporate better notions of change into planning.

Remote Sensing—the Big Picture

Airborne and satellite imaging have provided opportunities to examine the status, and the changes, in landscapes over spatial scales ranging from meters and kilometers to entire continents. Aerial photography became available in the 1940s and provided the means to see large-scale patterns on the landscape. Repeat photography has allowed us to monitor land use changes over five decades.

The spatial coverage of aerial photographs is typically limited to a few tens or hundreds of square miles, and photointerpretation is a complex art. Furthermore, land cover types are identified by characteristic "signatures" or patterns on emulsion-type photographs, and delineation of boundaries is often a matter of expert judgment. Satellite remote sensing and digital image processing have reduced these limitations. Data gathered by satellites appear in much the same manner as a video image—that is, by individual picture images or "pixels." Pixel size varies among remote sensing systems from diameters of 10 meters up to a kilometer or more. As pixel size decreases, spatial resolution increases—that is, we are able to resolve smaller and smaller features. However, smaller pixels mean that more data must be gathered per unit area; this may limit the total area that can be included in an image. Thus, there is a trade-off in remote sensing between spatial resolution and spatial coverage.

Satellite remote sensing systems may be passive, dependent on light from the sun reflected from the Earth's surface; or they may be active, emitting their own radiation and examining its "reflection." The Landsat Multispectral Scanner and Thematic Mapper images, which have become so familiar, are among the most widely used passive systems. For each pixel in such images, the satellite collects information on the reflectance of light energy at several different wavelengths or "colors." From these data, an image of the landscape can be generated that is very close to what the human eye would see.

However, certain landscape features or processes are especially prominent at particular wavelengths. For example, variations in hydrology are especially apparent in the infrared part of the spectrum, and images that are weighted toward that part of the spectrum are useful in mapping wetlands and other hydrologic features. Obviously, vegetation is most obvious in the green part of the spectrum. Indeed, the difference between light energy received in the green and infrared part of the spectrum has proved to be useful in mapping changes in vegetation according to the seasons and across landscapes.

One disadvantage of passive remote sensing systems is that variations in atmospheric conditions or cloud cover that affect the amount of light reaching the Earth's surface must influence what is sensed by the satellite. Thus, it is sometimes difficult to calibrate images from one location to another or from one time to the next.

Active remote sensing satellites emit light energy at precise wavelengths and energy levels and measure its reflectance or return to the satellite. Synthetic Aperture Radar (SAR) is the most widely used of such systems. In this system, light in the microwave portion of the spectrum (wavelengths of 1–100 cm) is "bounced" off the Earth's surface to form an image on its return to the satellite. Characteristics of the Earth's surface, such as the amount and structure of vegetation, hydrology, and topography influence the intensity of those returns. Microwave radiation is little affected by clouds or other atmospheric characteristics and thus provides a means of observing Earth's properties independent of weather. Furthermore, it is sensitive to structural features at the Earth's surface that are not apparent in images taken in the light spectrum visible to human eyes. Thus, it is possible, in theory, to calibrate images taken at different times, although this technology is still under development.

Geographic Information Systems—Being Spatially Explicit

Geographic Information Systems (GIS) provide the means to characterize landscapes by "layering" different kinds of data in a geographically explicit format. For example, vegetation, soils, transportation, hydrological, and socioeconomic data may exist in mapped formats in, say, a county or a state. Such data have been compared historically by overlaying transparent maps to identify preferred areas for development, transportation routes, or conservation. GIS technology provides the means to overlay multiple layers of data in a computer to produce a composite product that can be used for a variety of planning and decision-making purposes. For example, GIS can generate maps that classify the landscape based on vegetation, soils, and land use. The following examples illustrate the power of this tool.

Over the past two decades, we have come to understand the importance of wetland ecosystems to landscape-level regulation of hydrologic flows, to retention of nutrients and pollutants, and to the preservation of wildlife. Under the Clean Water Act of 1973, wetlands have been interpreted to be "waters of the United States" and, as such, are subject to the regulation of activities that might influence water quality. Such regulations seek to minimize dredge-and-fill operations associated with urban or transportation development that might adversely affect wetland functions. Unfortunately, information regarding wetland distribution is often introduced too late into the process of planning for development and transportation improvements, a delay that leads to inevitable clashes between the forces of economic development and ecological conservation.

Now, however, GIS technology is being used across the country to layer maps of vegetation, hydrology, soils, and transportation networks to develop a planning base for alternative road routings or development sites that maintain the integrity of wetland functions without prohibiting economic development. Often, maps for vegetation and soils are derived directly from aerial or satellite images. Thus, the flexibility of this tool permits advanced planning that minimizes conflicts between developers and land managers.

There is also widespread interest among a variety of state and federal agencies and nongovernmental organizations to identify unique habitats or ecosystems that may be threatened by fragmentation or development. Gap analysis, a special application of GIS, pinpoints such areas by overlaying information on land use, ownership, vegetation, soils, and the like and looking for "gaps" on the landscape where unique types are likely to exist and protection is absent. Such areas may then be acquired for permanent preservation or, increasingly, be protected by means of conservation easements.

Simulation Modeling—What If?

Land use management has often been compared to a gigantic wager. Given the inherent complexity of landscapes and ecosystems, we are often unable to predict the exact outcomes of particular actions and policies. Simulation modeling provides a tool for reducing the odds before proceeding with the implementation of policies on the ground.

In simulation models, key aspects of the behavior of a system are depicted, usually by mathematical relationships, in a computer. Ordinarily, such models seek to identify key processes or features that influence ecosystem behavior. Thus, a hydrological model might include information on rainfall, topography, soils, and seasonal vegetation patterns to predict stream flows. Climate, soils, and forest practices may be used to predict changes in tree composition and growth on forested landscapes.

Simulation models might be thought of as analogous to maps of a complex landscape. All maps are simplifications of the real world and their value as predictive tools depends on the scale to which they are drawn and the distortions associated with their projection. Similarly, predictions from simulation models must be interpreted with an understanding of the processes they include and the features they are intended to simulate. Nevertheless, simulation modeling provides a means of determining which activities are most likely to have positive or adverse effects on ecosystem processes, as well as a means of exploring the likely long-term outcomes of land use and ecological change.

A Synthetic Approach

One of the most daunting questions in wise land use management, as well as in ecology, might be framed as follows: "If I do something at a particular location, how far from that location must I be before there is no detectable effect?" In the broadest terms, the answer must depend not only on the nature and intensity of the initial action but also on the character of the landscape through which its effects are transmitted. A combination of all of the tools just described holds promise for answering this question.

Remote sensing provides a means for assessing and classifying landscapes over large areas and generates data that can easily be entered into GIS as a base-data layer. Successive images of the same location through time provide a means of examining patterns of landscape change. Thus, a pixel or a landscape patch may be classified as a particular land cover type (say, for example, a forest or agricultural field) at one point in time and may undergo change to some other cover type a decade later. By comparing such data, one can determine whether positional effects, the exact location of forests or fields relative to other land uses, influence patterns of change. Analyses might reveal, for example, that agricultural fields next to transportation routes or urban centers are more likely to be abandoned than those embedded in more rural settings, or that reforestation is more rapid in patches adjacent to other forest patches.

By including positional or spatially explicit effects, GIS and remote sensing data can be coupled to simulation models to predict landscape-level changes through time. The relationships among landscape change, wildfire, and human land use in the drier mountain ranges of California and the Pacific Northwest demonstrate the potential of this approach. Models that simulate the processes of forest succession provide the basis for predicting changes in forest cover and the extent of fuel available for wildfire based on current forest conditions. The likelihood of such fires is influenced not only by climate but also by the extent of landscape fragmentation and the available sources of ignition (lightning and people). Remotely sensed data can be used to initialize GIS data sets and simulation models to predict the frequency and impact of fires in association with scenarios of development and build-out into rural areas.

. . . .

Conclusions

Success in bringing the best science to bear on land use and land management depends on four important challenges: (1) setting sustainable and operational goals, (2) reconciling spatial scales, (3) reconciling temporal scales, and (4) educating the public to accept ambiguity and uncertainty.

Setting Sustainable and Operational Goals

Sustainable strategies for the provision of ecosystem goods and services cannot take, as their starting points, statements of need or want, such as mandated timber supply, water demand, or arbitrarily set harvests of wildlife. Rather, sustainability must be the primary objective, and the provision of commodities and amenities must be adjusted to meet that goal.

Nevertheless, we have learned that, however good our intentions, land use that focuses on commodity resources alone, that does not acknowledge the importance of diversity and complexity, that is not aware of influences and impacts on surrounding areas, and that concerns itself with short time frames is not likely to be sustainable in the long term.

Reconciling Spatial Scales

Sustainable land use and land management would be greatly simplified if the spatial scales and borders of ownership and management jurisdictions were congruent with the behavior of processes central to the sustained functioning of ecosystems. This is rarely the case for any particular ecological process, and, given the variation in spatial domain among processes, a perfect fit for all processes simultaneously is virtually impossible. Thus, reconciliation of the objectives and actions of various stakeholders within the domain of an ecosystem must be a central element in implementing sustainable management strategies.

Reconciling Temporal Scales

To be sustainable, land use and management must deal with timescales that transcend human lifetimes and almost certainly exceed the time lines for other political, social, and economic agendas. Public and private management agencies are often forced to make decisions each fiscal year whereas the behavior of the resources involved is better measured in centuries. Given sufficient time and space, unlikely events are certain to happen; managers, however, are rarely equipped to deal with surprises.

To implement ecosystem management, we must develop strategies that incorporate long-term planning and commitment, while recognizing the need to make short-term decisions. Wise land use and management is not an antidote for surprise; rather, it is an approach to management that acknowledges the certainty that unlikely events do, in fact, happen (Holling 1993).

Uncertainty and Education

Successful ecosystem management depends on institutions that adapt to variations and changes in ecosystem characteristics as well as to changes in our knowledge base. Ecological management demands ecological institutions. Land use planners and managers must acknowledge ignorance, and uncertainty and adaptive management must be integral components of ecosystem management. Planners and managers must recognize that knowledge and understanding are provisional and that their activities are experimental.

That management should be viewed as experimental is not to advocate capricious implementation of untried or gratuitous actions. It is, rather, to acknowledge the limits of our epistemology, of our understanding of the consequences of even the most conventional management procedures to the complex array of ecosystem components and processes necessary for sustained function. Lee (1993) outlines a number of institutional conditions that affect the implementation of experimental approaches to management. Decision makers must be committed to improving outcomes over biological timescales, be aware of the experimental nature of management, and be willing to accept the risk of perceived failures. To do this, managers and decision makers must have the understanding of stakeholders and a mandate for action in the face of uncertainty. Managers who feign certain knowledge engender like expectations from the public and justified condemnation when policies fail or actions result in unpleasant surprises.

Changes in organizational cultures and commitments will be critical to the implementation of evolutionary understandings of adaptive management (Lee 1993). Resources must be sufficient to implement appropriate monitoring systems, some of which may require measurements at very large scales of space and time. Furthermore, there must be sufficient institutional stability and sustained commitment to measure long-term outcomes. Monitoring and research programs are likely to add significant costs to management in many cases, and their added value may not be realized in the short term.

Institutional cultures must encourage learning from experience and research. Enhanced communication among scientists, managers, and decision makers is essential. Too often, data from monitoring programs are not analyzed promptly, and their results are not communicated to managers in a timely fashion. Improved means to communicate effectively the results of management experiments, as well as those of basic research, need to be developed. This may call for the development of a new type of professional with an understanding of the scientific, management, political, and social issues, and an ability to communicate with scientists, managers, and the general public. It is certainly a persuasive argument for a continuous training philosophy aimed at keeping managers and researchers informed as our needs and knowledge change.

Global Accounting

It is relatively simple to calculate the opportunity costs of not cutting a tree, of not building a highway, or of not exploiting undeveloped lands. However, it is critical to understand that decisions to exploit such opportunities also carry costs. The following quote (Christensen et al. 1995) captures the sense of intergenerational responsibility that should condition our view of land use:

> If the creator were a corporate manager, he or she might well pose the question, "Has human management added value to the earth's land?" From a purely human perspective, the reply would likely be an emphatic yes. After all, there are now 5.5 billion of us.
>
> But, any corporate manager knows that when inventories are depleted and the physical plant is allowed to deteriorate, it is possible to make money in the short-term while watching your net worth waste away. Such is the road to bankruptcy.

Businesses routinely make decisions with short-term costs, but obvious benefits to their long-term sustainability.

This metaphor captures the sense of intergenerational equity and the stewardship responsibilities that are central to a landscape perspective and ecosystem management philosophy. Such a perspective is the ecological analog to the economic stewardship of a trust or endowment dedicated to benefit all generations.

This is not a rejection of the anthropocentric for a totally biocentric worldview. Rather, it is land use that acknowledges the importance of human needs and, at the same time, confronts the reality that the capacity of our world to meet those needs in perpetuity has limits and depends on the functioning of landscapes and ecosystems.

REFERENCES

Christensen, N.L. 1989. Landscape History and Ecological Succession on the Piedmont of North Carolina. *Journal of Forest History* 33: 116–124.

Christensen, N.L., A.M. Bartuska, J.H. Brown, S. Carpenter, C. D'Antonio, R. Francis, J.F. Franklin, J.A. MacMahon, R.F. Noss, D.J. Parsons, C.H. Peterson, M.G. Turner, and R.G. Woodmansee. 1995. The Scientific Basis for Ecosystem Management. *Ecological Applications,* in press.

Holling, C.S. 1978. *Adaptive Environmental Assessment and Management.* New York: John Wiley & Sons.

Holling, C.S. 1993. Investing in Research for Sustainability. *Ecological Applications* 3: 552–555.

Lee, K.N. 1993. *Compass and Gyroscope: Integrating Science and Politics for the Environment.* Washington, DC: Island Press.

Likens, G. 1992. An Ecosystem Approach: Its Use and Abuse. In *Excellence in Ecology,* Book 3. Oldendorf/Luhe Germany: Ecology Institute.

Reilly, William K. (ed.). 1973. *The Use of Land: A Citizens' Policy Guide to Urban Growth.* New York: Thomas Y. Crowell Company.

Smith, K. 1995. Measuring Economic Values for Ecosystems. In *Ecosystem Health* (R. DiGiulio, ed.). New York: Chapman Hall.

Vitousek, P.M., P.R. Ehrlich, A.H. Ehrlich, and P.A. Matson. 1986. Human Appropriation of the Products of Photosynthesis. *Bioscience* 36: 368–373.

Private Property Rights, Government Regulation, and the Constitution: Searching for Balance

. . . .

Jerold S. Kayden

Jerold S. Kayden, a lawyer and city planner, is Associate Professor at the Graduate School of Design at Harvard University.

. . . .

> ". . . nor shall private property be taken for public use, without just compensation."
> —United States Constitution, Fifth Amendment

The close of the 20th century bears witness to increasing tensions between private property rights and government regulation. Landowners complain that, under the guise of environmental laws and land use regulations, public officials too often display gross insensitivity to constitutionally protected private property. If an endangered species, wetland, farmland, historic landmark, or similar asset located on private property is worth protecting, argue some owners, let the public pay for it. Equally assertive voices from environmental and planning camps frame the exercise of property rights in the context of broader public interests. They emphasize that the right to private property is not—indeed has never been—absolute, and that owners should use their property in ways that respect the needs of neighbors and society.

The battle cry of both sides has reverberated in all three branches of government, at national and state levels. After 50 years of relative quiescence, the Supreme Court of the United States revisited this debate with its 1978 opinion in *Penn Central Transportation Company v. New York City*,[1] and has not let up since.[2] Through the 1980s and 1990s, the Court has attempted to resolve what constitutes a taking of private property by government regulation, whether compensation must be paid for regulatory takings, when and where property owners must bring their lawsuits, and

similar issues. During its 1986 and 1991 terms, the Court granted review
in no less than three land use cases each, an unprecedented foray into the
arena; and in 1994, the Court decided yet another land use dispute pitting
owner against government (*Dolan v. City of Tigard*).⁰ Most knowledge
able observers expect the High Court to maintain an active presence, if
only to answer some of the questions posed in its own opinions. Lower
federal and state courts have taken their cues from the Supreme Court's
frenetic pace and issued their own statements on constitutional doctrine
governing the land use debate.⁴

Never content to be left out in the cold, the U.S. Congress and numerous state legislatures have joined the fray, enacting or considering
laws granting statutory protection to landowners well beyond that secured by the Constitution. Under so-called takings impact assessment
laws, government administrators have to conduct assessments of their
regulations before enactment to ensure that they do not transgress the
constitutional line. These laws mirror Executive Order 12630, adopted in
the waning days of the Reagan Administration in 1988, requiring federal
executive agencies to conduct such reviews.⁵ Under so-called compensa-
tion/diminution laws, government agencies pay monetary compensation
to property owners whenever government actions decrease by more than
a specified percentage the value of private property.

As development creeps steadily outward from central cities to environmentally sensitive places in the countryside, the conflict between property
rights and government regulation will only accelerate. This paper explores the constitutional framework for the property rights-regulation
conflict, with special attention paid to two recent U.S. Supreme Court
opinions. As the Court continues its century-long struggle to define an acceptable balance between individual and societal rights, it is apparent at
least to the justices that this constitutional riddle is not susceptible to
bright-line solutions and glib answers.

·   ·   ·   ·   ·   ·   ·   ·   ·

The Constitution's Compensation Requirement

Lodged in the Fifth Amendment of the United States Constitution as part
of the Bill of Rights, the Just Compensation Clause commands, "nor shall
private property be taken for public use, without just compensation."⁶
The purpose of the clause is to assure individuals do not bear public burdens that, in all fairness and justice, should be borne by the public as a
whole.⁷ With roots reaching as far back as King John's Magna Carta of

1215, this just compensation edict has protected property owners against arbitrary and uncompensated government seizure of property while implicitly endorsing government's authority to take property for the public good.

Indeed, in its most straightforward application, the clause has generated little controversy. To make possible the construction of highways, dams, and other public facilities, governments at national, state, and local levels have frequently exercised their power of eminent domain to seize land from private owners, even if they object. Disputes have involved questions about the amount of compensation offered, and occasionally about whether the purpose sought to be achieved by government is sufficiently "public,"[8] rather than about government's basic authority to take private property.

As America became more industrialized in the late 1800s, government found it increasingly necessary to impose regulations, especially on industrial activities, to protect the public's health and safety. Sometimes, such regulations severely impinged on an owner's use of property, and the question arose whether such restrictions contravened some aspect of the Constitution. During the late 1800s and early 1900s, the Supreme Court faced several of these conflicts and ruled in favor of the government. For example, in *Mugler v. Kansas*,[9] the Court upheld a regulation prohibiting the manufacture of alcohol, even though the effect of the law was to terminate the operation of a brewery. In *Hadacheck v. Sebastian*,[10] the Court approved a city law prohibiting operation of an existing brickyard in downtown Los Angeles, even though the law allegedly diminished the value of the property from $800,000 to $60,000, a decrease of more than 92 percent. In these and similar cases, the challenged land uses could easily be classified common law nuisances, and landowners for centuries had understood that their property rights were subject to the nuisance maxim, "*sic utere tuo ut alienum non laedes,*" translated "use your own property in such a manner as not to injure that of another."

The question whether a government regulation could ever contravene the just compensation clause, especially where it severely interfered with the owner's use of his or her property, nonetheless persisted. In 1922, the legendary Justice Oliver Wendell Holmes seemingly resolved this mystery when he announced in *Pennsylvania Coal Co. v. Mahon*[11] that, if a "regulation goes too far it will be recognized as a taking."[12] Justice Holmes fully understood the precarious balance between the needs of government and the rights of individuals. He observed that "[g]overnment hardly could go on if to some extent values incident to property could not be diminished without paying for every such change in the general law."[13] Indeed, he rationalized under his theory of "average reciprocity of advantage"[14] that, while an owner loses through restrictions on his or her property, the same owner gains from restrictions placed on neighboring owners. Still, Justice Holmes could not allow this principle to swallow the clause itself, and thus found himself enunciating a test that, with all its inexactness, made clear that there was, after all, a constitutional line not to be crossed.

For many years after the *Mahon* case, the courts, governments, and property owners operated under the "Model T" technology of Justice Holmes' "goes too far" aphorism. After several cases in the 1920s reviewing the constitutionality of zoning and its application under the Due Process clause,[15] the High Court effectively absented itself from the field for 50 years, leaving the lower courts and the parties themselves to tinker with the bare words of the Just Compensation Clause and Justice Holmes' gloss to govern property rights versus government regulation disputes. In 1978, however, the Supreme Court made up for lost time when it issued the most comprehensive judicial treatise ever on the Just Compensation Clause, in *Penn Central Transportation Company v. New York City*.[16] There, the Court upheld against a takings claim the constitutionality of New York City's landmarks preservation law and its application to the privately owned Grand Central Terminal. In so doing, the Court spelled out standards that guide to this day the constitutional analysis for takings challenges against land use and environmental regulations.

New York City enacted its landmarks law in 1965, authorizing a landmarks preservation commission to designate landmarks and historic districts having "a special character or special historical or aesthetic interest or value as part of the development, heritage or cultural characteristics of the city, state or nation."[17] Under this authority, the city's landmarks commission designated the 1913 Beaux Arts-style Grand Central Terminal a landmark, thereby requiring its owner to seek the commission's permission before altering or demolishing it. Penn Central, the railroad company and owner of Grand Central Terminal, applied to the commission to develop a 55-story or 53-story commercial office building directly above the terminal proper, requests denied by the commission in its belief that this would harm the landmark qualities of the terminal itself.

The Court prefaced its constitutional analysis with the candid admission that determining what constitutes a taking "has proved to be a problem of considerable difficulty"[18] and that "no set formula" exists to make such determination.[19] Instead, the Court announced an "essentially ad hoc, factual inquir[y]" focusing on three factors: first, "the economic impact of the regulation on the claimant"; second, "the extent to which the regulation has interfered with distinct investment-backed expectations"; and third, the "character of the governmental action."[20] Applying this three-factor inquiry to the facts of the case, the Court concluded that Penn Central's claim did not rise to the level of a taking.

First, the commission's actions did not interfere with Penn Central's long-standing "primary expectation"—operation of the terminal.[21] By inference, the expectation, if any, that Penn Central may have had in developing the air rights above its terminal held less weight. Second, Penn Central conceded that it earned a "reasonable return" on its investment.[22] Third, the landmarks law gave Penn Central the possibility of transferring the restricted development rights and utilizing them on eight adjacent parcels of land, an opportunity that produced some economic value to the company.[23] *Penn Central* thus makes clear that landowners are not entitled as a matter of constitutional law to the highest and best, most profitable use of their property. Although the landmark designation denied the railroad company millions of dollars in foregone revenue and dramatically diminished the value of its property, the constitutional line was not crossed.

Two years after delivering the *Penn Central* magnum opus, a unanimous Supreme Court composed a linguistic variation on the *Penn Central* theme, framing the analysis as an outcome-determinative test rather than an impressionistic inquiry. In *Agins v. City of Tiburon*,[24] the Court rejected a takings challenge to a local zoning ordinance limiting an owner to the development of one to five units of housing on a five-acre parcel. The justices pronounced that a regulation effects a taking if it "does not substantially advance legitimate state interests...or denies an owner economically viable use of his land [citing *Penn Central*]."[25] Because zoning for open space preservation represented a substantial advancing of legitimate state interests, and because on the facts before the Court it was not apparent that the property owner had been denied economically viable use, the Court upheld the zoning provision.

Both the *Penn Central* "ad hoc," "no set formula," three-factor inquiry and the *Agins* two-pronged disjunctive test have been cited, mantra-like and interchangeably, by literally thousands of federal and state court opinions. As applied, the constitutional hurdle for the property owner remains high. First, owners are not entitled to the most profitable use of their land. Second, substantial diminutions of value caused by government regulations are uniformly tolerated. Third, virtually all public interests sought to be achieved by typical land use and environmental laws are legitimate in the eyes of the Constitution. Fourth, the mechanisms embodied in such laws are usually found to substantially advance the articulated public interests.

What happens, however, if and when the constitutional line is crossed? Is the regulation merely invalidated, or must government pay compensation to the landowner? For many years, property owners and government regulators debated this point in and out of court. Public officials asserted that the existence of a compensation remedy would chill the proper exercise of authority on behalf of worthy public goals, and that judicial invalidation of the government action should suffice. Landowners countered that the nonexistence of a compensation remedy allowed government to violate the constitutional mandate without penalty, and to return time and again with new regulations to replace those invalidated by court action. The Supreme Court finally ended this argument in its 1987 *First English Evangelical Lutheran Church v. County of Los Angeles*[26] decision, holding that compensation must be paid to the landowner, but only for the period of time the regulation effects a taking.

. . . .

Doctrine Elaborated: The Lucas and Dolan Decisions

Two 1990s opinions from the Supreme Court have provided additional insights into the constitutional approach without altering the fundamental direction suggested by the *Penn Central–Agins* framework. In *Lucas v. South Carolina Coastal Council*,[27] the Court burnished the "economically viable use" test, while in *Dolan v. City of Tigard*,[28] it put flesh on the "substantial advancing" bones. David Lucas, a residential developer, purchased in 1986 two vacant parcels of land on the South Carolina coast for $975,000, with the intention of constructing two single-family homes permitted as a matter of right under then applicable regulations. In 1988, the South Carolina Legislature enacted the Beachfront Management Act, in part based on legislative findings that the "beach/dune system along the coast of South Carolina...protects life and property by serving as a storm barrier which dissipates wave energy and contributes to shoreline stability in an economical and effective manner," and that development along the coast "has jeopardized the stability of the beach/dune system, accelerated erosion, and endangered adjacent property."[29] The Act authorized the South Carolina Coastal Council, a state administrative agency, literally to draw a line in the sand, seaward of which new development of all types would be prohibited. Unfortunately for Lucas, his two lots fell on the seaward side of the line drawn by the council,

allowing him use of his lots for beachcombing, campfires, and construction of a deck and walkway, but preventing him from building his
houses.[30]

In court, Lucas conceded that the purpose of the South Carolina law to
protect the beaches was perfectly legitimate, but argued that he was
nonetheless entitled to compensation for the law's draconian effect on the
value of his parcels. A state trial judge agreed, finding that the law reduced
the lots' total value from $975,000 to $0, and that this effected a taking
requiring payment of compensation in an amount of $1,232,387.50.[31]
The South Carolina Supreme Court reversed, holding that when a regulation is designed "to prevent serious public harm," as this one concededly
was, then no compensation is owed to the affected owner even where application of the regulation results in an economic wipeout.[32] It is worth
remembering that the claim of serious public harm is hardly chimerical.
Hurricane Hugo swept into South Carolina causing substantial loss of life
and property in 1989.

In a closely divided 5–4 opinion, the U. S. Supreme Court overturned
the South Carolina decision, strongly suggesting, without formally
holding, that application of the Beachfront Management Act to Lucas'
property effected a taking.[33] First, the Court reaffirmed the *Agins* formu-
lation that, where a regulation denies an owner "all economically viable"
use of his or her property,[34] then it amounts to a "categorical" taking.[35]
For purposes of this analysis, a denial of "all economically viable use" is
synonymous with a complete wipeout of value, that is, from $975,000 to
$0. Second, the majority embellished its "categorical" takings rule by un-
dercutting it with an exception. As the Court explained, when "background principles of the State's law of property and nuisance" would have
authorized neighbors or other affected parties to bring a judicial action
against the landowner to stop certain uses of property, then the State may
accomplish the same result through, for example, newly enacted laws like
the Beachfront Management Act.[36] After all, the new law could not be
said to be "taking" anything at all, because the landowner was never entitled to conduct nuisance or other such uses on the property in the first
place. Put in terms familiar to lawyers, the newly prohibited uses were
never part of the metaphorical "bundle of sticks" that law professors are
fond of conjuring to define "property" during the first year of law school.

In Footnote 7, the Court muddied what many considered settled waters
when it pondered aloud the correct unit of "property" to be evaluated for
purposes of determining whether a regulation denies all economically viable use. Should courts focus exclusively on that portion of the property
burdened by the regulation, or should they look instead to the parcel as a

whole? In *Lucas*, the matter had resolved itself: both of Lucas' parcels were fully restricted. What would happen, however, when a regulation prohibited an owner from building anything on the proverbial "back 40," but allowed development of the "front 60"? Should courts find a "categorical" taking of the back 40, or consider the regulation in the context of its effect on all 100 acres? Think about the commonplace zoning ordinance that requires that buildings be set back 15 or 20 feet from the street. Should a property owner be able to claim a *Lucas* categorical taking on the basis that 100 percent of his or her land parcel in the 20-foot setback area is sterilized from development?[37]

In Footnote 8, the Court explored the flip side of the "denial of all economically viable use" coin, asserting that a taking may be found even when an owner has not been denied all economically viable use. In such a case, the majority suggested that property owners clothe their takings claim in two of the *Penn Central* factors, the economic impact of the regulation on the claimant and the effect on distinct investment-backed expectations. Property owners thus enjoy two bites at the economic apple: the first to prove a total wipeout; the second, if needed, to prove serious economic impact less than a total wipeout. Lower courts have already heeded this call, suggesting takings even where some economic value remains.[38]

In *Dolan v. City of Tigard*,[39] the Court reviewed a commonplace land use regulatory practice that requires property owners who want to develop new projects to set aside portions of their land for streets, parks, and other public infrastructure in return for government approval. The question in such cases frequently turns on whether the burden being imposed on the landowner reasonably addresses a harm or need generated by the proposed development, or whether it disproportionately burdens the landowner.

Mrs. Dolan owned a 9,200-square-foot plumbing and electric supply store on a 1.67-acre plot along the main street of Tigard, a suburb of Portland, Oregon. Part of her land fell within the 100-year floodplain for Fanno Creek, a waterway cutting through and bordering the parcel. Mrs. Dolan wanted to expand her store to 17,600 square feet and add a 39-space paved parking lot. The city agreed to grant development permission, as long as she dedicated to the city land falling within the floodplain and an additional 15-foot-wide strip adjacent to the floodplain for a pedestrian/bicycle pathway. The cumulative land dedication represented approximately 10 percent of her land parcel. The city rationalized these conditions on the basis that the expanded store and parking lot would create negative impacts on legitimate state interests—increased storm water runoff from the increase in impervious surfaces, and extra automobile traffic—and that the proposed conditions of the floodplain and pathway dedication could mitigate these impacts.

Seeking to build the expansion without these conditions, Mrs. Dolan challenged the city under the Just Compensation Clause and won in the U.S. Supreme Court. At its core, the Court's 5–4 decision asked whether it was fair to demand that Mrs. Dolan set aside parts of her property for public use. Because the conditions would deprive her without compensation of one of the most essential sticks from her property bundle—the right to exclude the public[40]—the city would have to demonstrate more to the justices than the simple importance of floodplains and pathways to the public interest. The Court announced two requirements to assure fairness: first, there must be an "essential nexus" between legitimate public purposes and the conditions imposed on the development permit;[41] second, there must be "rough proportionality" between the nature and extent of the conditions and the impact of the proposed development.[42]

The city easily met the "essential nexus" requirement, because the floodplain and pedestrian/bicycle pathway conditions were clearly related to the legitimate public purposes of preventing flooding and lessening traffic congestion. The city flunked the "rough proportionality" test, however, failing to show how the public access provision of the floodplain dedication would contribute to flood impact mitigation,[43] and demonstrating only that the pedestrian pathway "could" offset some of the traffic generated by the larger store.[44] "No precise mathematical calculation is required," observed the majority, "but the city must make some sort of individualized determination that the required dedication is related both in nature and extent to the impact of the proposed development."[45] For the pathway, the "conclusory statement that it could offset some of the traffic demand generated" would not suffice.[46] The Court's message to cities should not discourage land use planning and regulation. Indeed, the majority remarks on the "commendable task of land use planning, made necessary by increasing urbanization."[47] But the Court does serve notice on public officials that special burdens imposed on landowners must be demonstrably justified on the basis that such burdens proportionately address impacts springing from the new development. In short, cities must do their homework.

. . . .

Conclusion

Stepping back from the two-pronged disjunctive tests, the three-factor inquiries, and the important details that delight lawyers but elicit glassy
stares from everyone else, one conclusion stands out about the Court's
constitutional approach to the Just Compensation Clause. While the
Court's rhetoric may from time to time burnish the mantle of private
property rights,[48] its actual rulings give ample breathing room to government regulations in furtherance of land use and environmental goals. In
its view, the clause was not fashioned with a jeweler's hammer to protect
landowners against every downward fluctuation in value caused by government action, any more than it was designed to recoup from owners increments of value resulting from public investments and favorable regulatory actions. In the regulatory context, the clause is meant to safeguard
owners against government beyond the pale, acting as a check on actions
having an extreme impact on property use and value. For the rest, the political forces affecting the interaction between public officials and private
property owners will have to suffice.

And where does this constitutional jurisprudence leave the property
rights versus government regulation debate? Apparently not far enough
along for the property rights side. In search of more generous deference,
property owners have sought and received hearings in Congress and
many state legislatures on behalf of two species of statutes. Under the takings impact assessment laws, government agencies are required to assess
in advance whether their future actions and regulations may unconstitu-
tionally impinge on property rights. This idea mimics the "environmental
impact statement" assessment pioneered in the National Environmental
Policy Act of 1969,[49] which in theory does not stop government from
acting, but in practice can slow down or kill actions. Among the states
that have enacted such laws are Delaware, Idaho, Indiana, Kansas,
Louisiana, Missouri, Montana, North Dakota, Tennessee, Texas, Utah,
Virginia, West Virginia, and Wyoming.[50] The second type of legislation,
compensation/diminution statutes, requires payment of compensation for
government actions that diminish the value of property beyond a specified amount. Four states—Florida, Louisiana, Mississippi, and Texas—
have adopted such laws.[51] The Texas statute grants to property owners
the right to elect invalidation of the regulatory action rather than
compensation.

If takings impact assessment and compensation/diminution statutes
become the rule, rather than the exception, at national and state levels,

then the constitutional jurisprudence painstakingly elaborated by the Supreme Court will become temporarily irrelevant. Whether citizens over the long haul support ideologically and monetarily the practice of paying someone not to fill a wetland, develop a natural habitat, or tear down a historic landmark will in the end determine whether the Court's 70-year effort becomes historical backdrop or continues as vital law.

NOTES

1. 438 U.S. 104 (1978).
2. *See, e.g., Preseault v. ICC,* 494 U.S. 1 (1990); *Pennell v. City of San Jose,* 485 U.S. 1 (1988); *MacDonald, Sommer & Frates v. County of Yolo,* 477 U.S. 340 (1986); *Williamson County Regional Planning Comm'n v. Hamilton Bank,* 473 U.S. 172 (1985); *Loretto v. Teleprompter Manhattan CATV Corp.,* 458 U.S. 419 (1982); *San Diego Gas & Elec. Co. v. City of San Diego,* 450 U.S. 621 (1981); *Kaiser Aetna v. United States,* 444 U.S. 164 (1979).
3. *Dolan v. City of Tigard,* 114 S. Ct. 2309 (1994); *Lucas v. South Carolina Coastal Council,* 112 S. Ct. 2886 (1992); *Yee v. City of Escondido,* 503 U.S. 519 (1992); *PFZ Properties, Inc. v. Rodriguez,* 503 U.S. 257 (1992) (writ dismissed as improvidently granted); *Nollan v. California Coastal Comm'n,* 483 U.S. 825 (1987); *First English Evangelical Lutheran Church v. County of Los Angeles,* 482 U.S. 304 (1987); *Keystone Bituminous Coal Ass'n v. DeBenedictis,* 480 U.S. 470 (1987).
4. *See, e.g., Loveladies Harbor, Inc. v. United States,* 28 F.3d 1171 (Fed. Cir. 1994); *Florida Rock Industries, Inc. v. United States,* 18 F.3d 1560 (Fed. Cir. 1994), *cert. denied,* 115 S. Ct. 898 (1995); *Seawall Associates v. City of New York,* 74 N.Y.2d 92, 542 N.E.2d 1059, *cert. denied,* 493 U.S. 976 (1989).
5. Executive Order No. 12630, 53 Fed. Reg. 8859 (1988).
6. U.S. Const. amend V.
7. *Armstrong v. United States,* 364 U.S. 40, 49 (1960).
8. *See Hawaii Hous. Auth. v. Midkiff,* 467 U.S. 229 (1984); *Poletown Neighborhood Council v. City of Detroit,* 410 Mich. 616, 304 N.W.2d 455 (1981).
9. 123 U.S. 623 (1887).
10. 239 U.S. 394 (1915).
11. 260 U.S. 393 (1922).

12. *Id.* at 415.

13. *Id.* at 413.

14. *Id.* at 415.

15. *Nectow v. City of Cambridge,* 277 U.S. 183 (1928); *Gorieb v. Fox,* 274 U.S. 603 (1927); *Zahn v. Board of Public Works,* 274 U.S. 325 (1927); *Village of Euclid v. Ambler Realty Co.,* 272 U.S. 365 (1926).

16. 438 U.S. 104 (1978).

17. *Id.* at 110.

18. *Id.* at 123.

19. *Id.* at 124.

20. *Id.* at 124. As an example of the application of the "character" factor, the Court stated that a regulation authorizing a "physical invasion" would more likely constitute a taking than a regulation "adjusting the benefits and burdens of economic life to promote the common good." *Id.*

21. *Id.* at 136.

22. *Id.*

23. *Id.* at 137.

24. 447 U.S. 255 (1980).

25. *Id.* at 260.

26. 482 U.S. 304 (1987); *see also San Diego Gas & Electric Co. v. City of San Diego,* 450 U.S. 621 (1981) (Brennan, J., dissenting) (influential four-justice dissent presaging *First English* outcome).

27. 112 S. Ct. 2886 (1992).

28. 114 S. Ct. 2309 (1994).

29. 112 S. Ct. at 2896 n.10.

30. *Id.* at 2889-90.

31. *Id.* at 2890.

32. *Id.*

33. The Supreme Court sent the case back to the South Carolina Supreme Court, which consistent with the *Lucas* decision found a taking. *Lucas v. South Carolina Coastal Council,* 309 S.C. 424, 424 S.E.2d 484 (1992). Lucas and the South Carolina Coastal Council subsequently settled the case, with Lucas receiving over $1.6 million in direct compensation, interim interest, attorneys fees, and costs.

34. The Court inserted the word "all," and sprinkled the opinion with additional adjectives—"beneficial," "productive," and "feasible"—to join "viable," without any express indication that the supplemental words added new meaning to the test 112 S. Ct. at 2893, 2899.

35. *Id.* at 2893.

36. *Id.* at 2900.

37. For a recent journey down this road, see *Loveladies Harbor, Inc. v. United States,* 28 F.3d 1171 (Fed. Cir. 1994).

38. *Florida Rock Industries, Inc. v. United States,* 18 F.3d 1560 (Fed. Cir. 1994), *cert. denied,* 115 S. Ct. 898 (1995).

39. 114 S. Ct. 2309 (1994).

40. Under the Just Compensation Clause, the Court has invalidated regulations authorizing uninvited "permanent physical occupations" of private property by strangers, be they human or a half-inch cable wire and box. *See e.g., Loretto v. Teleprompter Manhattan CATV Corp.,* 458 U.S. 419, 441 (1982) (striking down New York City law authorizing television cable company to lay cable on private property against owner's will).

41. 114 S. Ct. at 2317. This requirement was originally announced in *Nollan v. California Coastal Comm'n,* 483 U.S. 825 (1987).

42. 114 S. Ct. at 2319.

43. In dissent, Justice Souter criticized this conclusion on the basis that, if anything, it described a failure of "essential nexus" rather than "rough proportionality." *Id.* at 2330 (Souter, J., dissenting).

44. 114 S. Ct. at 2321-22.

45. 114 S. Ct. at 2319-20 (footnote omitted).

46. 114 S. Ct. at 2322 (emphasis added). Justice Stevens' dissent tweaked the majority for its apparently decisive reliance on a single letter—a "c" for *could* rather than a "w" for *would*—to reach its conclusion. *Id.* at 2326.

47. 114 S. Ct. at 2322.

48. *See id.* at 2320; *Nollan v. California Coastal Comm'n,* 483 U.S. 825, 833-35 nn. 2, 3 (1987).

49. 42 U.S.C. Sections 4321, 4332(C) (1970).

50. *See* 5 CQ Researcher 513, 520 (1995).

51. *Id.*

An Economic Perspective on the Sustainable Use of Land

. . . .

John A. Baden
Research assistance by Tim O'Brien

John A. Baden is Chairman of the Foundation for Research on Economics and the Environment and an Affiliate Professor in the School of Business at the University of Washington.

. . . .

California's Central Valley was once an American Serengeti. It teemed with "thousands of grizzly bears and immense clouds of migratory waterfowl and . . . [a] million and a half antelope and tule elk" (Reisner 1986, 250). Today, little of that ecotopian past remains. Since European settlement, irrigation has made the Central Valley one of America's breadbaskets. It supplies roughly one-third of the food grown in the United States, especially avocados, artichokes, oranges, lemons, almonds, walnuts, tomatoes, lettuce, alfalfa, and other fruits and vegetables (Reisner and Bates 1990, 33). The valley's long growing season, heavily subsidized water (via the federal Central Valley Project and the California Water Project), and low elevation in a state otherwise dominated by mountains and high deserts combine to make it an attractive location for agriculture.

But there are serious problems in the Central Valley, problems of concern to conservationists and irrigators alike. The aquifer underlying the San Joaquin Valley (the southern portion of the Central Valley) is being overdrawn by nearly half a trillion gallons a year. Dams and diversions for irrigation have eliminated salmon runs on the San Joaquin and Sacramento rivers and killed tens of thousands of waterfowl by eliminating wetlands. Perhaps most serious of all, inefficient irrigation techniques are contributing to the salinization of soil, a process that makes land less valuable or worthless for agriculture and wildlife habitat (Reisner 1986, 483–4, 501, 503-4).

Arguing that the Central Valley's environmental problems are due to greed is partly true but analogous to complaining that falling is due to gravity. Greedy developers used land fraud to acquire large holdings and exerted their political and financial influence to obtain publicly funded water projects. The Central Valley's problems are also due to the climatic realities of California. California is a semidesert that gets little rainfall during key growing months. Irrigation is therefore essential for agriculture.

But, in a certain sense, greed and climate are not the most important factors in the unsustainable degradation of California's land. We cannot change the fact that people are self-interested anymore than we can eliminate the urge to eat or sleep. Even the Hutterites, who have practiced Christian communism for 20 generations, have found that they must make their institutions consistent with self-interest (Bullock and Baden 1977). And, in spite of our wondrous technologies, controlling California's climate is impossible. What we can change are the economic, legal, and political institutions that influence people's choices. By requiring people to bear legal and financial responsibility for their actions, we can adapt to the constraints of the natural world and vastly improve our ability to make sustainable use of scarce resources.

The most important issues affecting land use are poor information and incentives. If people lack access to the scientific and business knowledge of farming, logging, irrigating, grazing, mining, or otherwise using land sustainably, they cannot adjust their behavior. Even if they have good information, without proper incentives that ensure responsibility for the personal and social costs of land use, people will not act in a sustainable manner.

Economic science and political economy can help us explain and improve the operation of social institutions. They do so by focusing our attention and our policy reforms on accurate information and appropriate incentives. This paper will explore the economic approach to sustainable land use. It will examine how markets can help secure allocative efficiency and foster innovation through entrepreneurship. Markets also promote equity and environmental quality. Particular attention will be paid to the important role played by government and public, nonprofit, nongovernmental institutions.

. . . .

What Is Economics?

Many environmentalists are allergic to economics. They confuse the operation of markets and the advantages of voluntary exchange with a defense of commerce or big business. Worse yet, they may equate economics with a purely mechanistic, materialistic account of how the world operates. Devoid of values or of morals, the economic paradigm is dismissed, because it cannot comment on the beauty and "intrinsic meaning" of nature. These are indispensable values for environmentalism's aesthetic-preservationist and transcendentalist strands (Petulla 1977). Jack Turner captures the essence of this view:

> The word economics makes me hiss like *The Hobbit's* Golem: I hates it, I hates it, I hates it *forever*. For I do believe that classical economic theory, and all the other theories it presupposes, has indeed stolen the magic ring of life [1992].

But environmentalism's long-standing suspicion of economic analysis and market institutions is founded on myths. The first is that economics is primarily a defense of business (Lee and McKenzie 1993; Schumpeter 1962, 81-6). The second is that markets or economic institutions permit only commodity or narrowly utilitarian values. Correcting these errors is an important step in demonstrating how economics can promote environmental ends.

Economics is a discipline analyzing how people make choices in a world with scarce resources. The system it analyzes, the market, coordinates the actions of people who have different goals, abilities, information, and luck. Markets make the best of a world in which choices are inevitable and many wants are unsatisfied. Decisions made within markets are voluntary: No one may coerce another to act in a particular way.

Scarcity is a crucial feature of the economic world. In Eden or utopia, there is no economic system because there is no scarcity. Choices are unnecessary. But in the real world, people's wants usually exceed their ability to meet those wants. Nature imposes inherent constraints on us, and markets are merely a way of rationing scarce goods within those constraints. Because we cannot have everything we want, we must make choices. Do we prefer more food or better health care? Another car or new furniture? Every choice denies us other opportunities.

In studying people's choices, economics focuses on *marginal analysis*. In fact, the economic way of thinking is sometimes characterized as marginalism (Heyne 1987, 93-4). People are assumed to choose between incremental quantities of things at the margins rather than making all or nothing choices. This is commonly demonstrated through the diamond-water paradox.

Diamonds have a much higher market value than water, although

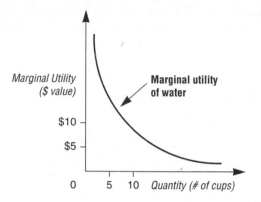

Marginal Utility ($ value)

Marginal utility of water

$10

$5

0   5   10   *Quantity (# of cups)*

FIGURE 1   Marginal Utility

water is clearly more valuable than diamonds—without it we would die of thirst. The key to understanding this apparent inconsistency lies in the relative marginal values of diamonds and water. Because water is relatively abundant most of the time, the first few gallons are valuable, subsequent gallons become progressively less so. Diamonds are relatively scarce, so they are more valuable. If we compared the first gallon of water to the first diamond, most people would choose the water, because water's initial marginal value is higher. We then continue to compare the value of additional gallons of water, the marginal additions, to additional diamonds.

Most goods conform to the law of diminishing marginal value. The first units are the most valuable, while successive increments are progressively less so. This is illustrated in figure 1.

Comparing goods at the margin and acknowledging the law of diminishing marginal value are critical in analyzing and designing environmental policy. For example, when comparing development and preservation, we only rarely choose all of one and none of the other. Instead, we select appropriate amounts of each, comparing the value, and not only the monetary value, of additional "units" of development or preservation.

Economics is a way of thinking about how people make choices. It is emphatically not a defense of business and commerce. Businesses are merely players within the market, much as organisms dwell within an ecosystem. Individual businesses must die if markets are to grow and adapt to changes in the real world, much as weak or uncompetitive organisms are culled from ecosystems. No one deserves special privileges in markets and if they get such privileges, it is often by obtaining government interference in the market process.

Nor do markets only favor the pursuit of monetary profits. The institution of private property ensures that many values are preserved and that people may do as they wish within their personal sphere of affairs. As long as the costs imposed on others are minimal, people may preserve their land's wilderness character or adopt sustainable farming practices, such as drip irrigation and crop rotation. By ensuring the pursuit and preservation of a variety of values, including environmental values, markets encourage innovation and hedge against unforeseeable circumstances, such as the unintended effects of a particular wildlife management or pollution control strategy.

* * * * * * * * *
Principles of New Resource Economics

New Resource Economics (NRE) emphasizes the constructive potential of private property rights, market incentives, and voluntary arrangements in integrating our economy and ecology. This perspective helps us understand how economic progress can be harmonized with demands for environmental quality. The NRE has strong ethical and philosophical foundations linked to the classical liberal ideals of America's founders, especially Jefferson and Madison. Today, it is identified with several schools of economics, including:

- *"Chicago"* economics, which provides the microeconomic foundation for policy analysis as applied to environmental matters;

- *Public Choice Theory,* which explains the workings of special interest politics and the way bureaucracies function in democracies;

- *Property Rights Theory,* which analyzes how institutions specify rights and responsibilities and evaluates the implications of those institutions and alternative arrangements;

- The *"Austrian"* approach, which emphasizes the importance of entrepreneurial responses to changing circumstances, the difficulties inherent in command-and-control style planning, and the importance of prices in communicating information and encouraging cooperation.

NRE assumes different institutions generate different information and incentives. Understanding these differences and the problems associated with each type of institution is critical if we are to choose institutions that promote sustainable land use.

. . . .
Institutional Variety

There are three types of social institutions important to analyzing environmental policy: for-profit firms (including corporations, partnerships, and individual proprietorships), government (including elected institutions and bureaucracies), and nonprofits. Businesses seek to maximize profits for shareholders and secure perks for managers. Government institutions respond to organized, informed constituencies and seek to maximize budgets (Downs 1957; Niskanen 1971). Nonprofits also seek to maximize budgets but are unable to use coercion to obtain funding or to achieve their goals. Let us consider each in turn.

For-profit Businesses: The Importance of Property Rights

While many go broke every year and few last more than two human generations, businesses are the most effective institutions ever devised for improving the efficiency of commodity production. When dealing with commodities, scarcity has never won a race with creativity. By concentrating profits on stockholders, entrepreneurs, and effective managers, businesses encourage innovation and the movement of resources to their highest valued uses. The effective operation of businesses depends on freedom of exchange, free movement of prices, and, to reduce uncertainty about the future, security of property and contract.

However, for-profit businesses are not very good at allocating, preserving, and nurturing noncommodity values or goods with high transactions cost.[1] Biotic diversity, nonpoint source pollution (such as auto emissions), and common pools (such as ocean fisheries) cannot easily be owned by any one person or business and thus are underprovided in markets.

Since each "good" is owned in common, anyone who degrades it for personal benefit receives all the benefits but bears only a small fraction of the costs. This is true even if the social or ecological costs of actions greatly exceed the social/ecological benefits. Each person acts rationally to further his or her own interests and thereby contributes to social harm. This calculus is illustrated by the prisoner's dilemma (figure 2).

The Prisoner's Dilemma is a two player "game" in which each player can either cooperate or defect. It is the best known game of strategy in the

Player A

		Stay Silent	Confess
	Stay Silent	A goes free B goes free	A gets 1 year B gets 10 years
Player B			
	Confess	A gets 10 years B gets 1 year	A gets 5 years B gets 5 years

FIGURE 2   Prisoner's Dilemma

social sciences. Here, we assume our players are indeed prisoners being questioned separately for their roles in a crime. Each can either confess, implicating the other, or remain silent. Neither knows for certain what the other will do. If both remain silent, they can go free. If A remains silent and B confesses, B may plea bargain and serve one year for a lesser crime; A goes to jail for 10 years. If B remains silent and A confesses, A can plea bargain and B goes to jail for 10 years. If both confess, both receive moderate jail terms (5 years).

Since neither can be certain what the other will do, there is a strong tendency for each to confess, thereby avoiding the worst possible personal outcome—a 10-year sentence. This is called a minimax strategy, minimizing the maximum possible loss. Players in this "dilemma" tend to gravitate toward undesirable situations (from both a private and social perspective) represented by quadrant four. Individuals' rational response to the uncertainty of others' behavior leads to socially suboptimal outcomes.

The logic of the prisoner's dilemma shows us why people tend to "free ride." People avoid the personal costs of acting in socially beneficial ways because they cannot be sure others will reciprocate. Just as neither prisoner can ensure his compatriot will stay quiet, no driver can ensure others will limit their driving to account for the social consequences of vehicle emissions. The private costs of not driving are large whereas the benefits one driver contributes to atmospheric quality are trivial, particularly if others do not follow a "socially beneficial" driver's lead. Therefore, each driver hopes that others restrain the amount they drive while doing little to alter his or her own driving habits. With most people adopting this strategy, driving and car emissions remain inefficiently high. Such dilemmas are most important in large, impersonal situations where people have few opportunities to meet, negotiate, and hammer out informal rules and customs that restrain rationally opportunistic actions. Virtually all national and regional problems fall into this category.

In such large-scale situations, we use political negotiations to overcome transactions costs and create mechanisms to constrain people's behavior. Perhaps we create tolls that induce people to pay for the social and atmospheric costs of driving. Or we use easements and covenants to encourage socially beneficial land use actions. Regulations are more problematic, for they often result in a partial taking of someone's property value.

Conservation through Property Rights

Businesses and the market system can only operate efficiently if there are well-defined, secure, and transferable property rights. Property rights induce people to account for future values. If owners degrade their land, perhaps by allowing extensive soil erosion, the expected decrease in the land's future productivity is capitalized into the land's present market value. Even people relatively insensitive to the future have a strong incentive to pursue conservation. However, acknowledging future values presupposes that both the owner and market understand the consequences of present actions on the land's future value (Baden and Stroup 1981).

A second reason property rights are valuable in conservation is that they support the development of market prices. Prices communicate information about the relative scarcities of goods, even unlike goods such as bananas, sheet steel, and computer software. Prices express, in a condensed form, a vast amount of information about how difficult it is to discover, process, transport, advertise, and sell a good or service. Prices also tell potential consumers how much *other* people value the resource and require them to consider interests of others as expressed through the price of a product. For example, coffee prices rise during a freeze in South America. The increase tells us that coffee has, at least temporarily, become more scarce and that we are imposing a greater cost on others when we purchase it. Higher prices lead people to reduce consumption, switch to substitutes, and seek out new sources,—for example, drink less coffee, switch to tea, cultivate more coffee in other areas. Without prices, complex market economies with extensive division of labor cannot exist (Hayek 1945).

Demsetz (1967) argued that property rights only evolve when the benefits of defining and enforcing them exceed the costs. This was the case in the rangelands of eastern Montana in the late 19th century. Until the invention of barbed wire, the range remained a commons because it was more costly to fence cattle in than to let them wander freely, even if this meant the number of cattle foraging on a particular stretch of land exceeded the land's carrying capacity. With barbed wire, property rights began to evolve but were thwarted by legislation such as the federal Homestead Acts and the Unlawful Enclosures Act of 1885 (Anderson and Hill, 1977).

It is when the costs of defining and enforcing property rights exceed the returns, as they do with rain-forest biodiversity or vehicular pollution, that significant externalities, or spillover effects (for example, pollution) arise. Such effects are common in the environmental arena and are the principal justification offered for government intervention.

Government and the Mirage of Scientific Management

The American model for green government originated in the Progressive era a century ago. Progressives saw many instances in which private initiative either failed to conserve or actively despoiled the environment. The destruction of the Great Lakes states' white pine forests, overgrazing on the western range, and the failure of irrigated agriculture west of the 100th meridian are examples (Dana and Baden 1985; Hess 1992).

The Progressives intended to remedy private abuses through government management of public domain lands. They would recruit a cadre of fine young men of good character and breeding, give them the best of scientific training, insulate them from political pressures, and send them out to manage America's public forests, range, and water. This was the model of "scientific management," a green incarnation of Platonism. The Progressives thought scientific management could ensure disinterested, expert oversight of America's timber, range, and water.

Scientific management is the philosophy underlying the federal resource management bureaucracies: the U.S. Forest Service, Bureau of Land Management, Bureau of Reclamation, and National Park Service. It is also the ideal sought in the Environmental Protection Agency, the Endangered Species Act, the Clean Air Act of 1970, and diverse state agencies and legislation. Scientific management assumes that people are basically good unless corrupted by the profit motive or political pressures. It also assumes that personnel in the agencies are beyond political corruption. Thus, federal bureaucrats are the ideal choice for impartial and efficient environmental management and regulation.

However, scientific management fails by any reasonable standard of environmental quality, efficiency, or equity. It fails because even the most enlightened and dedicated politicians and bureaucrats are: (1) self-interested; (2) ambitious in the service of their agency's mission; (3) myopic (believing that their agency's mission trumps all other considerations); and (4) lacking property rights to the resources they control. It is not enough to isolate bureaucrats from the profit motive and to give them the best technical information available. Without property rights, market prices cannot arise. Without prices, officials have only poor approximations of changing scarcities, production knowledge, and consumer preferences. An absence of property rights also greatly diminishes incentives to use resources efficiently (Anderson and Hill 1980).

Four phenomena explain why governmental agents tend to be largely ignorant of the need to balance costs and benefits at the margin: (1) rational ignorance and the special interest effect, (2) the bundle purchase effect, (3) the shortsightedness effect, and (4) little incentive for internal efficiency (Baden and Stroup 1979).

First, voters tend to be rationally ignorant of issues that do not immediately concern them (Downs 1957). Most Americans, for example, cannot name their own congressman. Average members of interest groups, however, are acutely aware of how public policy influences their well-being. The general public knows little about dairy price supports or Montana wilderness policy, but Wisconsin dairy farmers and Montana backpackers know a lot.

Because interest groups organize, become informed, and lobby for their preferred policies, while the general public remains rationally apathetic and uninformed, interest groups gain disproportionate influence over elected officials. And because Congress signs the checks for bureaucrats, bureaucrats are extremely sensitive to congressional pressures. Thus, scientific management does not isolate bureaucrats from politics, it merely makes them unaccountable for the consequences of their decisions (Baden and Stroup 1981; Olson 1971).

Second, because citizens cast only one vote for a representative who must speak for them on all issues, there is an inherent lack of precision in political decision making. Even well-informed voters have little hope of expressing all their preferences, and the relative value among those preferences, in a political setting. In direct contrast, a "voter-buyer" in the market can express his preferences on a multitude of "issues," such as which foods to buy in a supermarket.

Third, since politicians and bureaucrats must satisfy *current* constituents, they suffer from shortsightedness. Future generations cannot vote, and, though current voters are sometimes willing to sacrifice now for the future benefit of others, there remains a strong present-oriented bias among current voters and political officials. Speculators who personally benefit from conserving or hoarding resources for future use or sale are a more effective conservation tool. Speculators can gain by conserving a resource that is becoming scarcer and selling it later. By contrast, current politicians and bureaucrats can seldom gain political support by locking resources away from current voters to benefit the unborn. There is, at very least, no *a priori* reason to assume governments will pursue conservation more diligently than the private sector.

Finally, there is little incentive for internal efficiency in the public sector. Decision makers are not residual claimants; that is, they can rarely gain personal, material well-being from making efficient choices. Similarly, they lose little by choosing inefficient alternatives. The capitalization possibilities that exist with private property are absent in public institutions because authority and responsibility are separated (Baden and Stroup 1979).

The above four factors mean that political control of resources biases power toward special interests, bureaucrats, and politicians. It gives these groups powerful incentives to rent seek—that is, to transfer wealth from other segments of society toward themselves. Moreover, it is rare for a particular interest group to capture[2] a government agency for the long run. Instead, there is a continuing competition among groups to alter policies under existing laws or to change the laws themselves.

Competition to control resource policy occurs because trade-offs exist, for example, among various forest values, such as logging, recreation, and habitat preservation. Trade-offs make the simultaneous maximization of all values impossible (Stroup and Baden 1973, 304). Therefore, interest groups and bureaucrats cannot fully implement their agendas as long as other interest groups with different agendas exist. In short, any policy obtained by political influence is insecure because it lacks defensible property rights. Policies can be altered swiftly and without notice if an alternative group musters sufficient political power and attention.

Groups continue their attempts to influence environmental policy because they are insulated from the opportunity costs of their agendas. Most of a policy's costs are externalized. Once implemented, the costs are spread across the general public while the benefits are concentrated within a group. Here we have another example of the prisoner's dilemma: significant benefits for defection so long as no one else defects. But most people rationally defect to avoid becoming a "sucker," the losing player in quadrants one or three. Although everyone would gain by preventing special interests from manipulating the political process, no one can afford to go it alone. Anyone who abstains from the rent-seeking game loses wealth and opportunities to less principled constituencies.

The high returns to acquiring a favored policy coupled with persistent inability to secure such policies in the desired quantities virtually ensures an ongoing struggle for political control of resources. No group can "win" unless it achieves a disproportionately large political influence for a significant period of time. Politically obtained privileges are thus rented rather than bought. Interest group struggles are likely to become negative sum as interested parties expend resources until they just equal the expected private returns of a transfer. (Friedman 1986, 448-9; Gwartney and Stroup 1990).

Government Failure: The Historical Record

History as well as theory demonstrates the ineffectiveness and inefficiency of government management. Far from conserving, preserving, and efficiently managing resources, government agencies have engaged in and even encouraged ecological destruction, economic waste, and ethical erosion. Consider a few examples.

The Forest Service has become a budget maximizer driven by the receipts it retains from timber sales. Under the provisions of the Knutson-Vandenberg Act of 1930, the National Forest Management Act of 1976, and other legislation, the Forest Service has incentives to maximize revenues, not net value, from timber sales. "K-V" funds, highly discretionary monies the agency earns from selling public timber, induce the agency to subsidize clear-cuts on national forests and to make timber-oriented activities the dominant focus of the agency's agenda. (O'Toole, 1992).

One major subsidy to logging on the national forests is the construction of roads that give logging companies access to remote timber. The Forest Service has 8.5 times as many miles of roads as the entire U.S. Interstate Highway System. These roads cause significant erosion and ecological damage to streams and wildlife habitat. Erosion is particularly problematic because many national forests are located in steep, mountainous areas.

If the Forest Service did not subsidize logging by roughly $1 billion a year, logging operations would cease in virtually all national forests. Moreover, with a reduction in the quantity of publicly subsidized timber, private forestry operations would be encouraged to increase timber output on private lands or to increase the efficiency of their mills. If wood prices rose, consumers would have incentives to reduce their use of wood and to seek out substitutes.

The Bureau of Land Management (BLM) was created to end over-grazing on public range but has instead encouraged it. The BLM forces even responsible ranchers to overgraze because it wants to maintain control over its "public" lands (Hess 1992, 126-32). It keeps control by making it difficult for ranchers to retire or underutilize their public range grazing allotments, even if they are doing so to allow revegetation or to expand wildlife habitat. Excessively intensive grazing has caused great ecological damage, particularly in fragile riparian and wetland areas (Hess 1992, 124-32; Hess 1994).

The BLM uses range damage to obtain funding from Congress. This was one of its major accomplishments under the Public Rangelands Improvement Act of 1978. Since extensive range damage has proved to be a useful tool for obtaining larger congressional disbursements, the BLM has incentives to perpetuate damaging practices, to overstate the extent of existing damage, and to exaggerate the potential for amelioration (Hess 1992, 106-8, 119-20; Hess 1994, 41-2). This is true even if there is no conscious or clearly articulated policy within the agency favoring such an agenda.

Degradation of the public range is not caused by grazing fees that are set below market rates. It is the product of bureaucratic control and ranchers' incentives. To improve the long-term quality and management of western rangeland, it is necessary to change the incentives by creating secure and transferable property rights to the land.

If ranchers had a secure right to use public range, they would have strong incentives to acknowledge how their present actions affect the land's future value. Overgrazing today would reduce the land's value tomorrow, and this anticipated loss in value would be capitalized into the land's present market value. Even ranchers who cared little for the land or for the future would have strong incentives to pursue sustainable management.

In addition, by giving ranchers freedom from BLM oversight and control, property rights to public range allow those who care for the land to manage it in accord with their concern. At present, the BLM is an active impediment to sustainable range management. By freeing ranchers from BLM control, stocking levels could be lowered and riparian areas could be protected. Transferable property rights would also allow organizations such as The Nature Conservancy to purchase and preserve ecologically valuable areas. Until now, such purchases have been impossible.

The Bureau of Reclamation, created in 1902, also has undermined the sustainable use of land. Originally, dam construction was intended to help settle the West. The federal government financed projects through a Reclamation Fund and was repaid by selling the water to farmers.

But good intentions went awry, and water flowed uphill toward money. Dams were built to satisfy congressional constituencies while generating work for Bureau of Reclamation engineers. Arizona Senator Morris Udall's support for the Central Arizona Project; Senator Steve Symms' support for Teton Dam; and the near universal congressional resistance to President Jimmy Carter's effort to eliminate many bureau projects indicate the pervasiveness of politicized water (Reisner 1986, 317-42). Below-cost water encourages inefficient agricultural practices, such as rice and alfalfa growing in the semidesert Central Valley. Today, agriculture uses 80 to 90 percent of the water in most western states (Reisner 1990, 30).

Dams generate not only power but opportunism. For example, in 1982, then-Congressman Al Gore of Tennessee invited William Niskanen, an economist nationally respected for both his intelligence and integrity, to his office. Gore asked for a casual, informal meeting to discuss Niskanen's planned research into the pricing policy of federal power agencies. The Tennessee Valley Authority (TVA) was important to Gore, so he organized a manipulative ploy to protect his constituents' TVA pork. Niskanen arrived to find not the promised casual conversation but rather TV cameras and other congressmen. Gore staged the meeting as a Star Chamber interrogation for the consumption of home districts.

Bureau of Reclamation and TVA policies undermine the quality of America's environment. Inefficiently water-intensive agriculture contributes to the more than 20 million acre-feet of water lost annually to western stream systems, to salt accumulation and soil erosion in valuable farmland (Reisner 1986, 473-86; Wilkinson 1992, 260-4), and to agricultural runoffs that damage streams and kill fish. Erecting dams and filling reservoirs can destroy fish runs, submerge ecologically valuable riparian areas, and lead to substantial water losses through evaporation.

The final failure of government management is more general. It is the rent-seeking conflict between the professional environmental community and the Wise Use movement. Wise Use is an opportunistic response to the constraints imposed on private property through various environmental laws and regulations—for example, wetland restrictions, timber export controls, and the Endangered Species Act. Although parading under the banner of free markets, many Wise Users also defend their subsidies for grazing, logging, mining, and irrigation. These positions are in direct conflict with the economic theory of free markets.

Some green groups also manipulate and pervert environment protections, as did Natural Resources Defense Council with the Alar scare. Because the environment is protected politically, Wise Use and green groups often act in accord with the same political strategies. If forests, range, and water were privately owned, if perhaps a forest in the northern Rockies was owned by Rocky Mountain Elk Foundation, stakeholders would have to bargain with one another to obtain mutually satisfying decisions.

Sustainable Use of Land and the Need for Multiple Institutions

An understanding of political economy promotes sensitive and sustainable land use by identifying how different institutions harmonize liberty, prosperity, and environmental quality. We can make institutional choices at the margin, balancing the effects of given institutions in particular situations, rather than adopting an all-or-nothing embrace of government or markets. A mix of for-profits, state and federal agencies and regulation, and innovative institutions, such as public, nongovernment endowment boards or trusts, can allow us to address the particular circumstances of different land use problems.

Our first institutional reform must be to remove government impediments to private initiative and to eliminate subsidies that distort private decisions. Government should reemphasize its role as a monitor of general and impartial laws rather than a manager of resources. This is possible wherever resources can be privately owned and adequately priced.

One possibility is to end government's ineffective management of national parks and forests. Subsidized recreation in these areas makes it difficult to provide camping, biking, bird-watching, and similar activities on private land (O'Toole 1988). Private providers find it harder to attract customers when their fees are significantly higher than the fees charged on public lands. Thus, private conservation, and private innovations that may improve conservation, is reduced. We might privatize certain public lands or place them in trusts, an idea discussed below.

Federal agricultural subsidies are another clear-cut impediment to land conservation and sustainability. Price supports and base acreage provisions encourage farmers to emphasize price supported crops and to reduce the amount of crop rotation. Less rotation, particularly with corn and cotton, increases soil erosion and may degrade the land's agricultural productivity (Gardner 1995, 250-1).

Base acreage provisions, subsidized crop insurance, disaster bailouts, and certain tax provisions also encourage the elimination of wetlands and other wildlife habitat. Farmers try to maximize the year-to-year acreage being farmed because this increases the size of their subsidies. Crop insurance and disaster bailouts make farming on marginal lands less risky and thus encourage farmers to increase the number of acres they cultivate. Finally, federal subsidies may increase water pollution by promoting the use of fertilizers and pesticides. By using more of these inputs, the yields of price supported crops can be expanded and then maintained for many years (Gardner 1995, 241-90). Reducing or eliminating farm subsidies is one of the easiest ways to promote sustainable agricultural practices.

Our second reform is to recognize that the market process is strongly pro-environment, as long as prices are linked to social costs and decision makers are responsible for the consequences of their actions. For example, the profit motive encourages firms to reduce their waste when waste implies the loss of valuable materials, energy, and labor and when the firm is responsible for the consequences of external effects. In manufacturing, shipping, and storing products, the bottom line benefits by maximizing the final yield from a given set of inputs. Lynn Scarlett, vice president for research at the Reason Foundation, notes:

> Small changes can result in significant resource conservation. In one example, a 16% reduction in the cubic dimensions of a juice package, coupled with a 10.7% reduction in label size, saved for one producer nearly 20,000 pounds of material and more than 500 truckloads of outgoing freight, 20,000 pallets, 7,000 pounds of stretch wrap, and 250,000 square feet of chilled warehouse space. [Scarlett 1994]

What is true with packaging is true elsewhere: Incremental modifications in production technologies, coupled with changing resource scarcities, have gradually reduced our per capita consumption of natural resources. Products that are manufactured with less material or energy diminish humanity's impact on the land. For example, a building "that can be built with 35,000 tons of steel today required 100,000 tons 30 years ago." Sixty-five pounds of fiber-optic cable can replace one ton of copper cable and can carry 1,000 times more messages (Scarlett 1994, 24). And per capita use of "wood, cotton, specialty metals, lime, phosphorus, ammonia, minerals, concrete, potash, rubber, plastic, and virgin aluminum have been falling for a decade or more " (Easterbrook 1995, 259). Although groundwater pollution from fertilizers and pesticides remains an important problem, our increasing prosperity gives us ever greater resources to marshal against this challenge.

Less farmland, a sharp reduction in the per capita demand for wood, and changing public perceptions about the value of natural areas have contributed to a dramatic reforestation of the eastern United States and, to a lesser extent, Western Europe (Easterbrook 1995, 10; Lewis 1992, 136-7; McKibben 1995). Largely without government intervention, forests are expanding even as populations grow and urbanization spreads.

Consider two final instances in which private efforts have harmonized economic productivity, sustainable use of land, and conservation. The first is Simpson Investment Company, a leader in high yield forestry, which began a "fiber farm" near Corning, California, in 1988. Simpson's farm reduced the need for logging in natural forests in two ways. First, it used densely planted, fast-growing eucalyptus trees. This enabled Simpson to produce more fiber than a comparable section of natural forest. Second, trees were grown on land previously used for agriculture, so no new wilderness was eliminated and erosion was far less than that caused by logging in mountainous areas.

The second instance is equally impressive. Thanks to the nonprofit Wildlife Habitat Enhancement Council (WHEC), over 300 corporate sites are being managed to benefit wildlife. Companies such as DuPont, IBM, Ford, and Weyerhaeuser find they are saving money, improving community relations, and bolstering employee productivity by returning portions of their corporate estates to nature. This is a voluntary program wherein WHEC provides expertise and companies provide the land, time, and will (White 1994).

These examples from manufacturing, agriculture, forestry, and corporate property management demonstrate that markets often promote conservation. They are sensitive to changing values, particularly when prices reflect opportunity costs, property rights are secure and transferable, and entrepreneurship is free to operate. Thus, contrary to some people's perceptions, economic prosperity is often compatible with sustainable use of our land.

Our third reform is to adopt rules requiring less than unanimous consent in situations where there are large numbers of participants. Although we presumptively favor the use of markets and private initiative, political decisions are sometimes necessary to overcome high transaction costs and strategic behavior. In such instances, people must be coerced through political institutions into accepting group decisions. To control the abuse of political power we can create competition among the levels and branches of government—for example, federalism and separation of powers (Ostrom 1987, 1991). For problems that are inescapably national or international in scale, market-mimicking regulations, such as emissions trading, are probably unavoidable. Fortunately, these situations represent only a small fraction of environmental problems.

Finally, nonprofit, nongovernment institutions can address gaps in the management capabilities of for-profit firms and government agencies. Trusts, similar to those that manage nongovernment schools, nonprofit hospitals, and museums are familiar, time-tested institutions. Lacking the need to earn profits, trusts can promote and protect difficult-to-price values such as biodiversity, watershed preservation, and aesthetics. With legal liability, limited budgets (as opposed to budgets controlled by Congress), and flexibility in hiring and firing, trusts can avoid many of the problems associated with government resource management. Tax exempt status further lessens pressures to develop only commodity values.

Trusts encompassing U.S. public lands might be created by Congress and given one-time appropriations, then completely separated from government management. I have previously suggested this approach as a method of protecting endangered species (Baden and O'Brien 1993) and removing national forests from federal control (Baden and O'Brien 1994).

In designing trusts, we could draw on the conservation experience of the private sector. Ducks Unlimited, Trout Unlimited, the North American Elk Foundation, the Ruffed Grouse Society, Quail Unlimited, and the North America Wild Sheep Foundation have millions of members committed to preserving habitat for conservation purposes. The Boone and Crockett Club, founded in 1887, harbors elk, white-tailed deer, grizzly bears, cougars, eagles, falcons, and other wildlife at its 6,000-acre Theodore Roosevelt Memorial Ranch in Montana. These and other organizations provide many models for innovative, private-sector land conservation.

Privately organized trusts could also be created to preserve rather than conserve, once competition from "free" public lands is mitigated or eliminated. Pennsylvania's Hawk Mountain Sanctuary (Adler et al. 1994), the Audubon Society's Rainey Wildlife Preserve (Stroup and Baden 1981), The Nature Conservancy's 17,550-acre Pine Butte Swamp in Montana and 5,759-acre Pelekunu Valley in Hawaii, and many other private efforts have preserved environmental values (Reed 1993; Lucas 1994). Institutional experiments such as these are crucial to improving trusts' efficacy.

The important aspect of trust management that is lacking in the current system is the incentive to find voluntary, mutually beneficial opportunities for cooperation. Firms or environmental organizations that want to participate or use trust lands would only do so insofar as they are willing to pay and to promote the values protected by the trusts' charters. Cooperation would allow trade-offs among competing values to occur at the margins. Management extremes, such as clear-cutting a large area of forest, would occur less frequently because decision makers would bear the opportunity costs of their actions.

Good intentions, scientific and business know-how, and dedicated people are necessary but not sufficient conditions for promoting the rational, sustainable use of land. The critical factor often ignored by policymakers is getting the incentives right through careful institutional design. We have experimented with government resource management for nearly 100 years, and the experiment has failed. It has resulted in the degradation of ecosystems, and an inefficient emphasis on resource extraction, and has separated those best positioned to care for land from responsibility for outcomes. It is time to rediscover the virtues of the market, to decentralize political management and rule making, and to experiment with novel institutional designs. It is these reforms, aligning action with accountability, that can lead us to a sustainable future.

REFERENCES

Adler, Jonathan, Jennifer Green, Matthew Hoffman, Sam Kazman, Marlo Lewis Jr., James Sheehan, Fred Smith, Ike Sugg, and Jonathan Tolman. 1994. *Environmental Briefing Book for Congressional Candidates*. Washington, DC: Competitive Enterprise Institute.

Anderson, Terry L. and Peter J. Hill. 1977. From Free Grass to Fences. Pages 200–216 in G. Hardin and J. Baden, eds., *Managing the Commons*. New York: W.H. Freeman and Company.

Anderson, Terry L. and Peter J. Hill. 1980. *The Birth of a Transfer Society*. Stanford, CA: Hoover Institution Press.

Baden, John A. and Tim O'Brien. 1993. Toward a True ESA: An Ecological Stewardship Act. Pages 95–100 in W. Hudson, ed., *Building Economic Incentives into the Endangered Species Act*. Washington, DC: Defenders of Wildlife.

Baden, John A. and Tim O'Brien. 1994. *Political Management, Bureaucratic Incentives, and Forest Service Pathologies*. Unpublished paper. Foundation for Research on Economics and the Environment.

Baden, John A. and Richard L. Stroup. 1979. Property Rights and Natural Resource Management. *Literature of Liberty* 2: 5–44.

Baden, John A. and Richard L. Stroup. 1981. Transgenerational Equity and Natural Resources: Or, Too Baden We Don't Have Coal Rangers. Pages 203–216 in J.A. Baden and R.L. Stroup, eds., *Bureaucracy vs. the Environment*. Ann Arbor: University of Michigan Press.

Bullock, Kari and John A. Baden. 1977. Communes and the Logic of the Commons. Pages 182–199 in G. Hardin and J. Baden, eds., *Managing the Commons*. New York: W. H. Freeman and Company.

Dana, Andrew and John Baden. 1985. The New Resource Economics: Toward an Ideological Synthesis. *Policy Studies Journal* 14 (2): 233–43.

Demsetz, Harold. 1967. Toward a Theory of Property Rights. *American Economic Review* 57: 347–59.

Downs, Anthony. 1957. *An Economic Theory of Democracy*. New York: Harper & Row.

Easterbrook, Gregg. 1995. *A Moment Upon the Earth: The Coming Age of Environmental Optimism*. New York: Viking-Penguin.

Friedman, David. 1986. *Price Theory*. Cincinnati, OH: South Western Publishers.

Gardner, B. Delworth. 1995. *Plowing Ground in Washington: The Political Economy of U.S. Agriculture*. San Francisco: Pacific Research Institute for Public Policy.

Gwartney, James D. and Richard L. Stroup. 1990. *Economics: Public and Private Choice,* 5th edition. New York: Harcourt Brace Jovanovich, Publishers.

Hayek, Friedrich A. 1945. The Use of Knowledge in Society. *American Economic Review* 35 (4): 519–30.

Hess, Karl, Jr. 1994. The Western Public Range. *Different Drummer.* 1(2): 27–28.

Hess, Karl Jr. 1992. *Visions Upon the Land: Man and Nature on the Western Range*. Washington, DC and Covelo, CA: Island Press.

Heyne, Paul. 1987. *The Economic Way of Thinking,* 5th edition. Chicago: Science Research Associates, Inc.

Lee, Dwight R. and Richard B. McKenzie. 1993. *Failure and Progress: The Bright Side of the Dismal Science*. Washington, DC: The Cato Institute.

Lewis, Martin W. 1992. *Green Delusions: An Environmentalist Critique of Radical Environmentalism*. Durham, NC and London: Duke University Press.

Lucas, Eric. 1994. Successful by Nature. *Alaska Airlines Magazine.* August: 23–31.

McKibben, Bill. 1995. An Explosion of Green. *The Atlantic Monthly.* April.

Niskanen, William. 1971. *Bureaucracy and Representative Government.* Chicago: Aldine and Atherton.

Olson, Mancur. 1971. *The Logic of Collective Action: Public Goods and the Theory of Groups.* Cambridge, MA: Harvard University Press.

Ostrom, Vince. 1987. *The Political Theory of a Compound Republic: Designing the American Experiment.* Lincoln: University of Nebraska Press.

Ostrom, Vincent. 1991. *The Meaning of American Federalism: Constituting a Self-Governing Society.* San Francisco: Institute for Contemporary Studies.

O'Toole, Randal. 1988. *Reforming the Forest Service.* Washington, DC and Covelo, CA: Island Press.

O'Toole, Randal. 1992. *Citizens' Guide to the Forest Service Budget.* 12(9).

Petulla, Joseph M. 1977. *American Environmental History.* San Francisco: Boyd and Fraser.

Reed, Lawrence. 1993. Privatization: Best Hope for a Vanishing Wilderness. Pages 153–63 in *The Freeman: Man and Nature.* Irving-on-Hudson, NY: Foundation for Economic Education, Inc.

Reisner, Marc. 1986. *Cadillac Desert: The American West and Its Disappearing Water.* New York: Viking-Penguin.

Reisner, Marc and Sarah Bates. 1990. *Overtapped Oasis: Reform or Revolution for Western Water.* Washington, DC and Covelo, CA: Island Press.

Scarlett, Lynn. 1994. Packaging, Solid Waste and Environmental Trade-Offs. *Illahee: Journal for the Northwest Environment* 10(1): 15–33.

Schumpeter, Joseph. 1962. *Capitalism, Socialism and Democracy.* New York: Harper & Row.

Stroup, Richard L. and John A. Baden. 1973. Externality, Property Rights and the Management of Our National Forests. *Journal of Law and Economics* 16(2): 303–12

Stroup, Richard L. and John A. Baden. 1981. A Radical Proposal: Saving the Wilderness. *Reason* (July): 29–36.

Turner, Jack. 1992. Liberal Nature. Pages 15–20 in *Northern Lights* Volume VIII (3).

White, Daphne. 1994. Taking a Walk on the Wild Side. *Hemispheres.* February.

Wilkinson, Charles, F. 1992. *Crossing the Next Meridian: Land, Water, and the Future of the West.* Washington, DC and Covelo, CA: Island Press.

NOTES

1. Transactions costs are the costs of bargaining, negotiating, and exchanging. They tend to rise as more people become involved in decision making because it is time consuming and intellectually taxing to iron out differences among people with diverse interests. Not only must you identify and contact everyone involved, you must also find acceptable compromises and guard against people's efforts to exploit situations for personal gain. Ronald Coase made transactions costs a central issue in economics with his 1960 article "The Problem of Social Cost," *Journal of Law and Economics.*

2. Capture theory was developed by economist George J. Stigler in his 1971 article "The Theory of Economic Regulation." He argued that monopolies are created by government in response to interest groups who capture the regulatory agency and use regulation to prevent competition.

Selected Bibliography
and Further Readings

. . . .

Books

Antenucci, John, et al. *Geographic Information Systems: A Guide to the Technology.* New York: Chapman and Hall, 1991.

Arendt, Randall. *Rural by Design.* Chicago: APA Planners Press, 1994.

Calthorpe, Peter. *The Next American Metropolis.* New York: Princeton Architecture Press, 1993.

Carlson, Dan. *At Road's End: Transportation and Land Use Choices for Communities.* Washington, DC: Island Press, 1995.

The Conservation Foundation. *Creating Successful Communities.* Washington, DC: Island Press, 1990.

DeGrove, John and Deborah D. Miness. *New Frontier for Land Policy: Planning and Growth Management in the United States.* Cambridge, MA: Lincoln Institute of Land Policy, 1992.

Downs, Anthony. *New Visions for Metropolitan America.* Washington, DC: Brookings Institute, and Cambridge, MA: Lincoln Institute of Land Policy, 1994.

Echeverria, John and Ray Eby, eds. *Let the People Judge: Wise Use and the Private Property Rights Movement.* Washington, DC: Island Press, 1995.

Endicott, Eve. *Land Conservation Through Public/Private Partnerships.* Washington, DC: Island Press, 1993.

Flink, Charles and Robert Searns. *Greenways: A Guide to Planning, Design, and Development.* Washington, DC: Island Press, 1993.

Hough, Michael. *Out of Place: Restoring Identity to the Regional Landscape.* New Haven, CT: Yale University Press, 1990.

Kelly, Eric Damian. *Managing Community Growth.* Westport, CT: Praeger Publishers, 1993.

Kunstler, James. *Geography of Nowhere: The Rise and Decline of America's Man Made Landscapes.* New York: Simon & Schuster Trade, 1994.

Land Trust Alliance, *1995 Directory of Conservation Land Trusts.* Washington, DC: Land Trust Alliance.

National Commission on the Environment. *Choosing a Sustainable Future: The Report of the National Commission on the Environment.* Washington, DC: Island Press, 1993.

National Resource Council, Committee on Haze in National Parks and Wilderness Areas Staff. *Setting Priorities for Land Conservation*. Washington, DC: National Academy Press, 1993.

Felice, Neal. *Christics. How Urban America Can Prosper in a Competitive World*. Arlington, VA: Seven Locks Press, 1993.

Platt, Rutherford. *Land Use and Society*. Washington, DC: Island Press, 1995.

Portney, Paul, ed. *Public Policies for Environmental Protection*. Washington, DC: Resources for the Future, 1990.

Richmond, Henry. *Need Assessment for a National Land Use Policy Institute*, unpublished draft, 1994.

Rusk, David. *Cities Without Suburbs*. Washington, DC: Woodrow Wilson International Center for Scholars, 1993.

Smith, Daniel and Paul Hellmund, eds. *Ecology of Greenways: Design and Function of Linear Conservation Areas*. Minneapolis: University of Minnesota Press, 1993.

Smith, Herbert H. *Planning America's Communities*. Chicago: APA Planner's Press, 1991.

Stein, Jay, ed. *Growth Management: The Planning Challenge of the 1990's*. Newbury Park, CA: Sage Publishers, 1992.

Steiner, Frederick. *The Living Landscape*. New York: McGraw-Hill, 1990.

Van der Ryn, Sim and Peter Calthorpe. *Sustainable Communities*. San Francisco: Sierra Club Books, 1991.

Yaro, Robert, et al. *Dealing with Change in the Connecticut River Valley*. Cambridge, MA: Lincoln Institute of Land Policy, 1988.

Whyte, William H., Jr. *Cluster Development*. Washington, DC: American Conservation Association, 1964.

Whyte, William H., Jr. *Organization Man*. New York: Simon & Schuster Trade (Touchstone Books), 1972.

. . . .

Reports and Newsletters

"Beyond Sprawl." A joint report of the California Resources Agency, the Greenbelt Alliance, the Low Income Housing Fund, and Bank of America, February 1995.

Blakely, Edward J. "Shaping the American Dream: Land Use Choices for America's Future." Cambridge, MA: Lincoln Institute of Land Policy, 1992.

Common Ground newsletter. Arlington, VA: The Conservation Fund.

"Conservation Options: A Landowner's Guide." Washington, DC: Land Trust Alliance.

DeGrove, John. "Planning and Growth Management in the States." Cambridge, MA: Lincoln Institute of Land Policy, 1992.

Duerksen, Christopher and Richard Roddewig. "Takings Law in Plain English." Washington, DC: American Resources Information Network, 1994.

Growing Smart newsletter. Chicago: American Planning Association.
"Guiding Growth." Philadelphia: Pennsylvania Environment Council, 1992.
Land Economics magazine. Madison: University of Wisconsin Press.
Land Letter newsletter. Arlington, VA: The Conservation Fund.
Land Lines, newsletter. Cambridge, MA: Lincoln Institute of Land Policy
"Land Use in Transition," 1993. Washington, DC: Urban Land Institute.
Speare, Alden J. "Changes in Urban Growth Patterns 1980–90." Cambridge, MA: Lincoln Institute of Land Use Policy, 1993.

Advisory Committee Members for the Sustainable Use of Land Project

. . . .

Co-Chairs

Henry L. Diamond
Partner
Beveridge & Diamond

Patrick F. Noonan
Chairman
The Conservation Fund

. . . .

Advisors

Carl Anthony
President
Urban Habitat Program

Gus B. Bauman
Partner
Beveridge & Diamond

Gordon L. Binder
Senior Fellow
World Wildlife Fund

Robert L. Bendick, Jr.
Director of Natural Resources Planning
New York State Department of Environmental Conservation

Hooper L. Brooks
Program Officer for the Environment
Surdna Foundation, Inc.

David G. Burwell
President
Rails-to-Trails Conservancy

Norman L. Christensen, Jr.
Dean
School of the Environment
Duke University

Charles M. Clusen
Executive Director
American Conservation Association

Douglas M. Costle
Former Administrator, U.S. Environmental Protection Agency

William M. Dietel
Chairman
National Center for Nonprofit Boards

John D. Echeverria
General Counsel
National Audubon Society

Robert C. Einsweiler
Director of Research and Senior Fellow
Lincoln Institute of Land Policy

Charles H.W. Foster
Adjunct Research Fellow and Lecturer
John F. Kennedy School of Government
Harvard University

Robert W. Fri
President
Resources for the Future

Clayton W. Frye, Jr.
Vice Chairman
Jackson Hole Preserve, Inc.

William J. Futrell
President
Environmental Law Institute

Grenville Garside
Vice President
The Henry M. Jackson Foundation

Catharine M. Gilliam
Land Use Consultant

Robert E. Grady
Principal
Robertson Stephens & Company

Gilbert M. Grosvenor
President
National Geographic Society

Jean W. Hocker
President
The Land Trust Alliance

Charles Jordan
Director
Portland Bureau of Parks & Recreation

Jerold S. Kayden
Graduate School of Design
Harvard University

Thomas J. Klutznick
Thomas J. Klutznick Company

Christopher B. Leinberger
Managing Partner
Robert Charles Lesser & Company

Kathryn Jo Lincoln
Vice Chair
Lincoln Institute of Land Policy

Blaine Liner
Director State Policy Center
The Urban Institute

Edward T. McMahon
Director
American Greenways Program

James D. Maddy
President
National Park Foundation

James F. Murley
Executive Director
1000 Friends of Florida

John R. Nolon
Professor
School of Law, Pace University

George A. Ranney, Jr.
Partner
Mayor, Brown & Platt

Stephen Rattien
Executive Director
Commission on Geosciences, Environ-
ment, and Resources
National Research Council

William K. Reilly
Visiting Professor
Stanford University

Henry R. Richmond
Chairman
National Growth Management Lead-
ership Project

William D. Ruckelshaus
Chairman and Chief Executive Officer
Browning-Ferris Industries, Inc.

David S. Sampson
Executive Director
Hudson River Valley Greenway Com-
munities Council

H. Claude Shostal
President
Regional Plan Association

William H. Whyte. Jr.
Author

Douglas P. Wheeler
Secretary
The Resources Agency of California

Index

· · · · · · · · ·